BUILDING
A
MORAL SYSTEM

ROBERT B. ASHMORE

Marquette University

PRENTICE-HALL, INC., Englewood Cliffs, New Jersey 07632

Library of Congress Cataloging-in-Publication Data

Ashmore, Robert B.
    Building a moral system.

    Bibliography: p. 167
    Includes index.
    1. Ethics. I. Title.
    BJ1012.A73 1987   170   86-9502
    ISBN 0-13-086265-7

Editorial supervision and interior design: Serena Hoffman
Cover design: Lundgren Graphics
Manufacturing buyer: Harry P. Baisley

Parts of Chapter 4 originally appeared in Robert B. Ashmore, "Friendship and the Problem of Egoism," *The Thomist*, 41, no. 1 (1977), 105-130, and are included here with permission of the publisher.

Quotations from Aristotle, *Nicomachean Ethics*, translated by Martin Ostwald, are reprinted with permission of Macmillan Publishing Company. Copyright © 1962 by Macmillan Publishing Company.

ISBN 0-13-086265-7 01

Prentice-Hall International (UK) Limited, *London*
Prentice-Hall of Australia Pty. Limited, *Sydney*
Prentice-Hall Canada Inc., *Toronto*
Prentice-Hall Hispanoamericana, S.A., *Mexico*
Prentice-Hall of India Private Limited, *New Delhi*
Prentice-Hall of Japan, Inc., *Tokyo*
Prentice-Hall of Southeast Asia Pte. Ltd., *Singapore*
Editora Prentice-Hall do Brasil, Ltda., *Rio de Janeiro*
Whitehall Books Limited, *Wellington, New Zealand*

To My Mother
and the Memory of My Loving Father

Contents

Preface

Although a preface is perhaps the least read part of a book, I hope this will be an exception. The philosophical concerns that inspired the writing of this book are explained here, and I urge the reader to evaluate them. This book is a philosophical introduction to ethical theory. It presupposes neither acquaintance with other sources nor any formal coursework in philosophy, although both would be advantageous.

My purpose is twofold. First, I wish to introduce the various sorts of questions that must be decided if one is to have a consistent and comprehensive ethical theory. To this end, I discuss major alternative responses to these questions as they are found in the history of philosophy. I have tried to present as clearly as possible the strongest arguments on competing sides of an issue. The contributions of historical figures, though, should have a limited role: that of being instrumentally valuable in the development of one's own philosophical perspective. Second, we must not lose sight of the idea that the purpose of moral inquiry is practical. We cannot simply engage in the esoteric play of words and concepts, such that "In the beginning was the word. . . .and in the end too." The aim of moral inquiry is a noble, fulfilling life. Anything less than intellectual support of that objective would constitute an impoverished view of the role of the moral philosopher.

My purpose, then, has been not solely to identify major issues and historically significant responses to them. I have also *done* philosophy. It seems wrong to me to appear unmoved by every view. These are matters we do care about, and it trivializes the enterprise to treat all positions as if they were on a par. But there are opposite errors to be avoided as well. On the one hand, in a rush to judgment, no serious contenders should be denied a fair hearing. I must add, of course, that it is impossible in an introductory work to do full justice to any contender. Nevertheless, mature judgment must be sufficiently informed and tested in the encounter with opposing views. Propagandism ill serves the philosophical ideal.

The other extreme to be avoided is that of neutrality towards all principles and systems or, worse yet, viewing philosophical tools simply as sophistical weapons for the demolition of every theory. The end result of the solely negative employment of philosophical skills is cynicism on the part of the learner. Given the state of the world, we can little afford the reduction of philosophy to cleverness in attacking others' positions.

My own orientation is eudaimonistic; that is, actions, rules and institutions are justified by reference to an end or goal of human striving that can be called happiness or self-fulfillment adequately considered. Further, empirical evidence about human beings is relevant to specification of that end. I am philosophically indebted, above all, to Aristotle, Hume, Mill, and Dewey. Readers must, of course, think out their own answers to the questions and alternatives that are examined in these chapters.

The upshot is that, in this book, I have endeavored to offer both something old and something new. In building a moral system, we are not like engineers on shore, constructing a ship *de novo*. Because we find ourselves already immersed in a system, we begin with something—a ship already at sea. It can be overhauled only plank by plank. The accumulated experience of the human race provides us with a starting point, reflected in the practices and modes of thought to which we are exposed in early childhood. However, we must bring our theories, as Aristotle says, to the test of the facts of life. Consequently, our adherence to tradition or our reconstruction of any of its parts must be the result of critical thinking and fidelity to experience.

Distinctive features of this book reflect the beliefs just expressed. Someone has said that every important error contains elements of truth. I have tried to avoid traditional dichotomies which, in an attempt to simplify, seriously distort. The reader can judge my efforts to transcend rigid distinctions between facts and values, self-love and love of others, freedom and determinism, reason and desire, subjectivity and objectivity, rule and virtue ethics, deontological and utilitarian theories. Instead of creating Procrustean beds, I have tried to remain faithful to the complexity of lived experience. This is reflected, too, in the technique I sometimes employ of presenting arguments in claim/counterclaim format. Even where the immediate juxtaposition of counterclaims is not utilized, the same effect is intended by a movement back and forth from the consideration of one theory to its alternatives.

A serious omission in standard treatments of ethical theory is also corrected here. Modern thinking has focused exclusively on the articulation and criticism of rule theories. Neglected in the process has been the important ancient and medieval approach, a virtue-centered ethic. That tradition is given its due in Chapter 7 on The Life of Virtue.

Finally, this book is designed to be compact enough to be read in conjunction with primary sources, enabling the reader to experience first-hand the theories systematically investigated here.

I have tried to be "gender neutral" in my writing. However, the English language is not kind to such efforts, especially in the use of personal pronouns. When it was desirable to use such pronouns, the convention I have adopted seemed to me the least awkward. In four chapters I have consistently used masculine pronouns, and in an equal number of other chapters I have used feminine pronouns.

No prefatory remarks are complete without acknowledging indebtedness to others who have contributed to the success of the effort. Contrary to usual disclaimers, I should like to hold others also responsible for any errors that are found in this book. Understanding their reluctance to share the blame, I nevertheless offer words of praise to Mary Anne Siderits and Vincent Colapietro, colleagues with whom I have shared many thoughts over the years, and who have offered helpful comments on earlier versions of this book. I also wish to thank the administration at Marquette University for providing generous support of various kinds, including a Mellon research grant, so that this project could be completed. I am grateful to Kathy Hawkins and also to the philosophy department secretaries, who transformed the product into acceptable typescript. My one regret is that Bill Kestle, Prentice-Hall's long-time representative, is not alive to see his efforts bear fruit; he encouraged me in the earliest stages of this writing, and I am proud that his publishing house has seen fit to complete what he began.

Any book is infinitely perfectible. Since there is room for all words save the last word, I invite criticism. Your efforts to correct and improve my tentative offering would be deeply appreciated. In this as in every other dimension of the philosopher's vocation, it is well to bear in mind Aristotle's words in the *Eudemian Ethics*: "Every person has something of his own to contribute to the finding of the truth."

Robert B. Ashmore

*"How do most people live
without any thoughts?"*

Emily Dickenson

CHAPTER ONE

Setting
the Boundaries

Characteristic of Western philosophical thought from its beginnings among the pre-Socratic Greeks is the effort to understand human beings and their environment, and out of that understanding to fashion a way of life most in accord with human needs. Those first philosophers, whom history traces to the seventh century B.C., were distinguished by a turning away from myth and religion to a search for the natural causes and explanations of things. Aware of continual change ("All things are in constant flux," Heraclitus said), they searched beneath the surface phenomena for unifying and stabilizing principles, since it was apparent that there was order in the changes that occurred. The detection of regularity held the promise, then, both of understanding and ultimately of control.

In the case of humans, it became meaningful to distinguish between acting *according to* and *acting from*. Everything in nature acts *according to* laws, for example, the law of gravity. There is no question of physical objects exercising an option to obey the law of gravity; they just do. Such laws enable us safely to predict how natural bodies will act. However it is also the case that humans can act *from* a law; that is, they can deliberate and choose how they will act. The life of humans is not merely the expression of laws over which they exercise no control. They are able to reflect upon their situation, determine their goals (within limits), and formulate rules for the attainment of those goals. Of course, humans retain the capacity to violate the very laws they give themselves. The language of praise and blame, the reinforcements of reward and punishment, serve to strengthen conformity with those rules by which humans in society choose to describe their behavior. (We shall have occasion in Chapter 8 to discuss some of the problems associated with these claims.)

CUSTOMARY AND REFLECTIVE MORALITY

The concept of "ought" or "should" in a distinctively human sense arises, then, when we speak of behavior that can either conform to or deviate from norms that people in community devise for the moderation of their interactions, and for the guidance of their actions towards ends of which the society approves. The initial encounter with morality that an individual experiences is with those customary rules and instructions that form the mores of the community.

Note that the etymological meaning of *ethics* is customs or usages, coming from the Greek word *ethos*. Similarly, the word *morals* derives from the Latin *mores*, having the same meaning. Customs were not merely habitual ways of acting, but were ways approved by the group. They had a prescriptive force, not simply describing behavior in the community, but prescribing how it should be.

The possibility, however, that a customary instruction may itself be unwise (an issue to be further explored in Chapter 3), warranting reexamination by members of the community and possible reform, leads to a distinction between customary and reflective morality. *Customary morality* refers to those standards and rules found in ancestral habits. The individual accepts and acts according to those norms simply because they are the prescribed norms. At the extreme, customary morality tolerates no critical reflection or challenge of the socially accepted patterns of behavior. One is expected to act according to the way things are done. (Nietzsche's criticism of "herd morality" reflects the danger of too insistent a demand for obedience as the main virtue.)

Alternatively, *reflective morality* appeals to the reason or judgment of the individual. The essence of reflective morality is knowing reasons for or against customary instructions, leading to specification of criteria for judging various ways of acting. Justification of customary instructions is the important concept at this stage. No longer is it considered sufficient to conform to community practices; those practices must themselves be examined critically. Reflective morality insists upon reasons for observing customary morals, and upon acting from those reasons.

This distinction carries with it no assumption that customs are unjustifiable. Reflection may confirm them, and they may themselves be the product of previous reflections. The difference between customary and reflective morality, then, is not based on *what* is believed. The same tenets may be held by both. The difference turns on *why* the beliefs are held. Customary morality invokes such defenses as "It is traditional," or "This is how we do things," or "That's the way we were taught."

Moral theory, as a conscious and systematic way of deciding value questions, begins when we ask, "Why should I act in this fashion rather than otherwise?" Frequently, the need for reflection arises out of conflict in life situations. Old ways of doing things may no longer be relevant to present needs. Resources vary. Principles tug in opposing directions. Desires and values cannot be simultaneously satisfied. When conflict and novelty interrupt the flow of activity, we must pause and think about what has produced the blockage.

Thought as an instrument for the resolution of conflict is an enduring necessity for the effective human being, since no solutions are permanent and all-inclusive. The adequate human life has as an indispensable ingredient the continual operation of intelligence to guide habit and impulse. The alternative to reflective existence is either abandonment to the immediacy of blind impulse or to the rigidity of authoritarian habits. Neither impulse nor habit disengaged from the continuous scrutiny of intelligence serves humans well in meeting the uncertainties of their existence. It was Socrates who said, "The unexamined life is not worth living." And it has always been a primary task of philosophy to ask fundamental questions concerning what sort of life is indeed worth living.

These are not trivial matters that we treat of here. The question is how we should live our lives. The great philosophers of history are paradigms for all who seek answers to the problems of living since, as one author put it, "The goal of philosophizing has always been to form the best judgment we can of what man is, what kind of world he inhabits, and what kind of life he should lead."[1] That those judgments are interrelated will become clearer as we proceed.

THE AMORALIST

One possible way of clarifying what is requisite for a moral system is to proceed negatively, by asking what is characteristic of an individual who lacks a moral point of view. Let us use the term *amoralist* to name one who has no moral system. Perhaps you will conclude that no sane person could actually be such, but the question we are considering at the moment is simply, "What would qualify an individual as amoral?"

We might begin by focusing on just what it is to have a system, moral or otherwise. To act systematically means to act consistently or with regularity. If a person has reason to act in a certain way in a given situation, then that person will act in similar fashion in similar situations. What counted as a good reason for doing X in one circumstance should hold for other circumstances of the same or similar sort. If, on the other hand, there were no telling what a person might do from moment to moment, however much alike the circumstances might be, we would be inclined to conclude that the person was inconsistent or lacked a reason for what he did. To have a reason for doing X is to hold some general consideration that counts in relevantly similar situations.

By contrast, the amoralist would not be disposed to say that, if something is acceptable for him to do, then it is acceptable for others also. A person who lacks a system is without the means to draw any conclusions about the behavior of others from his own behavior, in addition to being unable to establish any consistency in his own behavior. If he had a system, of course, our hypothetical individual would be prepared to acknowledge that other people have a right to act toward him in the same way that he acts toward them. Reciprocity, then, appears as a formal aspect of a system.

What makes it exceedingly difficult to talk about the behavior of the amoralist is obviously the fact that he is not prepared to offer reasons for acting one way rather than another. It is not merely that he possesses a peculiar morality, but that he has no morality at all. As an amoralist, he cannot employ such concepts as "permitted" or "disapproved," if these terms are allowed to have any application to a variety of situations. To apply them in that way would be to have a moral system. The amoralist does not satisfy a condition that contemporary theorists call *universalizability*. That is, if one's behavior is governed by a rule or principle, then one is committed to behaving that same way in relevantly similar situations, and to acknowledging the right of others to do likewise. Acting "on principle" means acting from a general norm. Just as we cannot say that a law is made for just one particular act but for all acts of a certain kind, so also a moral principle or rule covers all acts identified by the principle. An inability to universalize behavior is a hallmark of amorality.

It may seem unclear whether any general terms are applicable to describe the behavior of the amoralist. Does he possess motivations? By definition he is at least indifferent to moral considerations. That would suggest that he cannot care about other people's interests, nor can he be relied upon to keep promises, honor contracts, or return favors. An inclination to behave with such consistency would manifest "acting on principle." Clearly, the amoralist cannot object to courses of action because they are selfish, unjust, or intemperate, for those are moral considerations.

Would such an individual even be able to live within a community? Any society must have rules, and those rules must take into account all members of that society. It would seem that a person without any morality at all could only be parasitic upon a society, trying by whatever means to get what he wants from others, but acknowledging no obligations to accept responsibilities, share benefits, or permit reciprocal treatment. Such a person violates our sense of fairness. But that, of course, is a moral consideration. And the amoralist is indifferent to such considerations.

In sum, what we find in the amoralist is the absence of any thoughts about *justification* for his actions. Being without principles, he is unable to generalize either about his own behavior or that of others. Certainly we can make no impression upon him with arguments such as, "But what if everybody did that?" Such an argument would invoke the universalizability criterion. By the same token, the amoralist may not complain that society has no right to ostracize him, punish him, or compel him to cooperate. For "right" is a moral category, like "duty" and "virtue."

What we are left with is not an individual who merely espouses a different form of life, but one whose life has no form. He fails to tempt us with an alternative to our own pattern of existence simply because we see the impossibility of any society, or indeed any individual, functioning for the sake of long-range objectives without system or principles. The amoralist, in short, inclines us to question his sanity.

Having a Moral System

Let us state in positive language the conclusions reached thus far. One who possesses a moral system recognizes behavior to be *rule-governed*; that behavior is rule-governed means that all acts of a given sort are judged the same way. Consistency and reciprocity mark the attitude of a moral agent toward successive acts of his own and of others. When challenged to justify his acts, the moral agent will appeal to general considerations (principles, rules, laws, etc.) that cover those kinds of acts. He will employ the "language of morals," which includes such categories as justice, honor, benevolence, and temperance. His moral system will contain both general and specific norms, ranging from the most universal and abstract prescriptions concerning goodness to very finely qualified applications of those prescriptions. The logic of his system is manifest in that qualified and particular rules are justified by appeal to more general rules, and conflict in the application of those more general rules is resolved by appeal to the most universal principles of the system.

The interests and needs of other people will be a matter of concern to the moral agent. Recognizing himself as similar to others in relevant ways, he will be influenced by sympathy (literally, "to suffer with") for their situation. Such an individual will recognize the need for humans in community to establish criteria for regulating their interactions, and will see that this consensus can be reached only on the basis of mutually shared desires and inclinations. Not only will possession of a moral system imply formal conditions such as universalizability, but substantive questions such as those concerning the goals of human striving will be answered through the identification of the ultimate values of that system. Some hierarchy of goods realizable through individual and communal activity will provide ultimate rational support for lower-level rules and judgments.

Partial Amorality

Although it would appear implausible to suggest that many people are completely amoral, a far stronger case might be made for the claim that partial amorality is commonplace. By *partial amorality* is meant a selective indifference to moral distinctions, a refusal to apply moral categories to one aspect of life, while retaining a sense of morality with respect to other areas.

It is not difficult to find examples of this suspension of the moral in one department of existence. The coach who maintains on the field that "winning is the only thing" exempts athletic competition from the ordinary rules of behavior that he observes on other occasions. The corporate executive brackets morality when he insists that "the only business of business is to maximize profits." Yet that same businessperson, who in his corporate suite fails to recognize another as his "neighbor" on Monday morning, will have listened approvingly on Sunday morning to the gospel message of love. The person in government who believes that "politics and morality make strange bedfellows" does the same. Various Watergate criminals, including Ehrlichman, Haldeman and Dean, acknowledged in various ways that their appetite for power and their unscrupulous desire to please Mr. Nixon made them indifferent to the morality of their acts. One of those criminals, Gordon Liddy, steadfastly defended his amorality with the assertion, "The proper response of a lieutenant to his prince is 'Yes, Sir.'" The soldier who in wartime will destroy people and property with an indifferent shrug that says "war is hell" has suspended the norms that govern his behavior in peacetime. The "godfather" who engineers the extermination of his rivals, even while he attends a baptism within the family he dearly loves, is a striking example of one who effectively compartmentalizes his morality.

What accounts for this split in the personality, so that both a moral and an amoral agent exist side by side? It would seem that each side of the person responds to a particular set of needs and aims that cannot be reconciled with the other. This lack of personal integration is fostered by the contrary messages an individual receives from his environment. For example, he is taught both that he should learn to cooperate with others and also that it is a "dog eat dog" world. This results in simultaneous approval of sharing and of hoarding, of respect for one's fellow man and of indifference to him in order to "get the job done."

The philosopher Thomas Hobbes (1588–1679) argued that human beings can afford to be moral only when they enjoy security in doing so. Similarly, the contemporary psychologist Abraham Maslow cites evidence that when safety needs are threatened, and until those needs are satisfied, the individual will not adopt a moral system. The businessperson who says it would be suicidal to mainfest "heart" in deciding company policy feels that threat. So does the politician who admits he cannot vote his conscience on a bill because it would cost him support back home.

It might be argued that we should have more sympathy for the predicament of an individual trapped in such situations. Should we expect that lawmakers be martyrs and that businesspersons lose their jobs for the sake of conscience? In the long run, we might ask, how much has been gained by losing a top-notch executive or legislator who bucked the system on a particular issue? "He's not going to do anybody any good once he's out." Jesus Christ accused the Pharisees of placing impossible burdens upon the people. Are we similarly guilty of imposing a morality people cannot live with, especially if their jobs, social status, and sometimes even their lives are in the balance when they act? Isn't it better to have a moral norm that is "realistic" than to have a double standard—one standard to which lip service is paid in the appropriate circumstances, and another by which "real life" decisions are made?

A truly practical point to be realized in these situational dilemmas is that institutional arrangements must be reformed if individuals are to act morally. It is quite clear that private and public morality are interdependent. We deal in foolish abstractions when we assume that individuals are not influenced by the environment that shapes behavior and reacts to behavior. There is something faulty in the evangelical message that a conversion of heart is sufficient for the salvation of the world; it is that the "inner person" cannot be segregated from the "outer." The tone of our social medium conditions our personal values. John Dewey has maintained that the neglect of environment implied in our separation of private from public morals is as unrealistic as expecting cars to race through jungles or tulips to grow in a desert. A path must be cleared through the jungle if cars are to make their way, and soil must be prepared if flowers are to bloom. By the same token, the reconstruction of social patterns is essential to effecting the conversion of individuals to moral conduct.

A compelling example of the incompatibility of the social environment with traditional moral values is documented in Michael Maccoby's *The Gamesman.*[2] His confidential interviews with executives at all levels of corporate life revealed their judgment that success was jeopardized by moral scruples. Those with ethical sensitivities simply could not make it to the top. The individual who says he must be amoral to survive because his competition lacks scruples presents us with a genuinely complex problem. The exhortation to heroism cannot be expected to move the many. Positive results are more likely to occur if institutional reforms transform the marketplace in which transactions occur. For example, the pressure to bribe customers in order to win contracts is lessened if laws are enforced that prohibit bribes. The pressure to vote according to the dictates of well-heeled special interests is lessened by public financing of elections. The pressure to deny blacks service at the lunch counter is reduced by enforcement of antisegregation statutes. The obvious point in all of this is that desired behavior is more likely to occur in an environment that supports such behavior.

It is ironic that social reformers are labelled utopian when they press for transformation of political or economic or educational structures. Rather, naive utopianism afflicts those who are optimistic about moral progress while negligent of the means by which that progress is accomplished. So long as suspending morality and compartmentalizing roles are the necessary conditions for retaining job and sanity, it is futile to preach dedication to lofty ethical principles. Only by healing the split in our public values will we overcome the dichotomizing that occurs in our personal lives.

Søren Kierkegaard (1813–1855), the Danish philosopher, went so far as to criticize his entire society for being amoral. Kierkegaard's claim was that, although people were formally committed to certain values, they did not in fact incorporate those values into their lives. The charge that one has objectively but not subjectively assented to moral truths is perhaps equivalent to the charge of hypocrisy. The evidence for such a charge lies in the failure of beliefs to influence conduct practically. Philosophers and psychologists alike have noted the neurotic tensions resulting from inability to integrate conflicting values. Ritualistic efforts to assuage conscience—for example, philanthropic activities, civic club memberships, and church worship—are ultimately ineffective so long as the underlying harmonization of public/private personhood is unrealized.

Kierkegaard noted the ease with which a person functions amorally when he is a member of the crowd. Who has not experienced the willingness to act in a group or in a social role in a manner totally at variance with one's behavior as an individual? Examples range from petty acts of personal vandalism to mob attacks on minorities. The loss of a sense of personal responsibility—sometimes unexpected, but at other times actually hoped for—is what attends this submersion in the crowd. "A crowd in its very concept is the untruth, by reason of the fact that it renders the individual completely impenitent and irresponsible, or at least weakens his sense of responsibility by reducing it to a fraction."[3] Partial or subjective amorality must be attacked at its roots if it is to be overcome. What protects those roots is pessimism concerning the amelioration of our social institutions.

MORAL AGENTS AND PATIENTS

A question to which we might now naturally turn is this: Who or what qualifies as a moral agent? And who or what is a moral patient? These are distinguishable questions. The former asks for the identification of those capable of *performing* moral acts, whereas the latter asks for the identification of objects or *recipients* of moral action. One view has it that, although the questions are separable, the answer to both is in fact the same. All human beings, and only human beings, are moral agents and patients, it is said.

Considering first the question of agency, does it follow from what was said earlier about the possession of a moral system that only human beings could qualify? Let us consider the example of a household cat. We might wish to make the case that cats are moral agents because their behavior can be described as rule-governed, and hence as systematic. They are capable, however, of violating those rules, and we describe cats as good or bad according to how their behavior conforms to rules. We teach cats, and we hold them responsible, for we reward or punish them in terms of their performance. When cats "break training," they manifest guilt; that is, they are aware that their behavior does not conform to norms. They will often hide to avoid the punishment they know attends the violation of rules. In other words, we might argue that, if we condition cats the same way we do humans, and we respond to their behavior in the same way, why maintain a difference as regards moral agency?

The opponent of such a position could reply that we do not really hold cats responsible for their acts, since they are not capable of deliberating and choosing how they will act. Their patterns of behavior are instinctual or, if acquired through training, are developed through specific stimulus-response sequences. What is lacking in the cat is the power of conceptualization, with the consequence that the cat does not understand why the act is right or wrong. Because cats lack this abstracting capacity, much of the language of moral agency is inappropriate if applied to them. We do not refer to their ideals or, for that matter, to any frame of reference that transcends the immediate environmental context. Surely, the argument goes, we cannot attribute to cats the considered selection of values from among alternatives, together with the formulation of rules governing exceptional circumstances.

However, a third party in this dispute might see the two previously described positions as needlessly extreme. Why not overcome this false dichotomy by acknowledging *degrees* of moral agency, just as we recognize degrees of moral responsibility among human beings? That is to say, the behavior and the capacities of cats are located on a continuum of agency. Along this continuum, some animate beings are found to be less capable and others more capable of behavior that is self-controlled, free, deliberate—or in other words, a moral action. (Chapter 8 will consider at some length the question of freedom.)

If we turn to the second question concerning moral patients, we encounter at least as many differences in point of view. One might wish to argue that only those beings who have moral rights deserve moral consideration. Moral rights and entitlement to respect are attributable only to those who are capable of asserting claims to be considered. Human beings alone are rational, and hence, alone the holders of rights. Therefore, it is possible to act morally or immorally only towards humans.

A contrary view is that of the contemporary philosopher G. J. Warnock, who says, "Just as liability to be judged as a moral agent follows from one's general capability of alleviating, by moral action, the ills of the predicament, and is for that reason confined to rational beings, so the condition of being a proper 'beneficiary' of moral action is the capability of *suffering* the ills of the predicament—and for that reason is not confined to rational beings, nor even to potential members of that class."[4] Although only persons or rational beings can be moral agents, according to Warnock, all creatures capable of suffering are moral patients.

Not all living things, however, are sentient beings and, hence, capable of suffering. What about flowers and trees? We might attempt to rule them out on the ground that moral considerability attaches only to beings having interests, and interests presuppose desires or wants. But can't it be argued that trees have interests—for example, in sunlight and moisture that would enable them to grow and maintain themselves? If so, moral respect might extend to all beings satisfying the condition of being alive.

An interesting argument that can be invoked to extend moral considerability even to nonliving objects such as rock formations is found in Christopher Stone's *Should Trees Have Standing?*[5] He maintains that, to be a holder of legal rights, four conditions must be satisfied:

1. Some public authority is prepared to review acts inconsistent with those rights.
2. The holder of rights can institute legal actions at its behest.
3. In granting relief the court must take injury to it into account.
4. The relief must be to the benefit of the holder of rights.

The holder of a right need not be able to speak for itself in court. Lawyers speak for infants, mental defectives, corporations, and estates. Consequently, the guardian of a natural object—for example, the Secretary of the Interior or the Sierra

Club—can sue to collect damages for injury to that object, and the court can determine reasonable claims on the basis of how much it would cost to restore that object to its former condition. Stone provides considerable evidence of the extent to which this "environmental ethic" is already operative in legal decisions.

What are some implications of Stone's position? To say that natural objects have moral and legal rights suggests that they have value independent of their usefulness to human beings. In other words, human advantage does not determine what has rights. "Useless" living and nonliving things can still satisfy the four conditions mentioned. How else do we explain laws prohibiting profit from the torture or neglect of animals? To whose advantage are statutes mandating adequate housing, food, and water for captive animals?

Is it a further implication of this view that the interests of nonliving things are on a par with human interests? Some would argue not, on the ground that having rights does not necessarily mean that those rights must prevail when they conflict with the rights of others. Therefore, the tree's interest in growing might yield to the human interest in building a road through a field. However, if this is so, aren't we back to saying that nonhuman objects have value in proportion to their usefulness to human beings and can be disposed of accordingly? Perhaps the environmentalist does not intend to deny the instrumental value of nonhuman beings, but only appeals for an attitude shift, so that we enlarge our sympathies toward other cooperating members in that ecosystem of which we are a part.

The consequence of this shift need not be that we stop all consumption of, or scientific experimentation on, living things. Rather, it might mean the development of a moral sentiment and of a corresponding body of law that gives more serious consideration to the interests of beings otherwise abused. In the words of one well-known environmentalist: "All ethics so far evolved rest upon a single premise: that the individual is a member of a community of interdependent parts. His instincts prompt him to compete for his place in the community, but his ethics prompt him to cooperate (perhaps in order that there may be a place to compete for). The land ethic simply enlarges the boundaries of the community to include soils, waters, plants, and animals, or collectively: the land."[6]

ABORTION AS A TEST CASE

A contemporary moral problem affected by one's conclusions about moral agents and patients is the abortion question. Some who defend abortion on demand maintain that the fetus has no rights because it has only the potentiality of human life. They find support for this view in the 1973 Supreme Court decision that held that "the word 'person' as used in the Fourteenth Amendment does not include the unborn." (Opponents of this source of appeal point out that it was also the Supreme Court which in 1857 declared that blacks were not persons protected by the Constitution.) It will help to sharpen our own thinking about membership in the moral community if we briefly consider some of the claims and counterclaims of abortion protagonists:

Claim: The issue is one of woman's right to privacy regarding her body. Her right here is no less absolute than her decision to have her ears pierced.

Counter: The issue concerns two bodies, not one. The fetus is a unique organism with distinct and separate genetic and hormonal constitution. What is in question is a decision to terminate a life other than the mother's.

Claim: Until the point of viability (usually twenty-eight weeks of gestation), the fetus is dependent upon the mother. Because it could not survive on its own, it has no independent right to exist.

Counter: Dependence does not end with viability. An eleven-month-old infant is absolutely dependent on the care provided by others. The location of the dependent creature has shifted from womb to crib, but what relevance does that hold for the right to exterminate?

Claim: Human life begins with birth. Prior to that time, what exists is only potentially human.

Counter: From the moment of conception, a distinct being is embarked on a continuum of development of potentialities toward full human existence. That continuous process of actualization does not terminate at birth, but is a movement that progresses through the entire natural life of the individual. Let's not forget that every human is a former fetus.

Claim: Although the fetus may be human in one sense, it is not a person, meaning "a full-fledged member of the moral community." Persons are conscious, reasoning, self-motivated, socially recognized participants in community life.

Counter: What percentage of actualized potential must human beings achieve before their right to continued life is recognized? Any decision on this question would be arbitrary. Infants, mental defectives, and many older people do not qualify under that definition of person. Moreover, history reveals the danger of denying human rights on grounds of social recognition as persons; for example, slaves, women, heretics, paupers.

Claim: The right to life of the mother outweighs the right of the fetus, for she is a further actualized human. Her diverse roles, responsibilities, and experiences entitle her to preferred existence.

Counter: In a case of genuine conflict between the two lives, one might convincingly argue that the mother's life should prevail. However, most abortions are for reasons of personal convenience or relief from embarrassing negligence. In these cases the fetal life should have a value greater than zero.

Claim: Why insist that a baby that is not wanted and will not be loved be brought into the world? Doesn't the mother have the right of self-defense against that which threatens her happiness?

Counter: Killing those we don't like is an extreme solution to social problems. The right of decision should be exercised before conception through the responsible use of contraceptives. Respect for life in process is the responsible posture after conception. Moreover, adoption is an alternative that provides love to the infant and also joy to those who want the adopted baby.

Claim: The decision of a mother is an agonizing one in any case. Why add to it the fear of breaking the law? Better to provide safe and economical conditions for abortions that will take place even though they are illegal.

Counter: Whether a decision is agonizing depends on the moral education of the individual. A permissive legal environment encourages a premissive moral attitude. Restrictive legislation helps to shape conscience and reinforce the seriousness of decision-making.

Claim: The decision to abort is a very personal one. It's easy to say what you would do when you're not in the situation. People cannot really decide until they find themselves in the predicament.

Counter: Every moral decision is a personal one, manifesting the kind of person you are. The issue concerns what criteria are appropriate to this sort of act. You don't wait until ''ou're in the situation to decide what are the relevant standards for conduct.

Claim: Among those relevant standards, shouldn't there be some concern for the woman who is a victim of rape? Why should she suffer the further trauma of carrying the product of sexual assault for nine months? Also, what if a fetal life is scientifically determined to be seriously defective? Even in the natural course of events there is often miscarriage of irreversibly damaged fetuses. Such cases indicate the irrationality of an absolute ban on abortions. Those who are "pro life" should recognize that there can be justifiable exceptions to general rules.

Counter: Even were one to concede the permissibility of abortion in cases like these, that would not be much consolation to "pro choice" people. What they advocate is abortion on demand. We need a public policy that recognizes that abortion is not merely an alternative form of birth control.

If we recall the discussion earlier in this chapter, several questions arise. Are fetuses moral agents? If not, at what point do they become moral agents? Can such a specification be made nonarbitrarily? Even if we grant that fetuses are not moral agents, that does not resolve the separate question of their possible status as moral patients. Many abortion advocates deny them this status also. However, as defined by Warnock and Stone, "moral patient" would seem to include fetal life.

Finally, as regards moral agency in abortion cases, is it sufficient to focus exclusively on the rights and responsibilities of the mother, to the neglect of the father? Does he also possess a right of decision as co-parent? And does he bear equal responsibility with the female for contraceptive precautions before pregnancy, as well as for parental care during and following pregnancy? Also, does the state have interests in this matter which, at some point, are compelling? The Supreme Court includes among state interests the mother's health, maintaining medical standards, and protecting the potential life of the fetus. Those interests, the Court argues, deny the mother's absolute right to abortion.

The abortion issue illustrates the importance in the development of a moral system for some clear determinations concerning the criteria for identifying moral agency and considerability.

REVIEW QUESTIONS

1. Distinguish between *acting according to* and *acting from*.
2. What are the differences between customary morality and reflective morality?
3. What factors give rise to moral theory?
4. What does it mean to act systematically?

5. Why is reciprocity a formal characteristic of a system?
6. Identify the characteristics of the amoralist.
7. Explain partial amorality, giving an illustration of your own.
8. Discuss John Dewey's criticism of the separation between private and public morals.
9. Why did Kierkegaard consider society to be amoral? What was his opinion of group behavior?
10. Identify different views concerning moral agency.
11. Explain the difference between the views of Warnock and Stone on moral patients.

NOTES

1. Keith Campbell, *Body and Mind* (Garden City, N.Y.: Doubleday & Company, Inc., 1970), p. 9.

2. Michael Maccoby, *The Gamesman* (New York: Simon & Schuster, 1976).

3. Søren Kierkegaard, *The Point of View for My Work as an Author*, trans. Walter Lowrie (New York: Harper & Row, Publishers, 1962), p. 112.

4. G. J. Warnock, *The Object of Morality* (London: Methuen and Co., Ltd., 1971), p. 151.

5. Christopher D. Stone, *Should Trees Have Standing?* (Los Altos, Calif.: William Kaufmann, Inc., 1974).

6. Aldo Leopold, *A Sand Country Almanac* (New York: Ballantine Books, 1970), p. 239.

CHAPTER TWO

Relationships

In order to develop clear ideas concerning what we are talking about when we discuss morality, it would be helpful to decide certain questions. To what extent, if at all, can we distinguish between morality and law, morality and religion, morality and science?

MORALITY AND LAW

On the one hand, the claim "You cannot legislate morality" reflects the view that morality and law are indeed distinct. On the other hand, there are laws that prohibit murder, rape, theft and any number of other acts that we consider immoral. Laws also mandate acts that we view as morally justifiable, for example, child support, water purification, elementary education, military service in wartime, and truth in advertising.

We obviously do legislate morality, inasmuch as we require or forbid by law what we judge to be morally right or wrong. So, what possible sense can be made of the claim that we cannot legislate morality? First of all, are there some areas of morality that the law cannot reach? The domain of one's inner thoughts, intentions, and affections would seem to be one such area. For example, although it might be immoral to harbor feelings of hatred toward others, there are no laws against having such feelings. Such feelings are inaccessible states of a person's inner life, rendering any legislation unenforceable. Thus, it is true that not *all* morality can be legislated.

Are there other aspects of a person's private life which, although they *can* be legislated, would be enforced at too great a price in terms of another value, for example, privacy itself? It is sometimes argued that what adults read in their own homes, or what sexual activity occurs privately between consenting adults, ought not to be legislated, in part because the enforcement of such laws would require intolerable invasion of privacy.

It was the contention of John Stuart Mill (1806-1873) that the only warranted grounds on which society might interfere with the liberty of any individual was the protection of society. In his words,

> ... the only purpose for which power can be rightfully exercised over any member of a civilized community, against his will, is to prevent harm to others. His own good, either physical or moral, is not a sufficient warrant. He cannot rightfully be compelled to do or forbear because it will be better for him to do so, because it will make him happier, because in the opinions of others, to do so would be wise, or even right. These are good reasons for remonstrating with him, or reasoning with him, or persuading him, or entreating him, but not for compelling him, or visiting him with any evil in case he do otherwise. To justify that, the conduct from which it is desired to deter him must be calculated to produce evil to some one else. The only part of the conduct of any one, for which he is amenable to society, is that which concerns others. In the part which merely concerns himself, his independence is, of right, absolute. Over himself, over his own body and mind, the individual is sovereign.[1]

However, as the contemporary legal philosopher H. L. A. Hart has pointed out, "Both in England and in America the criminal law still contains rules which can only be explained as attempts to enforce morality as such: to suppress practices condemned as immoral by positive morality though they involve nothing that would ordinarily be thought of as harm to other persons."[2] Mill, it might be argued, was not denying that some laws seek to regulate behavior that causes no harm to others. Rather, what he maintained was that this was an improper exercise of law. Legislation that compels the individual "for his own good" smacks of paternalism.

But, we might ask, should harm to others be the only basis of law? Consider the variety of laws not justified on those grounds: requirements for elementary education, fluoridation of water systems, wearing of seat belts or motorcycle helmets; prohibitions against bigamy and use of narcotics. If individual goals are not proper objects of law, should we strike down all such legislation? One response is that laws of this sort do *indirectly* prevent harm to others. For example, individuals who lack basic education or who are addicted to drugs become parasitic on society, unable to exercise sufficient self-reliance. Their excessive dependence on society creates an unjustifiable burden on other people. But then, we might counter, if indirect harm to others can justify legislation, no laws are excluded. A case can be made that whatever is done to promote good or prevent harm to oneself will have ripple effects upon society. It would be difficult to show that any law termed "paternalistic" has effects only upon individuals themselves. The appeal to indirect harm, then, can justify all law.

Another interpretation of "you cannot legislate morality" takes the form "You cannot make a person virtuous by act of Parliament." That is, you can mandate by law the performance of a right act, but you cannot legislate the motive or the disposition of the agent who performs that act. We might even go further and maintain that, when the threat of punishment is removed, the individual will return to the predisposed bad behavior.

Against this view we could argue that virtuous or vicious habits are the product of certain repeated acts. If laws effectively control behavior, in the long run they will also shape character and disposition. In other words, law is an important *educative* force. As an instrument for the establishment of patterns of behavior, it conditions inclinations and hence shapes character. Plato and Aristotle were so convinced of this that they declared the very purpose of law to be to produce virtuous citizens.

This view concerning the purpose of law might be opposed by those who assert the lack of a moral consensus in society. That is, we cannot legislate morality because there is no agreement on moral values. Countering this, someone might reply that, if we did not have some degree of moral consensus, how could we legislate at all? Laws presuppose consensus, for they reflect shared views concerning what is good or bad for people. There is no denying that on many moral questions we lack consensus, and in these areas the community is usually reluctant to legislate. Yet even here, a majority view can eventually produce consensus. Examples include desegregation statutes in the United States and laws prohibiting marriage dowries in India. Is it sound to conclude that some morality is legislated, but not all morality is, or even can be, legislated?

On the other side of the question of law's relation to morality, are there some laws which are merely penal, that is, which bind us simply because they are enacted, not because their specifications are morally necessary? For example, in deciding how to draft legislation, we might say that whether income taxes are to be paid by April 15 or March 15 is morally indifferent. The deadline is essentially arbitrary. However, what about the nature of the obligation to obey that April 15 deadline once the law is enacted? Can it be argued that it is *morally* wrong not to pay up by April 15, inasmuch as we have an ethical duty to obey valid laws? If so, does it follow that *all* valid laws are morally binding, for example laws against jaywalking, illegal parking, etc.? Perhaps the conclusion you have reached on the basis of the arguments thus far is that morality and law are not co-extensive. That is, although there is some overlap, certain areas of morality are outside the reach of the law, whereas other areas that are morally neutral have been legislated.

The co-extension question leads us into a related issue which has always been the subject of debate. Is it possible for a legal act to be nevertheless immoral, or for a moral act to be illegal? If so, does this imply that there is a standard beyond law by which we judge law to be good or bad? Is it our obligation to obey a law even though it is bad, or on the other hand, do we have a duty to disobey it? If bad law is not morally binding, does this imply that it really has no status as law?

In attempting to deal with these questions, some have made a distinction between law as it *is* and law as it *ought to be*. The latter is an expression of ideals or morality. The former, which is the actual statute law of the community, may or may not conform to those ideals. Some who recognize this distinction will insist, however, that statute law, even though it conflicts with morality, is still law and is obligatory. In other words, the existence of a law is one thing; whether it has merit is another.

Natural Law and Positive Law

Some who wish to challenge the status as law of unjust statutes, and thereby deny an obligation to obey them, make a distinction between *natural law* and *positive law*. Positive law is what legislative bodies have determined and the courts will enforce. Positive or human-made law, they say, is valid only when it is in conformity with natural law. The latter is *discovered* rather than made by humans. The basic principles of natural law specify what is required because of our human nature or constitution, if we are to achieve self-fulfillment or complete well-being. This assumes that objective facts about what humans need in order to realize their potential for happiness are as discoverable as what constitutes good health.

Natural law theorists may go further and locate the foundation of all law in God's eternal plan. Divine law, according to which God created natural beings with their specific inclinations and capacities, is for some the ultimate authority. Other natural law theorists do not find it necessary to decide whether God exists. For them it is sufficient to establish that human beings, like other natural beings, have requirements for survival and prosperity that are what they are because of the natural or genetic endowment of humans.

Thomas Aquinas (1225-1274), the most important philosopher and theologian of the Middle Ages, defined law as "an ordinance of reason for the common good, made and promulgated by him who has care of the community."[3] Consistent with this definition, Aquinas argued that a law could be unjust because: (1) its purpose is the selfish interest of the authority rather than the common good; or (2) the law exceeds the legislative authority of its author; or (3) it imposes burdens unequally on the community. Aquinas agrees with his predecessor, St. Augustine (354-430), that an unjust law is "no law at all," and hence does not bind us in conscience to its observance.[4] Martin Luther King, in his famous "Letter from Birmingham City Jail," appealed to the reasoning of Aquinas and Augustine in support of his civil disobedience to segregation statutes in the 1960s.

Opponents of natural law theory make a different claim. They maintain that it does not follow from the mere fact that a law violates morality that it is not a law. Nor does it follow that something is a law merely because it is morally desirable. Jeremy Bentham (1748-1832) protested that "law of nature" was nothing but a phrase employed to incite people to rebel against any law they happened not to like.

The contrast between a natural law theory and *legal positivism* becomes clearer when it is pointed out that the legal positivist holds one or more of the following propositions:

1. Concern with law is morally and evaluatively neutral, concerned not with ideal law but with actual or existent law.
2. No reference to justice or other moral values enters into the definition of law; law is simply the command of the sovereign.
3. The fact that a legal rule is morally wrong does not entail that it is invalid or not law.
4. Where a legal system is in operation, there is an absolute or unconditional obligation to obey the law, however unjust.
5. Although law and morals may often overlap, there is no necessary connection between them.[5]

Consider the merits of the opposing arguments in this exchange.

Claim: The law is not that which ought to be, but that which is. It is simply that body of rules which is recognized and enforced in the courts of law.

Counter: It is impossible to exclude morality from the definition of law. The ends of law are to further goals which we perceive as good. Moral principles in which we have active belief must support laws to make them effective in engaging our support.

Claim: It cannot be denied that the development of a legal system is influenced by moral opinion, and vice versa. However, the authority of law must not be dissolved into peoples' conceptions of what law ought to be. What is or is not law is determined by the sovereign legislative power in the community.

Counter: The fact is that legislative power must itself be exercised in accordance with fundamental rules. These rules specify essential lawmaking procedures. This is an acknowledgment that moral rules make law possible. That like cases should be treated alike, and that laws should be neither secret nor retroactive, are examples of natural procedural justice in the administration of law. This demonstrates that law cannot be morally neutral.

Claim: Natural law theory is not content to assert a minimum influence of morality in specifying formal conditions of good order. It also overextends itself to claims about the aims of all humanity. However, the purposes of human beings are too varied to allow such "natural necessities" to function as essential conditions for law.

Counter: There is no denying that people differ in their needs and also in their perceptions of their needs. However, there is abundant evidence of a common denominator of needs and interests which human beings everywhere experience. The people who founded this country appealed to the natural law, and the constitutions of countries throughout the world contain an enumeration of those rights and purposes which justify the exercise of political power. A document that dramatically enumerates these shared insights is the Universal Declaration of Human Rights adopted by the United Nations in 1948 (See Appendix). Violations of these rights have always been recognized as justification for disobedience and even revolution.

Claim: One may recognize a moral obligation to resist extremely immoral laws, but insist that laws in conflict with moral principles are still laws. It is better to say that "laws may be laws but some are too evil to be obeyed."

Counter: What is the force of calling them laws, if they deserve to be resisted? It is incoherent to claim that a rule is valid law, but that it does not bind us morally because it is wicked.

Claim: What makes a law valid is its enactment by a duly constituted authority. If a statute is sufficiently evil, however, it should not be obeyed.

Counter: The authority of law derives not merely from its authorship and its form, but also from its purpose. Respect for law must be respect for what the law does. Fidelity to law, therefore, must be related to the ends of human life. When statutes violate moral principles enabling people to live together harmoniously and successfully, those statutes should have no authority.

Claim: The refusal to recognize as law what conflicts with one's moral beliefs is an invitation to anarchy. Unless one defines law in a purely formal way, each individual is left to decide what is law. That situation is precisely the abandonment of the rule of law. No society can survive in which individuals are allowed to pick and choose what they shall recognize as valid law.

Counter: The dangers you describe are not avoided by claiming statutes "are still law" when you simultaneously claim that people have a moral obligation to violate them, and even to overthrow the authority which enacted them. Jim Crow ordinances, Nazi statutes, and the proclamations of madmen like Caligula are simply preversions of law. It is only by appeal to a moral order that they can be recognized as perversions. It is the superiority of moral claims that alone provides coherent justification for disobedience to measures that violate human dignity.

MORALITY AND RELIGION

Religion has historically been a powerful influence in shaping the behavior of human beings. Often what people have taken to be the will of God has functioned as the principal or exclusive norm for right and wrong. In building an ethical system, it is clearly important to establish whether there is any distinction between morality and religion. If there is, what is the relationship between them? Is it possible for the two to conflict and, if so, how do we resolve that conflict? Not only have basic disagreements over these questions been frequent, but, in what many find to be an incongruous consequence of religious belief, wars have been fought to decide what religion should prevail.

Extreme positions maintain either that religion alone illuminates the path of right behavior, or that religion is a primitive substitute for rational understanding and control of conduct. Moderate positions have claimed that both reason and faith can profitably assist humans in living well, and that it is possible to reconcile their demands.

Let us consider these various positions in a series of claims and counterclaims.

Claim: Religion is the only firm foundation on which people can build a sound ethical code. It has been well said that "if God does not exist, then anything is permitted." Religious belief, therefore, is essential to preserving the moral fabric of society.

Counter: Belief in God is not necessary for the construction of a workable system of moral principles. Experience in living and reflection upon the consequences of commitment to alternative life styles are sufficient to reveal how people ought to live if they are to be happy.

Claim: You assume that life here and now on this earth is the only concern of humanity. However, first of all, humans are created by God and are divinely directed to a supernatural end. That destiny exceeds the natural powers of humans to comprehend and to pursue. Hence, it is necessary that divine revelation guide us to an understanding of those things needed for our salvation. Second, even regarding truths which we discover naturally, more people will understand them, with fewer errors and with less effort and time expended, if God were to assist us in the acquisition of those truths.

Counter: The presumption here is that people share a belief in the existence of God and also agree on what God has revealed concerning the good life. However, neither presumption holds. Many people are atheists or agnostics. Are they necessarily without ethics? And even among theists there is an enormous diversity of religious belief. If religion, then, is to be the basis of morality, which religion? Radically different views have been defended by opposing religious sects. Moreover, there is a question concerning how we would "distinguish between the voice of God and the voices of our nursemaids (if we had them)."[6]

Claim: It is perhaps possible for a person to lead some sort of moral life without religious belief. But it will be a deficient kind of morality. William James (1842–1910), the American philosopher, argued that, in a world without God, life would be an ethical symphony "played in the compass of a couple of poor octaves, and the infinite scale of values fails to open up." He maintained that a "stable and systematic moral universe for which the ethical philosopher asks is fully possible only in a world where there is a divine thinker with all-enveloping demands."[7]

Counter: James did not claim any assurance about the thoughts and demands of this Creator, nor was he even sure about His existence. James simply argued that we needed to postulate God's existence in order to activate in us the "strenuous mood." In other words, James believed that we must assume God's existence in order to inspire our maximum effort in handling the problems of life. This smacks of playing "mind tricks" in order to get people to behave as they ought. Acting "as if" God existed is pretty much on a par with acting "as if" the bogeyman will get you if you do not behave.

Claim: You surely cannot deny that religion is a powerful sanction against being immoral. Apart from, and oftentimes prior to, any legal or natural moral systems, religion has motivated people because of the rewarding and punishing power of an all-knowing supernatural being. What can restrain human beings from the grossest immoralities of which they are capable if they have no higher goal than that of material well-being? The Russian writer Alexander Solzhenitsyn, in his 1978 commencement address at Harvard, found the roots of humanity's current moral weakness in the "humanistic autonomy of the Renaissance." He warned against viewing the world as creature-centered, with no task higher than earthly happiness. Otherwise, we succumb to a legalistic selfishness in which we worship our own material needs. What Solzhenitsyn laments is the loss of our concept of a "Supreme Complete Entity" that used to restrain our passions and irresponsibility. The return to a life of fulfillment of duty through self-restraint requires a "spiritual blaze."[8]

Counter: Solzhenitsyn is mistaken in thinking that loss of willpower attends abandonment of belief in God. There are countless examples of heroic lives lived by people without religion. It is a self-deprecating view of humanity to assume that we cannot use our own intellectual powers to discover norms for harmonious inter-action, and cannot be motivated to observe those norms unless God rewards and punishes. There are sufficient natural sanctions—namely, the happiness or unhappi-ness that results from living a moral or immoral life, and the approval or disapproval of our fellow humans—to establish the desirability of behaving ethically.

Claim: There is absolutely no assurance that living the moral life will produce happiness on this earth. On the contrary, many people who have chosen a life of virtue have suffered because of it. Furthermore, cruel and unjust individuals have frequently been successful and contented. Being moral is neither a necessary nor a sufficient condition for being happy. Immanuel Kant (1724–1804) argued that, "since human capacity does not suffice for bringing about happiness in the world proportionate to worthiness to be happy, an omnipotent moral Being must be postulated as ruler of the world, under whose care this (balance) occurs. That is, morality leads inevitably to religion."[9]

Counter: This demand that there is a life hereafter in which God gives each person what is deserved springs from an unreasonable craving for certitude in our life. It may take some courage to face up to the fact that a particular virtuous person may enjoy little happiness, but morality carries no greater guarantees than any other aspect of life. We do not follow the prescriptions of physicians because of any absolute certitude that life will be prolonged or improved. It would be ridicu-lous to argue that caring for our health is meaningless without complete assurance of a pay-off, or that all doctors are failures because in the long run we all die. We live with uncertainties in every area of our lives, not only in trivial choices such as where we should vacation or what we should have for a snack, but also in such momentous decisions as the choice of a mate or a vocation. Regarding each of these choices, who can predict the consequences with certitude? Moral rules are justified, not because they guarantee that each conforming act will produce desirable results, but because the general observance of those rules maximizes the probability of people living happily. Moreover, even when ethical individuals lack many conditions of a completely happy life, there is still one crucially important ingredient that no one can deny them, namely, the satisfaction of living a life consistent with their moral principles. To discount this is to be blind to what has motivated great people throughout human history.

Claim: This argument tends to maintain a false dichotomy in which each side defends either religion or an independent ethic as the only possible source of norms. Surely there is no inconsistency in maintaining that we can obtain knowledge both through divine revelation and through the unaided use of our natural intelligence and our senses. In the Middle Ages the distinction between philosophy and theology was based on the means by which knowledge was obtained. In some cases, it was asserted, the same facts could be proved either by use of natural reason (philosophy) or by appeal to revealed principles (theology). John Stuart Mill, who had no belief in the divine, also argued for the compatibility of both approaches. When Mill was attacked for propounding a utilitarian ethic that was "godless," he replied that, if God desires the happiness of His creatures, then "whatever aid religion, either natural or revealed, can afford to ethical investigation is as open to the utilitarian moralist as to any other."[10] In other words, the usefulness of a course of action in promoting happiness can be indicated either by the testimony of God or by human experience in living; the utilitarian who happens to be theistic can remain open to both sources of evidence.

Counter: It is true that a distinction between philosophy and theology does not compel us to choose either one or the other as the exclusive source of moral insight. However, there is a decided advantage in developing a science of morals which is independent of religion. First of all, by keeping clear the distinct sources of knowledge, we establish precisely what can be known by what means. Second, an ethic that appeals only to evidence available to both believers and nonbelievers provides a common denominator in moral discourse, enlarging the area of possible arguments which employ reason and empirical evidence. A philosophical defense of morality, then, will appeal to what is in principle available to all human beings, whatever their religious beliefs.

Claim: Reference to a "science" of morals that relies on empirical evidence looks suspiciously like a confusion between facts and values. The distinction between ethics and science also needs investigation. In building a moral system, it is important to decide the relevance of the social and natural sciences.

THE IS/OUGHT PROBLEM

During much of the twentieth century a dispute has raged among philosophers concerning the relation between "is" and "ought" claims. Some ethical theorists claim that a naturalistic fallacy is committed by those who in some way or other equate the two kinds of assertion. This issue is one among many which constitute what is called *meta-ethics*, in contrast with *normative ethics*.

Meta-ethics deals with three sorts of questions: (1) the definition of moral terms (What do such words as "good" and "ought" mean?); (2) the nature of moral judgments (Are they true/false statements, exclamations, or disguised commands?); (3) the methods of justifying or defending moral judgments (Can they be proved, and what counts as evidence?). As we shall see, these questions are interrelated, and often an answer to one will provide a clue to another.

Normative ethics, in contrast, concerns: (1) theories of right and of obligation (What is permissible to do, or more strongly, what is wrong not to do?); (2) theories of value (What things are good or desirable?); and (3) theories of responsibility (What motivates people, and what entitles them to praise or blame?). Normative issues are also interrelated. For example, a decision concerning what it is good to seek as an end in action can provide an answer to questions concerning what maxims are right or ought to be observed.

Textbooks in ethical theory often segregate normative and meta-ethical issues, treating meta-ethical questions after a full discussion of various normative theories. Other textbooks concentrate exclusively on one or another set of problems. The approach taken here is neither of these, for the reason that guidelines for building an ethical system, which is our project, do not permit it. That is, as we proceed logically to resolve the various questions that must be answered in constructing a viable moral system, an intermingling of meta-ethical and normative issues will naturally occur. An answer to the former is often required as a prerequisite for satisfactorily resolving the latter. We shall face these meta-ethical problems as they arise, so that what logically depends upon them can be seen in that relationship. (Such an effort cannot be entirely successful, since the various issues are so interdependent that it appears they must all be dealt with simultaneously. We shall try to overcome this difficulty when, after completing the analytic task of examining the various parts of a coherent ethical system, we attempt a synthesis in the concluding chapters.)

The meta-ethical issue at hand, concerning the distinction between facts and values, is illustrative. It is clear that what we decide about the relation of scientific facts to moral judgments crucially influences our normative claims about what is right and good. We must devote careful attention to this issue for, as one philosopher has put it, "The central problem in moral philosophy is that commonly known as the *is-ought* problem. How is what *is* the case related to what *ought* to be the case—statements of facts to moral judgments?"[11]

A useful distinction is made between *cognitivists* and *noncognitivists.* The former hold that moral judgments are true or false, whereas the latter deny this claim. Some noncognitivists under the influence of logical positivism maintain that moral judgments cannot be verified and, hence, that they are not meaningful. By contrast, the cognitivists claim that all moral judgments are statements, in the sense that they describe some feature of the world. As statements, then, moral judgments are capable of being objectively true, regardless of whether or not anyone knows them to be true. In the same sense that it may be true that asbestos material in hair dryers is harmful to human health, although no one may be aware of it, so it may also be true that "X is wrong" or "Y is good."

Three Views about Moral Judgments

One species of cognitivism that has figured prominently in recent discussions is called *ethical naturalism*. The naturalist holds that ethical statements can be confirmed by observation and inductive reasoning of the sort used in the empirical sciences. This is because of the meaning of ethical statements. Such statements can be translated, without change of meaning, into statements in the language of empirical science. For example, "Medical supplies should be distributed to these refugees" might mean, according to an ethical naturalist, "Distribution of medical supplies will reduce the pain and heal the wounds of these refugees." The latter statement can be experientially verified.

Objecting to ethical naturalism are those who analyze ethical utterances as commands, commendations, or expressions of feelings. The word *emotivist* is used to describe the view that identifies moral judgments with such expressions and commands. "Don't commit incest" or "Hooray for charitable donors" are not capable of being true or false, and such expressions are equivalent to moral judgments. An extreme version of this noncognitivism further contends that, since moral expressions are incapable of being objectively true, ethical principles must be arbitrary. The gap between facts and values is alleged to be such that one can only boldly assert ethical premises as a manifestation of personal wishes. Here there is no room for error, nor can individuals be contradicted in their affirmations. If I maintain that "X is right" and you maintain that "X is wrong," there is no real opposition. Each of us is simply exhibiting how we feel about X. Indeed, we are *both* "right" if we accurately report our state of emotion. Since these feelings are logically independent of facts about the world, we cannot infer conclusions about what should be from accounts of what is the case.

A third view may be contrasted with both the naturalist and emotivist positions just described. This view allows that moral judgments are not simply equivalents of scientific statements; neither are they causally unrelated to them. Rather, scientific facts provide "good reasons" for moral judgments. We can "justify" an ethical conclusion by appealing to the factual evidence from which it is derived. This derivation cannot be from premises that are "purely" factual. At least one premise must be ethical. For example, in the following informal argument, an ethical major premise combined with a factual minor premise yields an ethical conclusion:

> One should repay her debt by the due date.
> Today is the due date.
> Therefore, the debt should be paid off today.

If asked for justification of the ethical principle which functions in this argument as major premise, we might allege that timely repayment of debts contributes to harmonious societal interaction, and affirm the belief that societal harmony is a good thing. (The first support is simply that repayment was promised on time.) The process of appealing to further facts which are in turn combined with more general ethical premises cannot go on to infinity. Hence, the status of the ultimate moral principle(s) comes into question. Is a given principle itself arbitrary, or can it be proved by appeal to more facts? Perhaps neither alternative is the case. Justification must stop somewhere since, if everything has to be proved, nothing can be proved. On the other hand, in support of an ethical principle can't we muster evidence which, although it is not proof in the strict sense, establishes the principle as "reasonable"? In short, the "good reasons" approach affirms neither the equivalence of moral and scientific statements, nor an unbridgeable gap between *is* and *ought*. Rather, facts about the world provide rational support for moral maxims which are accepted nonarbitrarily because of our agreement about the ultimate purposes of moral existence.

This brief account of three different approaches to the fact/value problem lays the groundwork for an examination of the arguments mustered by proponents of these views.

Criticisms of Ethical Naturalism

An important criticism of ethical naturalism was put forth by the English philosopher G. E. Moore (1873–1958) in his well-known *Principia Ethica*.[12] Moore argues that "good" cannot be defined, since definitions require that the object be complex or composed of parts which we can substitute in our minds for the word defined. But "good" is a simple notion, like "yellow," and is therefore unanalyzable. However, "good" differs from properties like "yellow" or "tall" in that it is not a natural property of an object, capable of being investigated by the natural sciences. "Good" is thus a simple, indefinable, nonnatural property.

Moore went on to label as the *naturalistic fallacy* any attempt to define "good" in terms of natural properties which also happen to be part of an object. We commit the naturalistic fallacy whenever we confuse the nonnatural property "good" with such natural properties as "pleasurable" or "more evolved" or "loud" or "oblong." Moore proposed an *open question* test to determine when the fallacy has been committed. When some property is substituted for "good," is it meaningful to ask if that property is itself good? If so, we have obviously identified two properties which are not the same. For example, it is an open question whether what is normal or pleasurable or tall is really good. To say that an object is good is to say something different about it than to say that it is tall or productive of pleasure. Otherwise, it would be tautologous to say "Pleasure is good," or meaningless to ask if pleasure is good. "Pleasure is pleasure" and "pleasure is good" are not identical expressions.

More recently, another English philosopher, R. M. Hare, has sustained Moore's attack on naturalism by arguing that "what is wrong with naturalist theories is that they leave out the prescriptive or commendatory element in value-judgments, by seeking to make them derivable from statements of fact."[13] Let us assume that we are describing a picture in terms of such characteristics as its size, colors, composition, age, etc. Now, if we wished further to say of such a picture that it was a good picture, it is clear that "good" could not mean the same thing as these other characteristics. In other words, "Value-terms have a special function in language, that of commending; and so they plainly cannot be defined in terms of other words which themselves do not perform this function; for if this is done, we are deprived of a means of performing the function."[14]

Naturalistic Rejoinders

Several objections can be raised to the attacks on naturalism just outlined.

1. If "good" is a property as Moore described it, how do we come to know when an object possesses it? Moore said that we simply "intuit" its presence, meaning that we directly perceive the goodness of an object much as we perceive the yellowness of it. However, this contradicts our experience that we come to know a thing is good by knowing other things about it. For example, we judge that a woman is good because she moderates her appetites, pays her debts, manifests concern for the needy, etc. Moreover, if further evidence is offered which invalidates our initial judgment about a person, we change our valuation.

2. Either the moral property of an object is a function of its nonmoral properties, or it is not. The former constitutes the position of the naturalist. Now, if we claim that the moral property is not a function of nonmoral properties, then two things can have the same nonmoral properties but have different moral properties. But this is absurd. How is it possible to say, for example, that two acts are exactly the same (in terms of motive, agent, consequences, etc.) except that one is right and the other is wrong? This would be as ridiculous as deciding to buy one of two cars in the dealer's showroom, identical in all features, except that you judged one was good and the other was not.

3. We consider it appropriate to ask for and to propose reasons for moral judgments. That is, moral judgments are like scientific statements insofar as evidence can and must be presented for the decisions we make. For example, we want to know why we should think it unjustifiable for the United States to supply arms to the rebels in Nicaragua. The degree of probability that attaches to our moral judgments varies with the strength of the evidence that supports them. As a consequence, we acknowledge the relevance of discoverable circumstances about an act or object when we are forming or reforming our valuations.

4. Moore begs the question (assumes what really has to be proved) when he asserts that good is indefinable. If naturalists say, for example, that "good" means "what is sought by everyone," they contend that two sets of words stand for *one* property. Moore would object that he sees two properties. But in so doing, Moore is presuming without proof that ethical properties are unique. In any case, naturalists cannot be accused of committing a logical fallacy. At most they suffer a kind of moral color blindness. Moore, in contrast, might be suffering moral hallucination.

5. Can we know an object is good without knowing anything else about it, as we know an object is tall without knowing it is a rocket launcher? We always want to know what it is about an object that makes us call it good, that is, what other characteristics it has. The intuitionist claims that our concepts of ethical properties are not inferential, because they are not derivable from natural facts. But how can we account for the conflicting "direct intuitions" of people disagreeing about their obligation, for example, to fight in Vietnam? Is not such a decision vulnerable to facts?

6. Intuitionists might argue that one person's power of intuition is defective relative to another's. But, how do they establish which is the correct intuition? Can intuitionists account for the correlations between ethical opinions of children and those of their parents? Can intuitionists explain why needs, interests, and reasoning affect our ethical judgments?

The Emotivist Argument

Early emotivists reduced moral judgments to commands and expressions of feeling. Opponents charged them with unwarranted reductionism (collapsing distinctions). From the fact that we feel emotion in making moral judgments or that we try to influence others' behavior, it does not follow that moral judgments must be *equated* with ejaculations or imperatives. Among the many possible functions of moral judgments, might not one be to *state* how an act or object stands in relation to the needs or interests of an individual or community? Moreover, the opposition charged, people do argue about ethical beliefs. They consider it possible for moral judgments to contradict one another, and also possible for such disagreements to be resolved by appeal to weightier evidence. These commonsense attitudes of people cannot be accounted for by an emotivism which claims that moral judgments have no truth value.

Some later noncognitivists, like Charles Stevenson, admitted that people can argue about moral judgments, but they believed the relation between premises and conclusion to be merely a psychological one. Moral disagreements are basically disagreements in attitude. A good reason is simply one that succeeds in changing the attitude of an opponent. The effectiveness of a reason, then, in bringing about the desired change in attitude is sole criterion for a good reason. But, it was soon pointed out, this theory does not enable us to distinguish between rational and irrational persuasion. It is possible to change attitudes by playing upon the fears or exciting the prejudices of our listeners. It is also possible to effect change by offering arguments which distort facts and rewrite history. Are the effective methods of persuasion employed by Rasputin and Goebbels to be called "good reasons"? What we seek are ways of determining the *validity* of reasons and arguments. Ethically speaking, then, not all persuasion is on a par.

Cognitivists are quick to point out that, even if moral judgments are expressions of feeling or attitude, this does not render them immune to argument and factual inquiry. The critical point is that feelings and attitudes may or may not be grounded on good evidence. If someone ventures the judgment that "blacks should be segregated in their schooling," we are normally inclined to insist upon reasons that justify such a policy. When factual claims are offered as reasons, they need not be accepted at face value. They can be tested in the light of experience and scientific studies. We dismiss as "racist" such a judgment because those who make it are unable or unwilling to muster facts to support their conclusion. In the same way, expressions of fear, pride, hostility, remorse and the like are considered to be warranted or unwarranted, according to whether there is sufficient evidence for them. Fear is phobic if there is no real danger; pride is misplaced if the achievement is not the person's own; indignation is unjustified if the suspect is proved innocent, etc.

The noncognitivist rejoinder is that no relation of entailment can hold between factual reasons and normative conclusions. That is, a value judgment cannot follow with necessity from factual premises. Noncognitivists point out that it is a category mistake (failure to distinguish different kinds of things) to confuse descriptive and prescriptive language. Let us consider, then, the positive arguments of cognitivists in support of their position.

Closing the Fact/Value Gap

The most direct attack by naturalists on the fact/value "gap" is their claim that it is a false dichotomy. The distinction presupposes that we can neatly segregate elements of our language into pure descriptions and prescriptions. In reality, this is not the case. Illustrations of how the dichotomy is overcome include reference to *institutional* facts, to *bridge* concepts, and to *desire-dependent* or *valued* facts. We must examine the meaning of these concepts.

The claim, "She hit a ball over the fence," is a *brute* fact relative to the claim, "She hit a home run," which is an *institutional* fact. The latter presupposes the rules of baseball. Only within the context of a baseball game do such events as homers, balks, and no-hitters occur. Similarly, the physical acts of marking on paper or pouring water on peoples' heads are properly described as treaty ratifications or baptisms when they are performed in accordance with certain conventions. To say that someone undertook obligations as a consequence of these acts is to make a moral claim. But it is also a *fact* of the matter. "The president *ought* to withdraw troops from the border" is derived from "the president *is* a signatory to the treaty." And we must appreciate that such facts as "having gotten married" or "having been baptized" or "having hit a homer" can only occur within the context of institutions that prescribe how people shall act.

Regarding a description of events, we can ascertain what the brute facts are. These facts in a proper context determine whether a description is true or false. For example, it is a fact that the president promised (that is, became morally committed) to withdraw troops, if the president knowingly and willingly signed a particular document. In this case, "promise" is *both* an evaluative and a descriptive word. (R. M. Hare cautions us not to attempt a deduction of evaluative conclusions from purely factual premises by relying on naturalistic definitions which contain "covertly evaluative" expressions.[15] But he himself acknowledges that "almost every word in our language is capable of being used on occasion as a value-word.") If we accept the fact that certain events occurred, we accept the fact that certain obligations were created.

The peculiarity of the effort to maintain the is/ought distinction is revealed when realities become desiccated by an attempt to segregate their "moral" from their "descriptive" meaning. Baptism is an institutional fact, such that the proposal to analyze the "brute fact of baptism" causes it to disappear. What naturalists want to establish is that rigid categories of the purely factual and the clearly evaluative are inadequate to contain "moral facts."

Another way to approach the issue is to point out that within the realm of facts we must distingiush between those which "move" us and those to which we are motivationally indifferent. Values do not exist in the world independent of agents who have needs and interests. An act, an object, or a state of affairs is in itself value neutral. What meaning can there be in saying that any of these is good or bad in itself? They are good or bad *for* somebody or something. This view, that value is *relational*, derives from an analysis which identifies good as the object of appetite or inclination. (The preference for calling values *relational* rather than *relative* will be explained in the following chapter.)

What exists by itself, apart from its relation to any conative being, may be a value-free entity. However, it becomes an object that is evaluated insofar as it is judged relative to the needs and inclinations of a striving being for whom it is good or bad. In this context, then, "good" or "bad" signifies what fulfills or frustrates the need or inclination. The analysis applies not just to humans, but to all living things as well. Insofar as one can say that plants need water, then water is "good" for plants. From the perspective of a cat's well-being, there is a "wrong" way to feed and house a cat. Similarly, in the case of human beings, what they apprehend as an object of desire is what they consider will satisfy some potentiality or inclination.

The philosopher David Hume (1711-1776), who is much misunderstood on this point, used the word "passion" as a general term for all those affections and inclinations that draw us to certain kinds of objects and away from others. When he described reason as "the slave of the passions,"[16] what he meant was simply that people's reason or intellectual power does not discover or determine *a priori* what is good, independent of all reference to human needs and interests. Rather, the ultimate basis for value judgments is found in the suitability of any object to the passions of the agent.

Facts are relevant to value determinations, then, in important ways. What constitute the needs, appetites, interests or passions of plants, cats, and humans are *facts* about them. They are discoverable in the same empirical way that we come to know anything else about the natural world. These facts about agents will determine what objects in the environment are properly to be valued. Clearly, some will be beneficial, others noxious, and still others indifferent. Facts about objects will "move" us if they bear that relation to our interests which causes us to identify them as either harmful or beneficial; otherwise, they are morally indifferent facts. The defensible distinction, then, is not between facts and values, but between *brute* facts and *valued* facts. Both are facts. However, valued facts are those facts which are significant in that they move us. We cannot remain neutral to these facts, because they concern the fulfillment or the frustration of our inclinations. In short, facts about agents and facts about objects are inseparably joined to the correct use of moral terms. Facts which excite our appetites bridge the reputed gap between "is" and "ought."

We might begin to question this naturalistic theory. Does it suggest that whatever a person happens to desire or believe good becomes, by that very fact, morally acceptable? That this could not be the naturalists' position is manifest in their distinction between *real* and *apparent* needs or interests, and their distinction between *desired* and *desirable*. How these distinctions can be employed by naturalists will be developed in Chapter 3. Suffice it to say at this point that naturalists recognize our moral judgments can "go wrong" to the extent that they derive from inaccurate or incomplete awareness of the facts. That is, ignorance of relevant facts about agents and what they pursue can produce false moral judgments.

What the naturalists thus far have tried to show is that the false dichotomy between facts and values is overcome by such *bridge* concepts as wanting, intending, and needing. The language of morals, they contend, necessarily includes these words, which are both descriptive and evaluative. Further, there is an internal relation between notions such as needing or satisfying and certain objects. Not just any object will fulfill a need or satisfy an inclination. Also, we mistakenly describe an object as dangerous if it presents no real danger, and we falsely identify as a good person one who secretly murders little children. It is intelligible to speak of moral concepts as being appropriately or inappropriately applied. The possession of relevant facts is indispensable for this application.

Hume argued that wants determine what facts are relevant. Ordinarily our wants provide us with at least *prima facie* (presumptive) reasons for acting. This is not a peculiarly modern notion, however. In the Middle Ages, Thomas Aquinas defined "good" as "object of appetite." He argued that the precepts of the natural law derived from our natural inclinations. Among the ancient Greeks, Aristotle for example, the perfection of a thing consisted in the actualization of its potentialities, otherwise described as the fulfillment of its "function." For the Greeks, it was only common sense to decide the human good in the light of what a human is.

By nature, humans are active beings, tending to the exercise of their capacities and the realization of their possibilities. The purpose of moral striving, happiness, is naturalistically described as the harmonious fulfillment of human potentialities adequately considered. The touchstone for normative theory, then, is the nature of human beings as expressed in their basic needs, drives, or passions. The adequacy of an ethical system is judged in the light of experience concerning the extent to which life in conformity with that system is productive of happiness. It was Aristotle who observed in his *Nicomachean Ethics* that "when we are treating of conduct, it is experience of the facts of life that is the test of truth, for here it is experience that has the last word. We are bound then in our ethical studies to bring our preliminary statement of the case to the test of the facts of life. If this is in harmony with the facts, we can accept it; if it is not, we must look upon it as just a theory."[17]

Noncognitivism, then, is criticized because it abstracts feeling or state of mind from its empirical context of needs and the projected resolution of those needs in an environment interacting with them. The "vacuum-packed" feeling is assumed to be the valuation. But, as such, it cannot be evaluated. All such isolated value judgments are on an equal footing. The naturalistic critique of valuations occurs when they are judged in terms of their causes and their consequences. This is what enables them to be evaluated as warranted or unwarranted. When actual behavior and its consequences become the measure of feelings and subjective states, it is then possible to recognize idle fantasy, and intellectual controls over the life process come to have their place. When segregated from its existential context, valuation can only become hopelessly arbitrary.[18] That conclusion, however, is not altogether unpalatable to some theorists. As Brian Medlin has put it, "I believe that it is now pretty generally accepted by professional philosophers that ultimate ethical principles must be arbitrary."[19]

The Noncognitivist Argument

That quotation from Medlin causes us to think once again about the noncognitivists. Why are they not persuaded by the naturalistic appeal to empirical facts in justifying moral judgments? Recall the argument that derived moral obligations from the fact of having gotten married, or having been baptized, or having signed the treaty. What the critic can point out is that this argument does not really entail a derivation of normative conclusions from descriptive premises. What must intervene is the *acceptance* of a moral principle or the *commitment* to a social institution. The mere fact that certain words are uttered or certain physical motions occur does not necessarily lead us to the acquisition of any moral rights or duties. We might, for example, just be play acting. Or, more seriously, we may refuse to recognize the words or gestures as truly constitutive of acts of marriage or treaty ratification.

What the noncognitivist is reasserting is the duality of descriptive and normative elements in the meaning of words like "promise," insisting that the latter do not automatically derive from the former. In the descriptive sense "promise" merely means "uttering certain words." In the normative sense "promise" means "undertaking an obligation." Simply to utter the words does not entail anything evaluative. The words may be spoken by someone who does not accept the social institution of promising. It is also possible to use the word "promise" in a detached anthropological sense, as when a researcher reports the behavior of members of a tribe who are doing "what they call promising." For the normative meaning of "promise" to apply, additional circumstances are necessary. The words must be uttered without reservation by a committed participant. Thus, between the statement of purely descriptive conditions and the drawing of an evaluative conclusion there must come the acceptance of a social institution.

Another way to state the noncognitivist objection is to say that institutional facts can be derived from brute facts only if the relevant moral principles are accepted. In the example under discussion, it is necessary for people to commit themselves to the moral principle "We ought to keep promises" for any institutional fact about assumed obligations to come into existence. The reason is that such a moral principle is constitutive of the institution. Without it the words are mere words. In effect, an evaluative premise, which is really a substantial moral principle, is slipped in to draw the evaluative conclusion about what we are now under an obligation to do.

Cognitivists are not without a reply to these objections. In fact, they will point out that it is already part of their own argument that institutional facts come into being only under certain conditions that include the serious commitment to rules which define the institution. What the noncognitivist fails to appreciate is that there is no sense of "promise" in which the statement "She made a promise" states a brute fact. By definition, promising is undertaking an obligation to do something. In other words, this is internal to the concept of promising. So, when people literally and unreservedly make promises, they undertake obligations. To think otherwise would imply a self-contradiction. We do not first decide to make promising statements and then make a separate moral decision that they would be better if they were not self-contradictory. This situation is analogous to one in which a person says that "X is a triangle." In so doing she is committed to the view that X has three sides. This follows not from a separate decision, but from the meaning of the term "triangle." What is the relevance of talking about a "detached anthropological meaning" of "triangle"?

In conclusion, our language and our practice are everywhere permeated by moral realities which themselves give form and substance to our life. There is nothing subjective about the realization that a description of the structures of our life requires a recognition of the institutions and commitments that are integral to the life which is described.

For their part, noncognitivists might allow that a certain conceptual background is necessary in order to make sense of moral judgments. They need not deny, for example, that sticking out your tongue at another person is rude in the context of our societal standards concerning polite behavior. However, they may note that in another part of the world (for example, Tibet), sticking out your tongue is a friendly form of greeting. So, the act is rude only because a particular standard is assumed. To assert the "fact" that an offense has occurred must not blind us to the realization that such facts are dependent on the moral standard whch is chosen.

The naturalist will be suspicious of the possibility that this line of argument could lead to the view already cited earlier: that ultimate moral principles are arbitrary. For if claims about rudeness are relative to the standard chosen by a particular society, and if that standard is not grounded in any facts which are themselves independent of broader moral beliefs, then which moral facts are accepted by different individuals or groups will be a function of the standards they adopt. This is a matter of concern to the naturalist. It suggests that radical moral disagreement cannot be overcome by appeal to facts, experience, or scientific evidence. Whereas the naturalist has been maintaining that moral beliefs are vulnerable to facts, the noncognitivist rejoinder is that relevant facts in moral arguments are a function of our moral beliefs.

What the naturalist insists at this point is that some facts simply are not in dispute. All peoples seek happiness in living, and their moral views concern how best to accomplish that end. Moreover, what happiness consists of is not seriously in question. What constitutes human good or harm is decided by facts about human beings, and the facts about what we are can be discovered empirically. However, the noncognitivist might immediately point out that the theory which views happiness to be the purpose of moral obligations is just one among many ethical theories. Philosophers like Kant, for example, reject happiness as the justification for moral rules. Moreover, people very obviously do disagree about what constitutes human good or harm. The loss of eyesight may be judged harmful by one person, and not by another. For example, someone might consider being blinded a mark of distinction after having carried out a dangerous mission in defense of the homeland.

The noncognitivist defies us to identify a human good which is not so recognized because of the moral beliefs we hold. If anything is a fundamental precondition for possessing any other human good, it would seem to be life itself. But is life invariably viewed as good? Consider the Buddhist monks who immolate themselves in protest of the government in power. Or the spouse who commits suicide in the belief that this act hastens reunion with her deceased loved one. In short, different moral traditions generate conflicting moral beliefs. These beliefs in turn determine needs, wants, and perceptions of what is good. There is no such thing as what *all* humans want or need. We cannot rationally decide between fundamentally different systems of moral belief.

The point at which we have now arrived is pivotal in the task of developing a moral system, for we are here confronting the issue of moral relativism. Does our moral system rest upon a foundation no more objective than the customs that happen to prevail in our community? Must we conclude that, in the final analysis, moral beliefs are subjective? If so, the Latin adage, *"De gustibus non disputandum"* ("One does not argue about matters of taste") evidently would also apply to ethics. In that case, there would be no point in further efforts to construct a normative theory. The edifice is only as strong as its foundation, and the relativist finds no basis for objectively concluding that one foundation is better than any other. In Chapter 3 we will consider this issue in detail.

REVIEW QUESTIONS

1. In what respects can we, and can we not, legislate morality?
2. Contrast the view of Mill with that of Plato and Aristotle on the purpose of law.
3. What purposes are served by a distinction between positive and natural law?
4. How was the doctrine of Aquinas a support for Martin Luther King?
5. Explain the position of the legal positivist.
6. Enumerate the reasons for grounding ethics in religious belief. Then, state the objections to each reason.
7. Explain the medieval distinction between philosophy and theology.
8. What are the respective concerns of meta-ethics and normative ethics?
9. Define cognitivism and noncognitivism.
10. Contrast three different approaches to the fact/value question: naturalist, emotivist, and "good reasons."

11. Explain what Moore meant by the indefinability of good, the naturalistic fallacy, and the open-question test.

12. Summarize the objections to Moore's attack on naturalism.

13. What arguments are offered against emotivism?

14. What reservations are expressed about the view that moral judgments are expressions of attitudes that can be affected by arguments?

15. Explain how institutional facts bridge the fact/value dichotomy.

16. What is the significance of saying values are relational?

17. Contrast brute facts with valued facts.

18. Explain the relevance of facts to Aristotle's ethical theory.

19. What is the noncognitivist concern about appeal to institutional facts?

NOTES

1. John Stuart Mill, *On Liberty*, ed. David Spitz (New York: W. W. Norton and Company Inc., 1975), pp. 10-11.

2. H. L. A. Hart, *Law, Liberty and Morality* (New York: Vintage Books, 1963), p. 25.

3. St. Thomas Aquinas, *Summa Theologica*, trans. Fathers of the English Dominican Province (New York: Benziger Brothers, Inc., 1947) I-II, 90, 4, c.

4. Ibid., I-II, 96, 4, c.

5. For a discussion of these propositions, see H. L. A Hart, "Legal Positivism," *The Encyclopedia of Philosophy* (New York: Macmillan Publishing Co., Inc., 1972), IV, 418-20.

6. R. M. Hare, *Moral Thinking* (Oxford: Clarendon Press, 1981), p. 46.

7. William James, "The Moral Philosopher and the Moral Life," *The Will to Believe and Other Essays in Popular Philosophy* (New York: Dover Publications, Inc., 1956), pp. 213-14.

8. Alexander Solzhenitsyn, "A World Split Apart," *Vital Speeches of the Day*, 44, no. 22 (September 1, 1978), 683.

9. Immanuel Kant, *Religion Within the Limits of Reason Alone*, trans. Theodore M. Greene and Hoyt H. Hudson (New York: Harper and Row Publishers, Inc., 1960), p. 7.

10. John Stuart Mill, *Utilitarianism*, ed. Osker Piest (Indianapolis: The Bobbs-Merrill Company, Inc., 1957), p. 28.

11. W. D. Hudson, ed., *The Is/Ought Question* (New York: Macmillan and Co., Ltd. 1969), p. 11.

12. G. E. Moore, *Principia Ethica* (Cambridge: Cambridge University Press, 1959).

13. R. M. Hare, *The Language of Morals* (New York: Oxford University Press, 1964), p. 82.

14. Ibid,. p. 91.

15. Ibid,. p. 92.

16. David Hume, *A Treatise of Human Nature*, ed. L. A. Selby-Bigge (London: Oxford University Press, 1975), Book 2, Part 2, Section 3, p. 415.

17. Aristotle, *The Ethics of Aristotle*, trans. J. A. K. Thomson (Baltimore: Penguin Books, 1966), Book 10, Chapter 8.

18. Cf. John Dewey, *Theory of Valuation* (Chicago: University of Chicago Press, 1939), pp. 19-33.

19. Brian Medlin, "Ultimate Principles and Ethical Egoism," *Australasian Journal of Philosophy*, 35 (1957), 111.

CHAPTER THREE

Subjectivity, Relativity, and Objectivity

Everyone is at least confusedly aware of the problem to which we now turn; it is one of the most vexing in all of ethical theory. Are there such things as universally valid moral principles? Is there evidence that people everywhere hold some values in common? Or do moral codes vary from society to society and even from individual to individual? Who is to say what makes something right or wrong? In the final analysis, if I think something is right, then is it not right for me? Given the diversity of situations in which people live and the reality of change in their lives and circumstances, how plausible is it to defend objective moral norms? Does it even make sense to talk about "truth" in ethical decisions? Are not moral choices more like matters of taste than like scientific statements?

CULTURAL AND ETHICAL RELATIVISM

It is necessary to identify a number of different issues in order to achieve some clear thinking in this problem area. Those who are sensitive to a distinction between facts and values will want to sort out two kinds of questions that were intermingled in the previous paragraph. For example, the beliefs people hold about right and good are distinguishable from the beliefs they *ought* to hold. One can acknowledge that people in Puritan New England thought it proper to prosecute and execute "witches," while at the same time argue that this was an unjustifiable manifestation of mass hysteria. Similarly, a reporter might record the fact that racism prevails in South Africa, whereas that reporter's own value judgment might be that this practice is immoral. In short, assent to descriptive claims about what people value in different communities or cultures does not entail any acceptance of those values. We are led, then, to an initial distinction between two kinds of relativism, cultural and ethical.

Cultural relativism is the view that people in different cultures have different moral values and make different moral judgments about the same acts. This is a descriptive or scientific claim. *Ethical relativism* adds the claim that, in each culture, the judgment made by its members is correct; that is, if the community thinks something is right, it is right. This is a prescriptive or normative claim. Often there is an attempt to prove ethical relativism from cultural relativism, but this is an invalid inference, as we have just seen. We must return to this point shortly and consider an important objection to it.

Some of the difficulties associated with relativism are also raised with respect to subjectivism. *Subjectivism* can be defined as the view that moral judgments are simply judgments about the way individuals think or feel about behavior or states of affairs. That is, peoples' moral judgments merely state or express their own attitudes. Subjectivism can be linked to relativism insofar as, to the subjectivist, attitudes are determined by the community. If an individual's moral values are relative to the society, and if different societies have different moral values, then the possibility of "objective truth" in ethics seems unlikely. This is the contention of those who maintain, for example, that conscience or superego in an individual is an internalization of external authority.

There is a too facile tendency, however, to make an exaggerated claim here. We may admit the *influence* of parents, teachers, political and religious leaders in shaping the values of the individual. However, that is not equivalent to the claim that such prestige figures *determine* the individual's values, in the strong sense that individual values are necessarily those of the community. In fact, individuals frequently rebel against social pressures and influences. The idiosyncratic views of so-called "individualists" have often sparked reforms and even revolutions in society. We need not cite dramatic examples of such pioneers in order to illustrate the possibility of deviance from group norms; the individual who refuses to go along with "what everybody is doing Friday night" sufficiently demonstrates this point. The purported inevitability of individual behavior because of genetic and environmental causes will be examined at greater length in Chapter 8.

The Case for Subjectivism and Relativism

The plausibility of subjectivism and of relativism derives from some obvious facts about the human situation. Each person is a uniquely individual being. The mix of interests, needs, attitudes, physical characteristics, and acquired traits of that person creates a complex whole which is not identical to that of any other individual. Moreover, the circumstances in which these diverse individuals find themselves call for varying responses, depending upon the nature of the situation.

Since no two situations are ever exactly alike, it would appear unrealistic to assume that we could decide what is right or good outside the context of that unique relation of a particular person to a particular environment. Just as a physician must tailor the prescription of medicine and treatment to the requirements of the individual patient, so also must moral decisions be relative to the unique condition of the moral agent.

For example, consider the case of a child who ventured into deep water offshore, and suddenly cries for help. Can we decide without regard to individual circumstances what is the proper act for a person on shore who hears these cries? Whether the response of the onlooker is courageous or cowardly or foolhardy depends on the situation. If the child is only pretending to be in distress in order to draw attention, or if the onlooker is not a swimmer, this should clearly influence the decision about what to do. It would be foolhardy to attempt a rescue in exceedingly turbulent waters when one is not a skilled swimmer and others nearby are better able to make the attempt. However, not acting is cowardly if the onlooker is a skillful swimmer, the child is truly in distress, and the condition of the waters offers reasonable assurance of a safe return. In short, the morally proper response can be decided only in the light of a whole cluster of factors that are particular to the situation. We can leave it to the reader's own imagination to consider an infinitely large number of other circumstances which might occur in such a scene, each of which could have a bearing on the judgment concerning the morally right act.

As we enlarge the focus to include whole communities, a similar viewpoint holds. Different societies in different parts of the world labor to survive and prosper under sets of conditions unique to those societies. The size of the community, the climate, the stage of technological development, the quantity of natural resources, the history and experiences of the people, the proximity to or distance from other people—all of these and many more factors enter into a judgment about what is best for this society. Once again, it seems unreasonable to assume that we can make any universal claims about what ought to be done in abstraction from the peculiarities of the particular case. To frame a judgment in the light of particulars, it might be argued, is to abandon abstract universal moral principles in favor of essentially *ad hoc* decisions. That is, we can only decide what is morally correct on a case-by-case basis, with the uniqueness of each situation demanding a solution that is relative to that situation.

We can strengthen this line of argument by asking, "Who is to say what is right and wrong?" The implication is that the best judge is the individual or the community that is involved, and the notion that a moral authority can stand independent of the scene and pronounce judgment is rejected. An even stronger claim might be intended. Not only might we allege that only the people in the situation are the best judges of that situation, but we might further allege that there is no one correct solution. Regardless of who is deciding, we can never be certain of the circumstances, nor can we have complete awareness of the consequences of alternative courses of action which might be undertaken. Therefore, not even the individual or community involved can safely assume that a specific response to the problem is the best one possible. "It all depends."

Arguing Against Subjectivism and Relativism

What sorts of responses can be made to the claims of the subjectivist and the relativist? First of all, we might argue that the word "relative" is used confusedly. In one sense, every act is relative in that it has its identity in relation to a particular agent, objective, and environment. That is to say, acts can be described and evaluated only in relation to these factors. However, this does not require us to say that there are no similarities of situation that enable us to formulate general principles of action that can then be applied to future situations of a like sort. Indeed, without general principles of some sort, what is the basis for decision in a particular situation? Presumably we bring to bear on a concrete case the values and experience we have previously acquired. Experience of self and others facilitates recognition of the concrete case for what it really is, and values provide criteria for evaluating the factors which often clamor for priority. Justification of a particular decision is made by reference to what is general.

It may be granted that the application of general principles to particular situations requires consideration of the particular situation. However, that constitutes an acknowledgment of, rather than a denial of, general principles. Recall the medical analogy used earlier. A physician determines proper treatment only in the context of the individual diagnosis. Nevertheless, the recognition of the nature of the ailment and the presumption that treatments of specific sorts are appropriate for this or that ailment constitute a body of *general* knowledge. The patient would be unfortunate who had as physician someone who avoided medical training on the grounds that general principles derived from a history of medical practice are no substitute for on-the-spot diagnosis and treatment. In short, knowing what we are dealing with and how best to deal with it presupposes something more than mere encounter with it.

The reader is asked at this point to identify what considerations of a more general sort would enter into a decision concerning whether it would or would not be a moral duty to attempt to rescue the child in the water. It should be clear that these considerations can be brought under general rules applicable to the situation. Reasons for action have principles embedded in them. For example, to forego a rescue attempt because the water is shark-infested presupposes that it cannot be a moral duty to take a probably fatal risk.

To concede the relational character of acts in no way compels us to conclude that objective evaluations are impossible (*Objective evaluation* refers here to the fact that a moral judgment can be right or wrong independent of the persons making the judgment.) For example, a cashier in a grocery store is confronted with repeated opportunities to act justly or unjustly. A customer presents a basket of groceries and a $20 bill to pay for them. Is there any question that the just thing to do is to ring up each item as marked and return correct change by subtracting that total from $20? Assuming that an accurate tally of the price of the groceries is $15.40, the objectively just act is to give the customer $4.60 change. Although the correct change is relative to the groceries purchased and the dollar amount submitted by the customer, this does not oppose the claim that returning $4.60 is the morally right act *objectively*. If the cashier inadvertently overcharged one item, or misperceived the denomination of the bill, or in some other way innocently but mistakenly shortchanged the customer, she might be acting according to what she *thought* was right, but that does not affect the judgment that the just act was to give $4.60 change. It is even conceivable that the correct judgment is one which was not so perceived by anyone in the circumstance. Assume that both the customer and the cashier misperceive the money to be a $20 bill when in fact it is a $10 bill. The fact of the matter is that $5.40 more is owed by the customer, although neither the customer nor the cashier realizes it.

Furthermore, the fact that people often cannot claim certitude in their moral judgments does not invalidate the possibility of an objectively right claim. The state of knowledge of both customer and cashier affects what they *perceive* to be just, but their fallible perceptions may be at variance with the facts. Similarly, a jury may honestly come to the verdict that the defendant in a criminal trial is guilty and deserves punishment, when in fact the correct judgment is that the defendant is not guilty and ought not to be punished. Even the defendant herself might secretly but mistakenly perceive herself to be guilty of the crime. Psychological literature abounds with cases of self-deception in which individuals judge themselves deserving of punishment for wrongs they never committed.

Thus far, the response to the subjectivist has been that one can distinguish between what is "objectively" right and what is "subjectively" perceived to be right. Note how the question "Who is to say what is right and wrong?" misfires in the examples cited. Given the case as described, $4.60 is justly due as change, without regard to who is in a position to make that judgment. Similarly, the defendant may be innocent of the crime, despite the fact that no one is aware of it. The moral judgment, "She deserves to be punished," may be incorrect even though all accept it, because everyone may be mistaken in the belief that she is the murderer. Obviously, it is also possible that she is guilty and deserves to be punished, even though she is universally proclaimed to be innocent.

We might claim that these examples too neatly illustrate the objective/subjective distinction, since most moral decisions do not bear upon such clear-cut matters of fact as do determinations of justice. But we might just as well have said that an onlooker mistakenly decided it was courageous and proper to swim out to the child, when facts unknown to the onlooker would have modified her assessment of the situation. By the same token, a drinker's judgment that it would be temperate to have three shots might be incorrect if the drinker believes the whiskey to be 80 proof, when in fact it is 150 proof. What is courageous or temperate must be decided in relation to the facts of the situation. But this is not equivalent to the claim that no objective appraisal is possible. Perhaps, then, we can refine our terminology and say that, while value judgments are *relational*, they are not *relative*. That is, they must be made in the context of the act, but for all that, it is still possible for a judgment to be objective.

Some people are tempted to adopt the subjectivist view and deny the possibility of objective moral truth because of an error that takes the form of confusing two distinct moral judgments, one concerning the *act* and the other concerning the *agent*. Their reluctance to judge that an act is wrong can mistakenly result from a reluctance to blame the agent who performs the act. However, there is no necessary connection between the two. It is possible to perform a wrong act, but do so unknowingly or unwillingly. As a consequence, it may be that the individual is not responsible for an act done in ignorance or under compulsion. Conversely, an act can be judged to be morally right with no implication that the person who did it deserves praise. A vicious person can perform a right act, but do it by accident or with a bad motive.

This crucial distinction between judging the act and judging the agent who performs the act will be further developed in Chapters 5 and 7. The application here helps us to see that, in the examples just presented, decisions can be made concerning the correctness of what was done by the cashier or the jury or the swimmer, but that separate decisions must be made concerning whether they are worthy of praise or of blame. If we keep this difference in mind, we can avoid such incoherent claims as "I can't criticize what she did, because I know she meant well."

Some of the preceding arguments mustered in reaction to the subjectivist can also be brought to bear upon the contentions of the ethical relativist. The relativist assumes that, whatever the moral judgments of a given community, they are correct for that community. Accordingly, it would be wrong to interfere with another community's beliefs, imposing on them our own notions of right and wrong.

Two questions might be asked about this. First, is the relativist's principle of noninterference itself nonrelativistic? That is, does the relativist claim that *all* communities should practice tolerance or noninterference with regard to other communities? If so, the relativist is involved in a self-contradiction. An intolerant community must be as correct as a tolerant community, if the relativist is to be consistent. Consequently, if a community believes that it alone possesses true beliefs and then proceeds to exterminate other peoples who disagree, how is the relativist able to criticize that belief and practice? It would be incoherent for a relativist to say that all values are relative except one, namely, tolerance. Moreover, if tolerance were indeed a universal value, it would seem that other values linked with tolerance would also be absolute. For example, tolerance of other people's beliefs and practices presupposes respect for persons. That principle in turn finds expression in basic norms safeguarding the rights of minorities, ensuring democratic procedures for adjudicating disputes, and so on. It is important to understand that the general contention of a relativist is incompatible with advocating any of these values.

Second, what functions as the criterion for the correctness of a community's beliefs? Presumably, it is simply the fact that they are believed. This boils down to the claim that "X is right because the community thinks it is right." But once again, we can raise the objection concerning mistaken beliefs. If the community thinks Jones should be hanged because she is a murderer, the moral judgment relies upon a judgment of fact that may be erroneous. The same criticism applies to a general policy. A society's prohibition against masturbation on the ground that it produces insanity is vulnerable to evidence supporting or refuting the alleged causal connection. To make a judgment about the morality of slavery, we require proof that the individuals held in bondage are or are not in fact innately inferior in discernible respects. These and similar cases illustrate the general contention that "thinking something is so does not necessarily make it so."

The relativist might respond to the general contention by insisting that it holds with respect to scientific claims but not to moral claims. The relativist could admit that a community's belief that the earth is flat does not establish that the earth in fact is flat. But what has that to do with morality? The response might be, "A great deal." To the degree that acts, rules, general policies, and institutional arrangements rest upon judgments of fact, they are no more sound than is their foundation. What else accounts for the identification of some practices as superstitious? Despite the fact that an entire community accepts the appropriateness of acting in a certain manner, the practice may be based on a mistaken belief.

ANTHROPOLOGICAL EVIDENCE

Is cultural relativism itself supported by scientific evidence, since it is a descriptive claim? It is important to distinguish at what level we are considering the moral values of various communities. It is possible that particular beliefs and practices will differ, whereas the more general ethical principles that underlie those practices are common to the communities in question. For example, different societies may have individualized security systems for protection against fire, floods, crime within their borders, and invasion from without. But these systems which are specific to the various communities are nevertheless grounded upon many shared values regarding life, property, and a need to be protected against universal hazards that threaten those shared values. The important moral question, then, should be rephrased: "Do different communities have *fundamentally* different moral values?"

In Chapter 2 we considered the view that facts about human needs and interests are relevant to decisions concerning what is desirable and ought to be done. That view maintained that we are moved to act by what we perceive will satisfy or fulfill those needs. This relational character of values links the determination of good and right to the identification of requirements for survival and prosperity. At a very specific level these requirements will be affected by circumstances of geography, history, economic conditions, and other factors. However, is there empirical evidence that human beings in different societies around the world nevertheless do share *basic* needs and hence hold some values in common? It is not difficult to find anthropological evidence for such universal values. One need only consult the work of anthropologists such as Clyde Kluckhohn, Ralph Linton, George Murdock, and Alexander MacBeath.

For example, after surveying the findings in various sciences, Clyde Kluckhohn concludes:

Psychology, psychiatry, sociology, and anthropology in different ways and on somewhat different evidence converge in attesting to similar human needs and psychic mechanisms. These, plus the rough regularities in the human situation regardless of culture, give rise to widespread moral principles which are very much alike in concept—in "intent." These considerations make the position of radical cultural relativity untenable.[1]

Such investigators do not deny differences in detail among the practices of various societies. What they point out, however, is that "pan-human universals as regards needs and capacities" provide the invariant points of reference for people in different cultures. The specific and even unique patterns of behavior of a society constitute its own "distinct answers to essentially the same questions posed by human biology and by the generalities of the human situation."[2] Linton expresses this distinction in terms of conceptual versus instrumental values, providing a long list of conceptual values common to all cultures.[3] MacBeath does the same in distinguishing between formal and operative ideals. "The raw material of human nature," MacBeath states, "is the same everywhere for all people . . . In other words, the starting-point, the problem and the goal are the same for all. But between the starting-point and the goal there are the solutions at which different peoples have arrived in their attempts to give concrete expression to the ideal, and to embody it in a way of life."[4] This concrete expression, the operative ideal in each society, is measured in terms of its effectiveness by how well it meets the needs which are common to all human beings.

Since the conditions with which peoples cope do vary enormously, the adaptive responses to needs will take distinctive forms from society to society. What is clear is that at a fundamental level, the aim of these responses, as well as the limitations on the possibilities of response, reflect a sameness of nature. It was this claim, of course, that we saw so prominently featured in the natural law theory discussed in Chapter 2.

That claim is also reflected in the conclusions of another anthropologist, George Murdock. He argues that the many elements common to all known cultures suggest a common denominator.

The essential unanimity with which the universal culture pattern is accepted by competent authorities, irrespective of theoretical divergences on other issues, suggests that it is not a mere artifact of classificatory ingenuity but rests upon some substantial foundation. This basis cannot be sought in history, or geography, or race, or any other factor limited in time or space, since the universal pattern links all known cultures, simple and complex, ancient and modern. It can only be sought, therefore, in the fundamental biological and psychological nature of man and in the universal conditions of human existence.[5]

Lists of conceptual values or ethical universals include those which relate to satisfaction of biological needs, for example, a place to work and to live, food, shelter, clothing, a mate, and the securing of safety in the enjoyment of these values. Satisfaction of such needs requires the cooperation of others. Thus, the conditions of effective cooperation are valued. Good will, reciprocity, justice and fair dealing are viewed as so essential that rights and duties are defined, and submission to rules governing the behavior of those who cooperate are taken to be necessary.

In order to achieve the harmonious fulfillment of these needs, a network of institutions arises to provide organized response. But such institutions exist not merely to satisfy biological needs, for human beings everywhere have needs and interests which are also nonbiological and yet are equally essential to human well-being. (The term *need* can be used more or less restrictively. In the stronger sense, it is a categorical requirement that, if denied, causes degeneration. Beyond basic survival, there is a wider sense of *need* which includes what is important for well-being. Living and living well are not the same.)

The need for self-esteem, the need to love and to enjoy the favorable attitude of others in return, the values of hospitality and loyalty, the enjoyment of song and dance, the impulse to beautify oneself and the environment, the delight taken in games of physical and intellectual skill, the desire for knowledge which generates systems of education and communication of accumulated wisdom and practical skills, the urge to create artifacts of aesthetic as well as of utility value—these and many more are found to constitute a common denominator of values that spur the development of basic institutions everywhere. In order that satisfaction of these many needs may be achieved as harmoniously as possible with a minimum of conflict, a network of legal institutions arises. Within such networks, a hierarchy of values is established, authorities are recognized for adjudicating disputes, and penalties are prescribed for noncompliance.

Anthropological evidence suggests that the numerous elements common to all known cultures reflect deep-seated requirements of human beings as such, if they are to satisfy their potential. It has already been acknowledged that there is variation in details between cultures, but the recognition of diversity at an instrumental level is compatible with the recognition of universality at a formal or conceptual level. Indeed, were the latter nonexistent, physical and social science of human beings would be impossible. This last point should be pondered. What makes such sciences possible?

Often, there is a temptation to try to prove too much in the way of similarity among cultures. This derives from a mistaken belief that universal moral principles can be affirmed and justified only if they are universally accepted. However, there is no logical or empirical requirement for everyone to recognize what everyone needs. It is, for example, possible for human beings to have nutritional requirements of which they are not aware, just as they can do harm to themselves in ways that the state of the science does not enable them to know at a given time. Belatedly, human beings often discover that "X was desirable" even though they did not desire it. All sorts of factors can account for people not desiring what is desirable, for example, inculpable ignorance, force of habit, peer pressure, the stage of scientific development, or inadequate reflection.

We might also argue that the validity of a moral system does not depend upon universal observance, since deviance from normal patterns of behavior and development is found in every area of inquiry. No one suggests, for example, that the discovery of freaks in nature invalidates claims about normal patterns of development. In fact, the individual exception can be identified as freakish only by reference to the standard case. Therefore, evidence of aberrant behavior threatens no moral system which takes into account what happens for the most part, and is intended to be prescriptive for the *generality* of human beings. The fact that some few stand outside it may testify to the fact that, as Aristotle said, "they are either beasts or gods."

The possibility of exceptions to rules found in the rest of nature is predictably enlarged as we ascend the scale to the level of human beings, who are relatively less determined by instinct and who have the power to conceptualize the future as different from the present, as well as the freedom to act from those insights. The idea that "the exception proves the rule" applies here. What normal human beings require for fulfillment of their needs and interests controls the specification of moral principles and institutional frameworks for their implementation. That some are not, and perhaps should not, be covered by ordinary rules constitutes the basis for recognizing them as exceptions. Dealing with the extraordinary challenges normal procedures, but the presence of the defective and the gifted invalidates no claims regarding the standard case.

U.N. Declaration of Human Rights

Proponents of this point of view are frequently challenged to offer concrete evidence of at least quasi-universality of values on this planet. Some responses have taken the form of comparing constitutions or bills of rights in various countries. More dramatically, attention is directed to such achievements as the Universal Declaration of Human Rights, adopted by the General Assembly of the United Nations in 1948, or the Declaration of the Rights of the Child, proclaimed by the U.N. in 1959, or the Declaration of the Rights of Mentally Retarded Persons, 1979.[6] None of these documents claims that its prescriptions are universally observed, since a large part of the motivation to promulgate them derives from tragic abuses of these rights. Rather, as the U.N. Declaration of 1948 states, they are intended as

> a common standard of achievement for all people and all nations, to the end that every individual and every organ of society, keeping this Declaration constantly in mind, shall strive by teaching and education to promote respect for these rights and freedoms and by progressive measures, national and international, to secure their universal and effective recognition and observance . . .[7]

Specific articles in the Declaration condemn slavery, torture, application of *ex post facto* (retroactive) laws, and discrimination on the basis of race, color, sex, or religion. The General Assembly proclaimed as basic human rights the right to presumption of innocence when charged with an offense, the right to a public trial, the right to privacy and freedom of movement, the right to peaceful assembly and worship, and the right to participate in the political process with equal access to public service.

Cynicism about documents like the U.N. Declaration takes various forms. Some point to the widespread violation of its provisions and ask how meaningful a standard can be that is not observed. Others claim that the U.N. Declaration is "too idealistic," suggesting that it is somewhat utopian to advocate such lofty standards of conduct. However, *any* ideal is "idealistic." Ideals are not descriptions of how things are; rather, they provide a picture of how things should be. Of course, there will always be a gap between a moral ideal and its complete actualization. As Ralph Barton Perry noted, "It is of its very nature that there should be such a gap, that the 'reach' *should* 'exceed the grasp' . . . It does not mean that the ideal is too high, for all moral ideals are counsels of perfection . . ."[8]

An ideal might be "too idealistic" if it were humanly impossible to take steps to improve this world along the lines recommended by the ideal. However, there is no evidence that human beings are incapable of implementing measures that respect basic rights. In any case, the function of the standard is not to spell out the concrete means by which it can be realized. That is the day-to-day task of those who subscribe to the ideal. Moreover, it is important that the standard be set high. Henry David Thoreau said, "In the long run men hit only what they aim at. Therefore, though they should fail immediately, they had better aim at something high."[9] In another passage from *Walden*, Thoreau added, "If you have built castles in the air, your work need not be lost; that is where they should be. Now put the foundations under them."[10]

It is fair to level the charge of hypocrisy at member nations of the U.N. who violate its principles. However, the contrast between theory and practice should not be construed as justification for abandoning the ideal. Does anyone seriously suggest throwing out the Ten Commandments because people break them? Were the validity of moral ideals determined by their observance, none would pass the test. "Moral weakness" is a name for the character defect found in those who fail to act in conformity to values which they profess. However, when such failure occurs, it is the trespasser rather than the norm which stands accused.

However wise may be the provisions of a normative declaration, enforcement provisions are essential to its observance. A measure of any community's sincerity is its effort effectively to enforce the standards it proclaims. Member nations of the United Nations are vulnerable to criticism on this score. Whether due to the unwillingness of the superpowers to surrender some measure of national autonomy or due to other causes, the lack of effective enforcement provisions tempts us to question the earnestness of many nations' leaders. Once again, however, nonenforcement is no proof that the ideal is itself defective.

Whatever the skeptic may contend regarding the universality or enforceability of such declarations, what cannot easily be denied is the evidence they offer for transcultural values. The acknowledgment of universal needs and the widespread abhorrence of conditions at variance with the satisfaction of those needs is not easily dismissed. Only in the face of what is recognized on all sides as compelling necessity could it be possible, for example, for so many nations to gather together for a long series of "Law of the Sea" conferences and to agree to such international norms as territorial limits, fishing rights and conduct on the high seas.

The rather commonsensical conclusion of this extended argument is that the possibility and desirability of any cooperative effort at any level of human organization rests upon a recognition of mutual interest and need. Whether we are talking about a family, a bridge club, a political party, or an International Court of Justice, what is manifested by the etymology of the word "community" applies, namely, the requirement that some value or purpose be shared.

INDIVIDUAL FREEDOM
AND RELEVANT DIFFERENCES

Opposition to this line of thinking is often prompted by a concern with protecting individual freedom and also a recognition of important differences among persons and communities. Some fear that others might attempt to coerce conformity with their own notions of what all people need or how they should act. There are a number of ways in which this serious objection can be met.

1. The denial of relativism and the affirmation of ethical universals need not be combined with persecution of those who disagree. It is one thing to hold convictions about what is good, and it is another thing to coerce others to share those views. In a democratic society the effort to resolve differences, when it is necessary to do so, is characterized by rational discussion, respect for the dignity of all participants, and tolerance of those differences which do not compromise the safety and well-being of other members of the community. But it is muddled thinking to confuse democracy as a form of political organization with subjectivism or relativism as an intellectual posture. That individuals are treated with deference to their political equality carries with it no assumption about the correctness of their views. We are familiar with an assertion attributed to Voltaire, "I disapprove of what you say, but I will defend to the death your right to say it." Consistent with this point of view, the nonrelativist in ethics might insist that: (a) there are objective facts about the human situation which are relevant to moral decision; (b) individuals and societies may make mistaken judgments about what is really for their long-range good; and (c) it is absurd to believe that contradictory moral claims can all be correct. None of these views requires the nonrelativist to seek the elimination of opposition by force or by coercive legal action.

2. The acknowledgment of a moral rule is compatible with recognition of exceptions to that rule. It was earlier pointed out that rules can take account only of what usually happens. While prescribing what ought to be in view of what generally is the case, there always remains a possibility that the individual case is relevantly different and thus deserves to be treated differently. (This point will be developed at length in the discussions of universalizability and of justice in Chapters 5 and 8. It should be pointed out here, however, that similar treatment is assumed only when there are relevant similarities.) It is impossible for a statement of principles and rules to include all qualifying conditions, especially as they become more specific in their application. This gap in the formulation of a moral rule must be compensated for by the prudent judgment of those applying the rule. A classic example concerns the unobjectionable moral rule that "borrowed property should be returned to

the owner upon request." While this is a sound general principle, a moment's reflection indicates that it requires qualification. Imagine the lender arousing a neighbor in the middle of the night to request return of a hunting rifle, because the lender wants a permanent settlement of a domestic dispute. Clearly, the neighbor is under no moral obligation to return the weapon in such circumstances. This need not even be seen as a case of breaking the rule, since any reasonable interpretation of the rule recognizes this as a legitimate limitation on the application of it. However, not all exceptional circumstances can be explicitly incorporated into the statement of the rule; otherwise it would become infinitely long. To prevent abuse of the rule, the most common kinds of exceptions might be incorporated into the rule, provided that the result is a norm which is still concise enough to be teachable and learnable. For the rest, one must be content to state that, "under ordinary conditions, do . . . ," with discretion supplying the needed corrective to a too literal application of the letter rather than the spirit of the rule. In short, the soundness of general moral norms is consistent with the recognition of justifiable exceptions.

3. It follows from the above that sometimes it makes no sense to claim that there is one correct moral evaluation. Variations in individual situations give some intelligibility to the phrase, "It all depends." Aristotle's example about temperance in food and drink makes the point that moderation is relative. What is a reasonable amount of food for one person may be excessive for another and inadequate for a third. However, particular sorts of confusion must be avoided here: (a) It is possible for one standard to apply to all, even though individual circumstances warrant different acts in the application of that standard. For example, the moral requirement that people who drive should not drink alcoholic beverages to the point of intoxication may be absolute. However, what constitutes excessive consumption of alcohol may vary from person to person. Therefore, what is moderate for one individual may not be so for another. (b) This should not be further confused with the untenable position that it is impossible to determine what is moderate for the individual. With due allowances for a certain range, it is clear that there are limits for an individual which, when exceeded, create hazardous driving conditions. The law recognizes this in its tests for drunken driving. (c) Finally, the agent is sometimes the poorest judge of what is morally sound reasoning and correct behavior. The victims of an automobile accident would be disinclined to believe a drunken driver's insistence that she did not have too much to drink. The belligerent question, "Who's to say what is moderate?" loses strength as one reflects on the objective evidence which establishes correlations, for example, between body weight, amount of alcohol intake, and loss of motor skills. The subjectivist can find little comfort here. Admission that the moral mean is relative is quite compatible with objective measurements to determine that relative mean.

We have seen that objectivity of morals is compatible with acceptance of relevant differences. Thus, the dichotomy between moral relativism and absolutism can be overcome. Moral judgment is relative to the condition of the agent and the environment. In this sense, moral arguments are always *ad hominen* (personal). But this requires only that all the facts of the case be carefully examined; it does not require the untenable view that there are no facts at all. Moreover, that moral judgment is relative in this sense carries with it no assumption that the agent is correct in judging what is right relative to the circumstance. The relational character of moral truth is compatible with the objectivist contention that the truth of moral judgments is independent of the person making them.

REVIEW QUESTIONS

1. Distinguish between cultural and ethical relativism and subjectivism.
2. What facts lend credibility to subjectivism and relativism?
3. Why is the relative character of a particular judgment no argument against general moral principles, nor against the objectivity of moral judgments?
4. How is objectivity of moral judgments compatible with imperfections in human knowledge?
5. What is a response to the ethical relativist's contention that moral claims are unlike scientific claims?
6. In response to the cultural relativist, what is the significance of distinguishing levels of moral value?
7. What anthropological evidence is there for pan-human values?
8. Why is universal acceptance not a necessary condition for universal moral principles? Give two arguments.
9. What are three responses to the fear that acknowledgement of universal values will threaten individual freedoms and differences?
10. What replies can be made to charges that the Universal Declaration of Human Rights is too idealistic and that its provisions are often violated by member nations?

NOTES

1. Clyde Kluckhohn, "Ethical Relativity: Sic et Non," *Journal of Philosophy*, 52 (1955), 673.

2. Clyde Kluckhohn, "Universal Categories of Culture," *Anthropology Today*, A. L. Kroeber, ed. (Chicago: University of Chicago Press, 1953), p. 520.

3. Ralph Linton, "The Problem of Universal Values," *Method and Perspective in Anthropology*, Robert F. Spencer, ed. (Minneapolis: University of Minnesota Press, 1954), p. 150.

4. A. MacBeath, *Experiments in Living* (London: Macmillan and Co., Ltd., 1952) p. 68.

5. George Murdock, "The Common Denominator of Cultures," *The Science of Man in the World Crisis*, Ralph Linton, ed. (New York: Columbia University Press, 1945), p. 125.

6. *International Human Rights Instruments of the United Nations 1948-1982* (Pleasantville, N.Y.: UNIFO Publishers, Ltd., 1983), pp. 57 and 117.

7. See Appendix for complete text of this United Nations document.

8. Ralph Barton Perry, *Realms of Value* (Cambridge, MA; Harvard University Press, 1954), p. 90.

9. Henry David Thoreau, *Walden or Life in the Woods* (New York: Harper and Row, Publishers, 1965), p. 20.

10. Ibid., p. 240.

CHAPTER FOUR

Egoism

In constructing a moral system, we must decide important questions concerning the criteria for right and wrong action, who is to count morally, and the relevance of rules to the assessment of actions. Generally, normative ethical theories are distinguished on the basis of their responses to these questions.

Normative means that the theory is not merely descriptive of the way certain people, or even all people, think about moral questions, as might be the work of an anthropologist gathering and summarizing data concerning the moral code of an Indian tribe. Normative implies that the theory is *prescriptive*, making claims about how people *ought* to act, and presenting arguments to justify certain rules about human conduct.

Normative theories are classified as either *teleological* or *deontological*. The former are sometimes called *consequentialist* theories, and the latter *nonconsequentialist*. This gives us a clue concerning the different emphases in these theories. Teleological theories argue that what count morally are the consequences of acts or rules, that is, how much good is brought about by behavior. Etymologically, the word comes from *telos*, the Greek word for goal or end. Therefore, a teleological theory justifies acts and rules on the basis of some end or purpose that they bring about. Nonconsequentialist theories reject the claim that consequences decide rightness, or at least insist that other considerations are important as well. The investigation of both kinds of theory should help us come to some conclusions about the major issues we must decide in choosing one or another moral system as preferable.

It is common to divide teleological theories into *egoistic* and *utilitarian* theories, depending on what consequences they take into account. Utilitarianism takes everyone into consideration, arguing that what count are the consequences for all those who can be affected by the act or rule. Egoism, on the other hand, maintains that only self-interest matters. That is, the rightness of action is a function solely of the consequences for oneself. Detailed consideration of utilitarian theories will be found in Chapter 5; this chapter will consider egoism.

PSYCHOLOGICAL AND ETHICAL EGOISM

It is important not to confuse *psychological* with *ethical* egoism. Psychological egoism is a descriptive theory, asserting how people do act, whereas ethical egoism prescribes how they ought to act. Often, psychological egoism is presented as a justification for ethical egoism, but we should by now be in a position to judge the validity of such reasoning. Psychological egoism of a strong sort maintains that people always act exclusively from concern for self, because this is all that they can possibly do. That is, the strong form of psychological egoism alleges that people act selfishly because they cannot act otherwise. Now, if this were the case, it would seem that discussions about how people *ought* to act would be useless. If people can act *only* in the way that they do, then it is idle to argue about the merits of alternative ways of acting; a choice of alternatives is in principle impossible. The question of determinism and freedom will be considered in detail in Chapter 8. For now, it is enough to say that strong psychological egoism is incompatible with ethical reasoning, since the latter assumes there can be a difference between what people do and what they should do.

However, weak psychological egoism will not do as a justification of ethical egoism either. The weak form merely asserts that people generally act selfishly, that is, exclusively out of concern about the consequences to themselves. What people may do, frequently or infrequently, is not in itself a sufficient argument to prove anything about what they ought to do. That people should pollute the environment is not established by the fact that many of them do. Consequently, whether in its weak or strong form, psychological egoism provides no adequate basis for ethical egoism. Because we have already seen that facts about human beings are relevant to judgments about what is desirable, in what follows we shall carefully consider the egoist's views about human nature and the alleged facts that support the attractiveness of egoistic moral theory.

At the outset, we should clarify the definition of terms. Egoism derives some initial plausibility from verbal ambiguities and misunderstandings. A case in point is Ayn Rand. In her introduction to *The Virtue of Selfishness*, Rand states that "the exact meaning and dictionary definition of the word 'selfishness' is: concern with one's own interests."[1] Dictionaries do not support her claim. For example,

Webster's Third International Dictionary defines *selfishness* as "concern for one's own welfare or advantage at the expense of or in disregard of others." Similarly, *selfish* means "seeking or concentrating on one's own advantage, pleasure or well-being without regard for others."[2] The danger in permitting Rand's stipulative definition to pass for an ordinary meaning is that it confuses what is really at issue. The question does not concern the acceptibility of a theory of self-realization. Rather, the issue is whether integral fulfillment of human needs and interests entails exclusion of regard for others. If egoism merely means a theory which aims at self-realization, then it becomes a net so wide that it catches virtually every ethical system.

However, common sense discriminates between those who devote their lives to caring for lepers and those whose career is loan-sharking. The ordinary person perceives a difference between sharing books with others and pilfering books from the public library. Few people confuse the motive of a parent assiduously attending to a sick child with the motive of one who beats a child that disturbs his sleep. Our customary use of the terms *selfish* and *unselfish* is intended to mark the real difference between these sorts of actions, motives, and states of character. Were we to abandon that vocabulary, reducing everything to selfishness, it would be necessary to invent new language to reflect our everyday experience of these differences.

Factors Encouraging Egoism

That anyone should adopt such a monistic interpretation of human behavior and motivation and then devote endless labor to explaining away plain facts which obviously conflict with it challenges us for an explanation. The possibilities are various. One is the very simplicity of the theory. Reducing all impulses to forms of self-love is attractive when priority is given to economy of explanation. Longing for simplicity can override the most compelling evidence that motivation is complex, that constituents of the self are diverse, and that a plurality of objects motivate our impulses.

Another possibility derives from the influence a social environment can have upon the individual's values. John Dewey has pointed out that our moral judgments, our habits, and our conduct are socially conditioned. At a time when thought is decidedly individualistic and social arrangements are judged to be secondary and artificial, it is not surprising that people should try to find egoistic justifications for the behavior of individuals, who are presumed to be naturally isolated. Moreover, when this prevailing individualism is expressed in an economic theory that maintains that each person can only survive if he is a rugged individual seeking his own profit in competition with others, social approval will erect egoism into a virtue.[3]

Many have recently called attention to a current trend in psychological therapy toward a deification of the isolated self. The "new narcissism," as it is termed, arises from our desire to defend ourselves against feeling shame and guilt because of routine inequities of consumption and distribution that may benefit us and condemn others to misery. So we struggle to convince ourselves that our privilege is earned and deserved. The ground of community disappears in the face of growing solipsism, and the hunger for relation is suppressed in the name of selfishness posing as enlightenment.[4]

A third factor that encourages egoistic theory is the type of psychology that assumes inflexibility in basic motives and drives. Psychoanalysis and other genetic accounts assume that every motive of personality traces back to infancy. Against this, Gordon Allport has argued that we cannot assume motives operative in the infant or the small child to be identical with those of an adult. It may be granted that the child starts life as an unsocialized horror; it is thoughtless and demands immediate gratification of its desires. However, these egocentric beginnings are not consciously referred to self, and as the self matures and becomes socialized, a genuine transformation of motivation occurs.[5] With extension of the ego, an individual can come to find it intolerable to seek happiness at the expense of others. What Allport terms the "functional autonomy of motives" expresses this possibility of change and evolution in the motivations of the individual. The same act, at different stages in a person's life, can be inspired by different motives. For example, going to sea at first may be done solely to earn money. However, over time the adult might cultivate a love of the sea, and thereafter enjoy sailing for its own sake. The later motive is "autonomous" from the earlier. "Motives being completely alterable, the dogma of Egoism turns out to be a callow and superficial philosophy of behavior, or else a useless redundancy."[6]

A fourth and perhaps most significant encouragement to egoism, rests upon two commonplace confusions, each often intertwined with the other. The first maintains that whenever we act, we are simply doing what we most want to do. That is to say, our wants, desires, and interests prompt us to act. Allegedly, the crucial fact is that, whether we are helping an elderly person cross the street or stealing coins from a blind beggar's cup, it is self-interest that determines the act. In the final analysis, all acts are selfish because what motivates us is the interest or desire that we happen to have and that we want satisfied.

The problem with this argument is that it confuses the *ownership* of an impulse and its *object*. It was Joseph Butler who pointed out that "although every particular affection is a man's own," we require language to express "the difference between the principle of an action proceeding from cool consideration that it will be to my own advantage, and an action . . . by which a man runs upon certain ruin to do evil or good to another."[7] The appetite or the passion is in each case distinct, and the object of the one is not the same as the object of the other. The fact that both acts proceed from inclinations in the self cannot be denied. The relevant point is that in the one case our inclination is to assist the elderly pedestrian, and in the other our inclination is to obtain money at the expense of the blind beggar's own needs.

Selfishness and unselfishness are terms that mark this real difference in the kinds of character traits that produce acts of the one sort or the other. Indiscriminately to label all acts as selfish merely because they are our own is of no interest either psychologically or morally. What is important is to distinguish between behavior that is considerate of the needs of others and that which is not. Undoubtedly, it is our own desire that is satisfied when we assist the elderly pedestrian, and it is our own desire that is satisfied when we steal the beggar's coins. The egoist's contention boils down to the trivial truth that it is we who are acting whenever we are acting. What is morally significant, however, is the kind of person who is acting: whether that person is sensitive to the interests of others, or whether he is obtuse to those interests. Either disposition is obviously a constituent of the self, and the interest of the self is involved in action springing from that disposition. But, as Dewey has pointed out, "the different selves have different values. A self changes its structure and its value according to the kind of object which it desires and seeks; according, that is, to the different kinds of objects in which active interest is taken."[8]

A second confusion closely related to the first has it that everything we do has pleasure as its goal. All agents act to attain what they expect will give them the most pleasure. Since we all are pleasure-seekers, apparently altruistic acts are as much a manifestation of underlying egocentrism as any other acts. That some derive their pleasure from tending lepers and others derive pleasure from stealing beggar's coins, it is said, should not obscure the fact that seeking our own pleasure is the common denominator.

In response, it is once again necessary to point out how little is asserted in a claim of this sort. It goes without saying that performance of an act for which we have some appetite is attended with pleasure. Indeed, pleasure is the satisfaction experienced in fulfilling an appetite. We would hardly expect a person not to experience pleasure in the performance of an act towards which he is disposed. But what is important here are the sorts of things that give an individual pleasure. It has been on the record at least as far back as Aristotle that what distinguishes the good person from the evil person is not that one rather than the other finds pleasure in what he does, since both do. Instead, the distinction derives from the activities which characteristically are a source of pleasure to each. The just person will experience pleasure in doing just deeds. The unjust person will experience pleasure in doing unjust deeds. And each would experience pain were he to perform the kind of act pleasurable to the other.

What someone finds pleasurable or painful, then, will depend on his character. Consequently, it is the prior suitability of an object to an interest that determines its pleasurableness. What objects are suitable to given individuals are contingent upon the interests of those individuals. As those interests obviously vary, the thrust of moral education is to discourage the formation of interests which disregard the welfare of others (which are selfish), and to encourage the formation of interests which are considerate of others (which are unselfish). In sum, an unselfish interest is one of a person's *own* interests but not one of his *selfish* interests. It is not made less moral by the fact that it gives satisfaction to the agent.

It should also be noted that pleasure is not itself the object of our acts, whether selfish or unselfish. A cup of tea, the relief of a child's distress, the publication of an article, may each be the object of one or another act. It is because we desire an object that we will have a pleasant experience in attaining it. But the pleasure presupposes the existence of the appetite, and the appetite is specified by its object. Were pleasure itself the object of desire, what would differentiate our desires?

An earlier example should illustrate this point. When we assist the elderly person across the street, what we seek is not pleasure, but the safe passage of the elderly person. That we experience pleasure in the fulfillment of that purpose is to say little more than that our purpose is accomplished in a manner that conforms to our character. There is nothing but confusion in the egoist's claim that we did the act in order to receive the satisfaction, and that we would give up doing it if that act gave us no satisfaction. Satisfaction is not the object of the act, but a sign that the object is appropriate to our dispositions. The ethical problem is not that a self is satisfied, but what *kind* of self is satisfied. It is on this issue that the egoist's view is impoverished.

> In morals, the concrete differences between a Jesus, a Peter, a John and a Judas are covered up by the wise remark that after all they are all selves and all act as selves . . . . The fallacy consists in transforming the (truistic) fact of acting as a self into the fiction of action always for self. Every act, truistically again, tends to a certain fulfillment or satisfaction of some habit which is an undoubted element in the structure of character . . . . But theory comes in and blankets the tremendous diversity in the quality of the satisfactions which are experienced by pointing out that they are all satisfactions. The harm done is then completed by transforming this artificial unity of result into an original love of satisfaction as the force that generates all acts alike . . . . In reality the more we concretely dwell upon the common fact of fulfillment, the more we realize the difference in the kind of selves fulfilled.[9]

EVIDENCE FROM HUMANISTIC PSYCHOLOGY

The fact that the *self* is fulfilled when acts of an unselfish nature are performed indicates the error that underlies the separation of self from others. Historically the egoism problem has sprung in part from the false assumption that a strong disjunctive choice is necessary in determining our life's course. Either we act to realize our own interests and potentialities, or we act self-sacrificingly to satisfy the interest of others. One or the other, but not both. Not only have philosophers such as Aristotle and Dewey attacked this misconception, but contemporary humanistic psychologists have as well. Personality theory, which seeks to explain the development of the individual from infant beginnings toward full maturity, supports the philosophical thesis that humans are social beings, and that egoism fails precisely because it is unfaithful to this ego-transcending dimension of the self, which is constitutive of our human nature.

Philosophers today can neglect the evidence of psychology and the other social sciences only at the risk of rendering groundless their own reflections on the human condition. Although some philosophers do recognize the relevance of psychological and other empirical data, the predominant tendency is to shy away from such "naturalistic" orientations and, in the process, ensure the sterility of philosophical deliverances. However, philosophers have no privileged access to reality.

The study of humanity advances most fruitfully when barriers erected between the disciplines are dismantled in the interest of restoring unity to the complex object of investigation.

Abraham Maslow is one of many contemporary psychologists studying personality development who deplore the false distinctions that do violence to the human situation. Maslow insists that experimental and clinical evidence compels us to think holistically rather than atomistically. "Dichotomizing seems now to be characteristic of a lower level of personality development and of psychological functioning; it is both a cause and an effect of psychopathology."[10] Direct study of psychologically healthy individuals reveals that in them the satisfaction of basic needs prepares them to move toward a higher level, termed *self-actualization*. At this level there is integration of motivations and inclinations that are viewed as, and also function as, opposites at a lower level. Relevant to our purposes is Maslow's finding that in self-actualizing people the dichotomy of selfishness and unselfishness is resolved into a higher unity. (Thus the term *holistic*, referring to a perspective that considers the *total* organism, and studies parts in their relation to the whole.)

Growth emerges only from safety. If basic physiological and safety needs are not gratified, the individual will remain preoccupied with self. The growth pattern of a healthy child indicates an initial movement outwards to the environment. If not crippled by fear and frustration, the child will continue to try new things. Egocentricity at first is only a prereflective appetite for immediate gratification of impulses. It will emerge as the dominant, conscious tendency only when the environment confronts the developing personality with a conflict between safety and growth. Study of free choices in both healthy and sick individuals leads to the conclusion that, in those whose capacities are developed and fully functioning, there is an egoless or self-transcending interest in others. Self-love and altruism are not opposites. Rather, love in self-actualizing people involves a free giving of oneself, without reserve, wholly and with abandon. The needs of the other become one's own needs. For psychological purposes, we are no longer separate egos, but a single unit. The psychology of personality suggests that "this need to go out beyond the limits of the ego may be a need in the same sense that we have needs for vitamins and minerals, i.e., that if the need is not satisfied, the person becomes sick in one way or another."[11]

The social parallel of this holistic psychological theory is the perception of culture itself as a potential method of gratifying needs. The interests of the individual and of society are not necessarily exclusive and antagonistic. The challenge is to create social conditions which foster universal self-actualization. The age-old problem of reconciling personal good and common good is attacked at its root when the person is revealed as an organism whose needs instinctively draw him forward to seek others, and in the further reaches of that growth to identify with others. If the culture is itself healthy, the good pursued through collective effort will be synonymous with the requirements for psychological maturation.

Maslow's claims find support in the research of another psychologist, Andras Angyal. Life may itself be defined as "a process of self-expansion."[12] This life process embraces both organism and environment, tending toward an increase of autonomy, that is, toward self-assertiveness, freedom, and mastery. However, equally basic to human existence is what Angyal calls the "trend to homonomy." Humans strive for a place in larger units of which they wish to be a part. (This is why Angyal uses the term *homonomy*, which has a Greek prefix that means "one and the same" or "shared.") The search for integration into superindividual units indicates that life is not contained within the individual self. The homonomous tendency satisfies that level of human existence in which we need to mean something to someone else. We want to exist in the thoughts and feelings of others, so that our own life is reflected in an understanding and affectionate way. Theories that presume an egocentric organization of the individual conflict with evidence that we not only have needs, but we also want to be needed. Homonomous integration can be toward another person, toward a group, or toward a cause. In any case, the need to belong forms a community or a unit towards which our attitudes are quite unlike the self-assertive tendency toward autonomy.

> While the trend toward increased autonomy aims at the domination of the surroundings, the characteristic attitude toward superindividual wholes is rather a kind of submerging or subordination of one's individuality in the service of superindividual goals. In this latter trend a person seeks union with larger units and wishes to share and participate in something which he regards as being greater than his individual self.[13]

Personality development requires integration of the individual into the social group, and psychological theory cannot neglect this powerful source of human motivation. Homonomous expression is essential for normal adjustment. "Self-centeredness, being wrapped up in oneself, inability to 'loosen up,' to get out of oneself, is a well-recognized characteristic of many forms of personality disorder. . . . The merging into superindividual wholes, the sharing and participation in larger units, is a powerful support of mental health."[14]

Although the autonomous and homonomous trends are distinguished and can be opposed to one another, in a well-integrated person the two orientations are complementary rather than conflicting. An attempt to master the environment uncovers the need for a homonomous attitude in understanding and respecting the laws of that environment. By the same token, a loving relationship lacks quality when a partner is deficient in resourcefulness and self-reliance. For Angyal as for Maslow, at a higher level of personality development the apparent opposition of egoism and altruism dissolves in the perception of the self as one whose essential nature is expressed in tendencies to incorporation.

Gordon Allport, a major figure among humanistic psychologists, is even prepared to say on this score that true neuroses are best defined as stubborn self-centeredness. We have already looked at Allport's description of the asocial beginnings of the child. The first stages of growth are devoid of altruism. However, as the person matures the preponderance and intensity of personal inclinations diminishes, and feelings toward others grow. This is accounted for by the fact that, in all forms of human association, we want not only to preserve self-esteem, but also to establish relationships with others. Enlarging our interests to include our fellows is a natural bent of human beings.

In the process of maturation we move away from the unit of self as a center to increasingly large social units. Egocentricity gives way to reciprocity and inclusion. However, this process can be arrested at any point, especially when our affiliative inclinations are frustrated. Often the clamorous manifestations of egotism gain the upper hand when we are denied a proper continuation of the originally friendly and symbiotic relationship with family, friends, and neighbors. When affection or love is rebuffed, then hostility as an emotion of protest may ensue. However, it must be borne in mind that our original striving is toward affiliation. Encountering the environment is at first positive; we feel a zeal for approach. Anxious fear, aggression, and hostility arise only to the extent to which these affiliative needs are threatened.

Adolescent love is one example of youthful experience that rapidly extends the boundaries of the self. The welfare of another becomes not only as important as, but identical with, our own welfare. As we develop more and more interests outside of ourselves, whether in friends, ideas, associations, hobbies, or a vocation, the self expands. It is Allport's contention that we cannot qualify as mature personalities unless we have experienced this development of automonous interests in significant areas of human endeavor. "Maturity advances in proportion as lives are decentered from the clamorous immediacy of the body and of egocenteredness. Self-love is a prominent and inescapable factor in every life, but it need not dominate. Everyone has self-love, but only self-extension is the earmark of maturity."[15]

Allport is aware that a philosophy of egoism will argue that motives that at first are judged to be self-sacrificing and other-regarding are in reality merely selfish. However, consistent with his thesis of the "functional autonomy of motives," Allport insists that socialization is not simply a varnish laid over personality, but involves, at least much of the time, a genuine transmutation of interests from the egoistic to the altruistic. This is not merely a movement from unenlightened to enlightened self-interest. Ego-expansion causes us actually to lose ourselves in the objects of our interests, to go outside of ourselves and to become absorbed in persons, causes, and pursuits that cannot be accounted for in terms of self-seeking. The extension of the self which identification with these goals implies is, for Allport, the first requirement for a mature personality.

Finally, social and political implications are to be drawn from this psychological account. What Allport names *propriate striving* is distinguished from other forms of motivation in that it results in unification of personality. (The *proprium* identifies what is peculiar to the individual, central to one's own sense of existence.) Integrating drives and the various subsystems of inclinations is what characterizes maturity. Harmonious integration of interests resolves conflicts and reduces the possibility of such conflicts within a given individual. And in similar fashion, the enlargement of interests which causes the individual increasingly to identify with the needs of others reduces the possibility of conflict in social intercourse. As a consequence, the ethical ideal, both on a national and on an international level, is the resolution of conflict through progressive enlargement of interest systems. The United Nations, Allport points out, is organized expressly for that purpose.

There is an impressive list of other contemporary psychologists whose theories of personality development bear strong family resemblances to those of Maslow, Angyal, and Allport. Perhaps it is not necessary for our purposes to do more than suggest the areas of agreement. Carl Rogers, for example, indicates that from his experience of engaging in therapy with disturbed and troubled people, he has learned of their deep need for affiliation and communication with others. Once such individuals are freed from defensiveness, they exhibit increasing openness to the whole range of their needs. The problems of socialization and control of aggressive impulses diminish. As a disturbed person becomes more fully himself, that is, "as he becomes more open to all his impulses, his need to be liked by others and his tendency to give affection will be as strong as his impulses to strike out or to seize for himself."[16]

Similarly, as a consequence of her psychoanalytic work with neurotic persons, Karen Horney has written extensively on healthy human growth and its opposite. Because of unfavorable environmental factors, especially those which discourage a feeling of belonging, neurotic individuals develop a basic anxiety, or a sense of isolation and helplessness, in a world they view as hostile. Out of these feelings they develop an urgent need to lift themselves above others. Thus they become alienated from their real selves, concerning which they feel no self-confidence. Instead, neurotics construct idealized images of themselves endowed with exalted powers. The hopeless attempt to actualize this fictitious self has been labeled by Horney as the "search for glory."[17]

Not suprisingly, then, a characteristic of neurotic claims is egocentricity. Neurotics, torn by conflicts and driven by unrealistic psychic needs, *must* be the most intelligent, the most attractive, most entitled to special attention, victorious in any argument, and least at fault for any mishap. Neurotic selfishness places continual and exorbitant demands upon others who, however, are not seen to have needs and desires which establish any legitimate claims on their parts. After all, the neurotic sees himself as so far superior to everyone else that his rights take precedence, and his needs are more deserving of immediate attention.

In sum, the pride system of neurotics removes them from other human beings by making them egocentric. Unrealistic about themselves, they are also unrealistic about others. Horney concludes:

> the inner psychic process which is the neurotic equivalent to healthy, human striving is tragic. Man under the pressure of inner distress reaches out for the ultimate and the infinite which—though his limits are not fixed—it is not given to him to reach; and in this very process he destroys himself, shifting his very best drive for self-realization to the actualization of his idealized image and thereby wasting the potentialities he actually possesses.[18]

Erik Erickson, another leading figure in the field of psychoanalysis, identifies eight stages of development in describing the lifecycle. In so doing he emphasizes the growth toward ego-transcendence which has been stressed by all the other researchers we have discussed. Thus, in stage six Erickson finds that young adults, emerging from the search for, and the insistence on, identity, are eager and willing to fuse their identities with those of others. Ready for intimacy, they are willing to commit themselves in ways that may call for significant sacrifices. In the next stage, what Erickson terms *generativity*, or a concern to establish and guide the next generation, displays itself. However, the "ability to lose oneself in the meeting of bodies and minds" with its consequent "gradual expansion of ego-interests" and "libidinal investment in that which is generated" can be retarded. Once again, defective childhood experiences, especially "self-love based on a too strenuously self-made personality" can block development of this essential stage in psychosexual and psychosocial actualization.[19]

In concluding this discussion of psychological theory on the nature and origin of egoism as an aberrant maturational phenomenon, it is important to note what is *not* being asserted. Nowhere is the claim made that ego-expansion, propriate striving, homonomous tending, or the like imply a denial or rejection of self in favor of others. Instead, egoism's presumption of a dichotomous conflict between self and others is viewed as a symptom of psychopathology. In healthy human striving, the real potentialities of the individual are gradually brought to actualization. It is indeed the self that is realized, but this self is one whose natural tendency is towards identification with others. The love of self, unless neurotic, is not opposed to, but rather is fused with, love of fellow beings.

Erich Fromm in *Man for Himself* has argued that "love for oneself and for others in principle is conjunctive," so that "the affirmation of one's own life" is "rooted in one's capacity to love."[20] Selfishness should not be confused with self-love, for they are actually opposites. The selfish person in fact hates himself. Were he to possess an adequate self-concept, he would not hesitate to exercise his capacity to love others. In short, traditional doctrines that have identified virtue with self-denial or self-sacrifice or selflessness have presented a false dilemma.

Humanistic ethics builds upon psychological awareness that integrated personality development implies no disjunction of self-interest and interest in others. The bottom line is that human nature is a social nature. Individual fulfillment cannot in principle be opposed to regard for others, since the needs and interests of individuals necessarily carry them beyond themselves and toward community with fellow humans. This conclusion contends that both psychological egoism and ethical egoism are unacceptable. Neither do people in fact always act selfishly, nor should they. The latter claim follows from all that has been said concerning the failure of such behavior to promote self-fulfillment. If this "fact" is considered by some to be insufficient to ground a "value," then they are left with the difficult task of establishing a credible set of norms that ignores what people want and need because of their species characteristics.

FRIENDSHIP AS A TEST CASE

That this reading of various philosophical and psychological theorists should take us back to a thesis which appears to be little more than a quote from Aristotle should cause no discomfort to the unprejudiced mind. If it is human nature we are talking about, observations made by a Greek over 2,000 years ago should not be falsified merely by the passage of time. Of course, it would be absurd to maintain that there has not been scientific progress in knowledge of the human species. Nevertheless, many of the insights grounded in experience which Aristotle has left us seem only to be confirmed in the findings of contemporary social science. Aristotle devoted two sections of his *Nicomachean Ethics* to a discussion of friendship, and it is there that we find a paradigm of the mature human being similar to the one humanistic psychologists describe. For it is in Aristotle's doctrine of friendship that we find admirably reconciled the apparent duality of the individual's striving towards self-perfection with that individual's nature as a social being. The good person is the same as the true friend, so that to fail to appreciate the role of friendship in Aristotle is to lack understanding of virtue in operation. It is in the activities of virtuous friends that we may discover the most sublime achievement of human potential. The claim of the contemporary psychologists that we have just considered are fully confirmed in Aristotle's analysis of love in friendship of virtue.

Aristotle defines three kinds of friendship early in Book VIII of *Ethica Nicomachea*, indicating immediately his belief in the non-egocentric nature of true friendship. *Friendship of utility* and *friendship of pleasure* differ from *friendship of virtue* inasmuch as the former love "for the sake of what is good for themselves."[21] The friend is loved because he is pleasant or useful, and such friendship easily dissolves when this service to self is no longer needed or available. Even vicious persons can enjoy friendships of these sorts. Virtue is not requisite, for example, if people are friends because of their usefulness to one another in business deals. The same is true when pleasure is the object, as when we value a friend because he is a good drinking companion. In contrast, perfect friendship can exist only between good people. The distinguishing characteristic of this kind of friendship is that a friend is loved for his own sake (1156b9). The friend is good and, hence, what we love in the friend is intrinsic rather than incidental.

Of course, goodness or virtue may vary from individual to individual. Consequently, even within character-friendships there will be differences of degree, and friends of this sort are prepared to assist one another in becoming more virtuous. We must keep in mind, however, the purpose of this assistance, "for in purpose lies the essential element of virtue and character" (1163a23). In a true friendship, we desire the other's good for his own sake. This is why in true friendship, the friends have little cause for complaint. Who can complain of a friend who wills our own good? Lesser friendships are full of complaints because "they use each other for their own interests" and each wants "to get the better of the bargain" (1162b16).

Noble or virtuous friendship rises above such wrangling, for the essence of this relationship consists in loving rather than in being loved (1159a33). What is of value in lesser friendships is not sacrificed in noble friendship, however, inasmuch as "the good man is at the same time pleasant and useful" (1158a33). Delighting in the admirable qualities of the beloved, noble friends naturally wish to spend their time in one another's company, since "there is nothing so characteristic of friends as living together" (1157b19). Preferring the society of one another to all other things, noble friends clearly utilize one another. The friends seek to transfer to themselves the traits they admire in each other, and in this case those traits are truly admirable. It is in association with virtuous friends that we ourselves grow in virtue. The good will of virtuous friends is unquestionable, for their character requires that they seek others to be the object of their beneficence. The subtle reconciliation of self-love and love for another reveals itself once again. The "good man will need people to do well by" (1169b14). Consequently, in conferring benefits upon another he is satisfying his own needs.

In Chapter 8 of Book IX Aristotle tackles the problem of egoism. "The question is also debated," he says, "whether a man should love himself most, or some one else" (1168a28). He responds to this question with a distinction. The prevailing type of self-love is rightly a matter of reproach, for lovers of self in the bad sense "assign to themselves the greater share of wealth, honours and bodily pleasures" (1168b16). However, true lovers of self, unlike most individuals, will assign to themselves "the things that are noblest and best" (1168b29). Good people wish to excel in virtuous deeds. What are objects of competition for most people are of no consequence to them. They gladly dispense with these in order that they may accomplish that which is finest in their nature. What good people *want* to do in life is identical with what people, morally speaking, *ought* to do. It follows that good people should be lovers of self, for their nature is lovable. In fulfilling their wants, which are to perform noble acts, they simultaneously profit themselves and benefit others.

It is no mystery, then, why good people will sacrifice so much for a friend. They identify their own good with the good of the one they love. Their unselfishness is exhibited, first of all, in the willingness to share material possessions. "What friends have is common property" (1168b7). But it extends beyond this. Good people make the best friends, because in each partner there is so much that is worthy of love. The things of which they approve are the same. Whether in times of good fortune or in times of adversity, friends will seek out one another, for they are prepared to share sorrows as well as joys. What strikes the egoist as most paradoxical—the willingness of a noble person even to die for the sake of a friend—presents no problem to Aristotle. It has already been established that the good individual loves in himself the disposition to virtuous acts. Therefore, he will choose nobility before all else. If circumstances require that his life be lost in the service of those he loves, then a good person will choose the greater prize. In sacrificing his life for his friend, he becomes noble (1169a18-36).

That this doctrine of friendship should be judged by some as unacceptable or even impossible of implementation would not strike Aristotle as surprising. Fundamental to his ethical theory is the conviction that people's habits determine what they find desirable. The sources of pleasure of a good person differ from those of an evil person. Ideal friendship will not attract a person lacking in those qualities by which Aristotle defines virtuous living.

Indeed, we must concede that for some individuals it is not possible to be a noble friend. Recall Maslow's point that a person will not attempt or be capable of transcending the self unless deficiency needs are satisfied, unless basic needs for security and a sense of belonging are fulfilled. Similarly, Aristotle would argue that unselfish friendship is an attainable good only for those properly disposed. This "peak experience" is not species-wide, but rather is idiosyncratic in the sense that only when requisite qualifications are fulfilled does this higher value become desirable, pleasurable, or even possible.

Aristotle maintains that "as a man is to himself, so is he to his friend" (1171b32). If an individual does not find his own self desirable, he will not be able to find a friend's self desirable. Now, some people have good reason not to love themselves. A loveable self is created through the cultivation of praiseworthy qualities. Psychology reveals how significant early childhood experiences are in the development of wholesome personality characteristics. If Fromm is correct in arguing that the selfish person is actually one who hates himself, then surely for him to expand the boundaries of self into the relationship of friendship which Aristotle describes is impossible. However, even people who are properly disposed for noble friendship will not have many friends. It is Aristotle's belief that love, an emotion of affection carried to a point of intensity, can only be felt for one or at most a few. A considerable investment of time and attention is necessary to acquire experience of the other and to become familiar with him. Finally, the intimate manner of their living together, sharing so completely their interests, their joys, and their griefs, means that "great friendship can only be felt toward a few people," and that "the famous friendships of this sort are always between two people" (1171a13-15).

In conclusion, friendship of this sort could only have been described, as Aristotle has done it, by someone who has had that experience. Readers of Aristotle's account are likely to be skeptical unless they too have shared a similar experience. Nevertheless, whether attested to by Aristotle or by the self-actualizers of Maslow's clinical practice, the experience establishes the possibility of genuine unselfishness in human relations. That the experience is desirable is premised upon the idea that a harmony of interests between people provides hope for human happiness in society.

As Ralph Barton Perry has put it, "It is not to be supposed that personal integration or even self-love is necessarily selfish. The several interests of the same subject may be interests in the interests of another subject." Perry goes on to point out that conflicts in society can be reduced when love establishes an integration of wills which are social in their object. "What we require is a *personal* integration that shall be *socially qualified*, or that shall guarantee a harmonious fulfillment of all interests."[22]

Perry's call for love and universal benevolence creates uneasiness in many philosophers as well as in many social scientists. Allport has found "a persistent defect of modern psychology" to lie in its "failure to make a serious study of the affiliative desires and capacities of human beings." Allport explains this "flight from tenderness" by the feeling that it is "more tough-minded to study discord. The scientist fears that, if he looks at affiliative sentiments, he may seem sentimental; if he talks about love, he may seem emotional; and if he studies personal attachments, he may appear personal." [23]

Perhaps, if this is an age of liberation from sexism, the chauvinistic attribution of "femininity" to such characteristics as considerateness, benevolence, or sympathy will slowly erode. Perhaps, too, we shall overcome the assumption that survival and prosperity in this world require "manly" traits of power-seeking, impassivity, and egocentrism. Dewey is correct in arguing that "the very problem of morals is to form an original body of impulsive tendencies into a voluntary self in which desires and affections center in the values which are common; in which interest focuses in objects that contribute to the enrichment of the lives of all." [24]

The viewpoints of Aristotle, the Gospels, and humanistic psychology converge in affirming the ideal that we "should love others as we love ourselves." It is the practical task of our social institutions to generate the kind of self that finds this ideal both possible and appealing. To the extent that social institutions, whether political or economic or educational, are not constituted so as to accomplish this purpose, a more radical reform is needed—a reconstitution of our institutions so that they present models expressive of this higher potential in our human nature.

FURTHER ARGUMENTS AGAINST EGOISM

Before concluding this chapter on egoism, we will briefly consider other arguments that have been raised against the psychological and ethical egoist. Recall that one claim made by psychological egoists in defense of their theory is that "everybody always does what he wants to do." We have already seen that one objection to that line of reasoning is the triviality of the assertion, since what is morally significant is the nature of the desire. That we are agents whose wants are fulfilled in action does not alter the fact that those acts are morally distinguishable by way of the objects of those wants.

A further objection to this claim of the egoist takes the form of showing that it is not an empirical thesis. That is, we may ask what would count as observational evidence against the theory. Presumably nothing could. Whatever example of non-egoistic behavior were proposed, the theory would insist upon its being egoistic simply because it was done. The fact that, in principle, it is impossible to disprove the hypothesis proves that it is not an empirical psychological theory at all. The egoist has tried to win the argument simply by a definition of terms. This is a hollow victory, however, since it renders evidence irrelevant and reveals the theory to be only *a priori*.

If we do proceed empirically, however, the egoist is confronted with a third difficulty. In ordinary language we often speak of doing not what we *want* to do, but what we think we *should* do. For example, someone might say, "I don't really want to stay home and babysit with my little brother, but I ought to, since I promised my parents I would." The egoist would be quick to point out that he is still acting on a want, namely, to keep a promise. So, he is simply acting on the basis of the stronger want. However, this will not do, since it once again confuses the issue. There is a straightforward sense of "wanting" such that, if we promise to do X, and yet we do not want to do it, it is false to say that we want to do it. In other words, in our ordinary experience there can be a conflict between wanting and feeling obligated. If the egoist tries to collapse the distinction by treating "feeling obligated" as just another want, we must insist that some other language be agreed upon that expresses this distinction, real enough in daily life, which explains the act of fulfilling a moral obligation that is in conflict with another kind of want. Even if we allow all these promptings to be gathered under the umbrella of wants, this does not render moral discrimination impossible. We can still describe a want as selfish (reneging on the promise to babysit in order to go out to a party) or as unselfish (sticking by a promise to help our parents, thus sacrificing a Friday night out with the gang). In contrast, what we find in the egoist is an attempt indiscriminately to gloss over real differences in behavior and motivation that ordinary language identifies by means of a distinction between selfishness and unselfishness.

An attack on egoism from another direction seeks to show that it lacks a necessary feature of any moral system, namely, *general applicability*. Just as it makes no sense to talk about a legal system that applies to just one individual, so too we cannot talk of a moral system that is applicable only to one agent. Consistency requires that in applying any principle or set of principles we treat similar cases similarly. Can the ethical egoist's principle be universalized? The prescription of universal ethical egoism would read something like, "Everyone ought to act selfishly,"—that is, exclusively from self-interest as opposed to the interests of others. However, it cannot be in the self-interest of the egoist to promote universal ethical egoism. For he would be encouraging others to act in their own self-interest when that would conflict with his own. It is not in his own selfish interest publicly to express support for behavior that opposes his own interests. In short, the inconsistency of the egoist is revealed in the attempt to universalize his maxim. The egoist does only what is in his own self-interest. That cannot include advising others to act in their own self-interest, rather than his.

Finally, an essential purpose of a moral system is to provide solutions to conflicts of interest. Were everyone to act consistently without regard for others, and were everyone exclusively concerned with promoting selfish interests even at the expense of others, life together on this planet would be, in the words of Hobbes, "solitary, poor, nasty, brutish, and short."[25] It is, then, in our interest as social beings to devise and observe rules that are superior in an important sense. They override reasons of self-interest in those cases in which everyone's behaving according to his own self-interest would be harmful to all. A moral system must contain principles that everyone observes, because they are in the interest of all members of society. The egoist might argue that it is self-contradictory to urge the overriding of self-interest in the name of self-interest. But the paradox can be easily explained.

Once again, what must be distinguished are two kinds of self-interest. On the one hand, there is the self whose long-range, integral fulfillment requires the cooperation of others, their love as well as their division of labor. An interest in the self so conceived (let us call it self-interest #1), prohibits behavior that tramples upon the legitimate expectations of others who are similarly striving for self-fullfillment in the community. This view of self-interest is in opposition to the egoist's view that we should pursue our advantage in disregard of, or at the expense of, that of others (let us call that self-interest #2). In other words, it is not in our self-interest #1 to act from self-interest #2.

An illustration will highlight the contrast. Every society recognizes that an important function is served by a judicial system of some sort. There must be provision for judges, jury, or some structure to mediate disputes and determine priorities when conflicts arise. It is in the interest of all that an orderly and peaceful mechanism be in place to deal with these situations. However, it is accepted by all who understand how such a judicial system works that decisions rendered by those arbitors may not always be to our own advantage, insofar as it may be in conflict with another's advantage. One litigant will win the case, and the other will lose. It is foolish to claim that we are obligated to accept the decisions of judge and jury only when we win. That implies the abandonment of a system of peacefully adjudicating disputes. Notice what we have, then. It is in our self-interest #1 to accept an institutional arrangement, the effect of which may be to require submission to decisions unfavorable to our self-interest #2.

We should not find this too perplexing. A moment's reflection will show that many advantageous societal arrangements are similar. It is in the interest of all, for example, to develop a mutual defense system. However, the necessary condition for fulfillment of that interest is that each of us be prepared to risk personal safety when called upon to be a defender of the community. There are, then, rules which require subordination of self-interest when it conflicts with an important good for the entire community. Only by the general observance of such rules does each of us stand a better chance of living a peaceful, happy existence. However, the egoist is at a loss to provide such a solution to conflicts of interest. If you doubt this, try to formulate the egoist's advice to the unsuccessful litigant in a court case, or to a citizen drafted to fight at the front in wartime.

A refutation of egoism is not an attack on self-love. Rather, self-love and the love of others are, in principle, *conjunctive* rather than *disjunctive*. Consistent with this view, the kind of denial of self that has sometimes been perceived as a virtue is actually a character defect at the opposite extreme from selfishness. In Chapter 7 there will be an explanation of the classical theory of moral virtue, which represents moral virtue as occupying a mean or middle position between opposing extremes, both of which are vices. Applied to this discussion, unselfish self-love is a virtue located in the mean between the extremes of selfishness and self-hate.

The vice of self-hate may motivate someone to subordinate his own interest to that of others at every turn. He perceives the self as unworthy, and others as fitting objects of service. Even the logic of this position is faulty. How can we regard it as virtuous to love humanity and yet despise ourselves? After all, the self possesses the same qualities of personhood that inspire love of others.

Psychologically, the person who finds it most difficult to love others is the person who hates himself. Low self-esteem is an impediment to generous sharing of self with others, since the self is perceived as lacking in anything that deserves to be shared. Spiritual writers and moralists who have counselled thoroughgoing self-denial are guilty of false dichotomizing. It is not true self-love but rather self-hate that opposes love of others. In short, the worthy interests of others are not best served by becoming a "doormat." This is apparent in child education, where parents sometimes view their self-denial as manifesting genuine love of their children. Opposed to this tendency is the insight that wholesome childhood development includes learning self-restraint in the demands and expectations placed upon parents. Children acquire a more balanced view of relations with others when they see others as persons to be served as well as persons who serve them. The person who is "all bleeding heart and no bloody head" serves no one's interests well.

REVIEW QUESTIONS

1. Distinguish between teleological and deontological theories.
2. What is the difference between ethical and psychological egoism? Distinguish weak and strong forms of the latter.
3. Why is neither form of psychological egoism a basis for ethical egoism?
4. What is an objection to Ayn Rand's definition of selfishness?
5. What factors encourage egoistic theories?
6. Explain the significance of distinguishing between ownership of an impulse and its objects.
7. For what two reasons is it misleading to argue for egoism on the grounds that everyone seeks pleasure?
8. What false dichotomy is overcome by emphasis on humans as social beings?
9. Explain the following concepts:
   Maslow: holistic self-actualization
   Angyal: homonomous tending
   Allport: propriate striving
   Horney: search for glory
   Fromm: the conjunction of loves
10. What is meant by claiming that egoism is an "aberrant maturational phenomenon?"
11. Distinguish three kinds of friendship in Aristotle. What are the characteristics of noble friendship?
12. What are three objections to the claim that "everybody always does what he wants to do"?
13. What is the difficulty in universalizing ethical egoism?
14. Explain the kind of self-interest found in providing for a jury system and a mutual defense system, as contrasted with egoistic self-interest.

NOTES

1. Ayn Rand, *The Virtue of Selfishness* (New York: The New American Library, Inc., 1964), p. vii.

2. *Webster's Third New International Dictionary* (Springfield, Mass.: G. and C. Merriam Company, Publishers, 1967), p. 2060.

3. John Dewey, *Theory of the Moral Life*, ed. Arnold Isenburg (New York: Holt, Rinehart & Winston, 1960), pp. 163-4.

4. See Peter Marin, "The New Narcissism," *Harper's*, 251, no. 1505 (October 1975), 45-49. Also, Christopher Lasch, *The Culture of Narcissism* (New York: W. W. Norton & Co., Inc., 1979).

5. Gordon W. Allport, *Becoming* (New Haven: Yale University Press, 1955), pp. 28-30.

6. Gordon W. Allport, *Personality* (New York: Henry Holt & Co., 1937), p. 206.

7. Joseph Butler, *Fifteen Sermons Preached at the Rolls Chapel* (London: G. Bell & Sons, Ltd., 1914), pp. 168-9.

8. Dewey, *Theory of the Moral Life*, p. 159.

9. John Dewey, *Human Nature & Conduct* (New York: The Modern Library, 1957), pp. 136-7.

10. Abraham Maslow, *Towards a Psychology of Being* (New York: D. Van Nostrand Co., 1968), p. 207.

11. Abraham Maslow, *Motivation & Personality* (second edition; New York: Harper & Row, Publishers, 1970), p. 194.

12. Andras Angyal, *Neurosis and Treatment: A Holistic Theory* (New York: John Wiley & Sons, Inc., 1965), p. 5.

13. Andras Angyal, *Foundations for a Science of Personality* (New York: Viking Press 1969), p. 172.

14. Ibid., p. 179-80.

15. Gordon Allport, *Pattern & Growth in Personality* (New York: Holt, Rinehart & Winston, 1961), p. 285.

16. Carl Rogers, *On Becoming a Person* (Boston: Houghton Mifflin Co., 1961), p. 194.

17. Karen Horney, *Neurosis and Human Growth* (New York: W. W. Norton & Co., 1950), p. 24.

18. Ibid., p. 377.

19. Erik H. Erikson, *Childhood and Society* (second edition; New York: W. W. Norton and Co., 1963), p. 267.

20. Erich Fromm, *Man For Himself* (Greenwich, Conn.: Fawcett Publications, Inc., 1947), p. 135.

21. Aristotle, *Ethica Nicomachea*, trans. W. D. Ross (New York: Random House, 1941), 1156a15. For the remainder of this chapter, all quotations from Aristotle will be immediately followed by Bekker numbers for purposes of locating passages in the Ross translation, which is the standard method of citing specific lines from Aristotle's works.

22. Ralph Barton Perry, *General Theory of Value* (Cambridge, Mass.: Harvard University Press, 1967), p. 676.

23. Gordon Allport, *Personality and Social Encounter* (Boston: Beacon Press, 1964), p. 220.

24. Dewey, *Theory of a Moral Life*, p. 168.

25. Thomas Hobbes, *Leviathan*, ed. Michael Oakeshott (Oxford: Basil Blackwell, 1960), Part 1, Chap. 13, p. 82.

CHAPTER FIVE

Utilitarianism

In Chapter 4 it was argued that an essential fact about the self is its *social* character. We need to relate to others, not only in order to satisfy our material interests, but also to satisfy a compelling psychological inclination to create bonds of affection with others. Given this fact, it is possible to establish that enlightened self-interest disposes us, not to egoism, but to an ethical theory that incorporates the affiliative dimension of the self. This leads us to a discussion of *utilitarianism*. Utilitarianism is a teleological theory which regards the end of action to be "general happiness" and which judges praiseworthy those acts, dispositions, rules, and institutions which maximize the happiness of all who are affected by them.

Some philosophers have argued that the very object of morality is to extend our sympathies.[1] That is, the sufferings and deprivations to which humanity is vulnerable can be mitigated by the cultivation of benevolent sentiments. A tendency to be concerned exclusively with ourselves or with only a limited number of others contributes to a human situation in which there are uncertainties and frustrations. If our sympathies are restricted, there can be no assurance that when we are in need there will be others to respond to that need. Also, when it is to the advantage of one party to act aggressively against another, the likelihood is that there will be aggression. Indifference to the needs and interests of others will encourage discrimination, the infliction of needless pain, and neurotic insecurity all around. The great concern of morality, then, is to combat this propensity to exclusivity of concern. A direct way to counter exclusionary tendencies is to cultivate and inculcate *sympathy*, the etymological meaning of which is "to feel with." This is the thesis of utilitarianism—that we should be concerned with, and endeavor to promote, the welfare of all. What has utility or is useful to that end is morally right.

ACT AND RULE THEORIES

A distinction is sometimes made between two kinds of utilitarianism—*act* and *rule*—although later we shall discuss whether that distinction holds up. *Act utilitarianism* prescribes that we perform that act the net consequences of which are the greatest happiness for all who are affected by the act. Note that the emphasis is on judging the individual act and on calculating the effects solely of that act in deciding whether it is right or wrong.

　Rule utilitarianism is the view that we should obey rules whose general observance maximizes happiness for all concerned. The difference here is that an act is not to be judged directly by its results, but rather by whether it conforms to a moral rule. What justifies rules is the general principle of utility. That is, the point of morality is to bring about the greatest good for the greatest number of people. This end functions as the criterion for testing rules and practices. Approval is given to those rules which are most useful in promoting the end. Individual acts are only indirectly evaluated in terms of the general principle; they are immediately judged by their conformity to the rules.

　This distinction is thought to be important because different acts can result from the application of one or the other norm. Act utilitarians emphasize the fact that often the observance of a rule does not increase happiness. In contrast, rule utilitarians are fearful of the consequences when general guidelines for actions are not inculcated and scrupulously observed. Whether these two viewpoints are reconcilable is a matter of dispute. Before we deal with that issue, perhaps an illustration will make clear the alleged differences.

　Act utilitarians suggest that sometimes we ought not tell the truth. In some situations it may be better to lie, since telling the truth could do more harm than good, for example, when a thug seeks directions to innocent prey. Consequently, we should decide whether or not to tell the truth on a case-by-case basis. The same is said for other rules, such as those regarding the keeping of promises, killing or injuring other persons, or sexual fidelity. Which act is *optimific*—produces the best consequences—depends upon the individual circumstances. Although it may be the case that observing a rule will be the best thing to do in a given situation, we cannot presume this with respect to every case. Slavishly following rules ignores the diversity of particular situations. It also threatens to produce results that frustrate the utilitarian objective of welfare maximization.

Rule Observance

　Rule utilitarians stress a number of facts about the human situation that support rule observance. First of all, rules contain a distillation of accumulated human experience concerning the consequences of acting this way or that. Over a long period of time we have learned by trial and error that certain kinds of behavior are likely to produce good results or bad results. We can never be certain that in performing an act consistent with the rule we are doing that act which has the best consequences. But neither can we be certain that violating the rule is better. What we are dealing with are probabilities. The *likelihood* is that in observing the rule we shall be doing the best thing in the long run. This follows from the fact that so much experience supports the rule. In other words, it is presumptuous to suppose that our own case is sufficiently unlike most cases that we can gamble on the likelihood of greater good resulting from violating a rule. The odds favor the rule.

Second, since it is not merely the immediate consequences of acts that are of concern morally, but also their long-range effects, we are wiser to respect those guidelines which have survived the test of time. In the effort to assess beforehand all the consequences of a particular act that violates a rule, we are necessarily going to suffer from limitations of time, intelligence, and breadth of experience. Moreover, we will be strongly tempted to lose objectivity because of our own involvement in the act. Personal advantage will encourage rationalization concerning the desirability of the act for others as well. Rules preserve impartiality in decision making.

Third, the peace and efficiency with which people interact in society is enhanced by the predictable expectations they can have of one another. When people make promises, we assume they will be kept. When they sign contracts, we assume that terms will be fulfilled. Imagine the precariousness of human existence if there could be no guarantee that rules would be respected. If physicians are not bound by their code of ethics, we have no assurance that their effort is to save lives. If motorists are not bound by traffic rules, we cannot confidently enter an intersection. If parents respect no obligations to their offspring, then children will grow with the insecurity of vacillating responses from those upon whom they are dependent. If politicians are not faithful to their oath of office, we are never assured that the public interest is being served. It is obvious that human interaction requires respect for rules.

The unsettling consequence of everyone's always functioning as an act utilitarian is that we could never be sure whether, for example, a secret told under a pledge of confidentiality would be kept secret. After all, act utilitarians are prepared to violate confidentiality if they think it better to do so in a particular situation. A military officer could not predict the behavior of his troops, since they might decide that in some cases orders ought not to be carried out. Not only our happiness, but even our sanity depends upon our being able to count on others to stick by their commitments, fulfill their roles, and respect the institutional arrangements that facilitate interaction—all of this without the fear that each person is calculating at every moment whether or not it is wise to do so.

Finally, the rule utilitarian points out the advantages of rules when it comes to educating the young or the inexperienced. Exhortations simply to "Try your best" or "Do the most loving thing" remove no perplexity regarding what is "best" or "loving" in specific cases. Presumably, there is something in the experience of previous generations that can profitably be passed on to succeeding generations. This is conveniently communicated in the form of rules. But such rules are neither teachable nor learnable if they include a full range of exceptions. Parents are inclined to say "Don't play with matches–period!" or "Never accept a ride from a stranger." What would it be like to instruct children in all the possible ways that they could justifiably act in exception to those rules? Once again, can't we argue that, in the long run, we are all better off if everyone faithfully observes those rules which have stood the test of time? If there are changes in circumstances or enriched community experience, then rules should be revised, rather than each individual abandoned to a solipsistic assessment of every situation as it arises.

Naturally, this enumeration of the benefits that can be achieved through rule observance does not quiet the act utilitarian's concern about a deficiency in the statement of *any* rule, namely, that it cannot accommodate the infinite variety of circumstances we may face as moral agents. Since building all the exceptions into the rule itself is impossible, there can be no substitute for the prudence of the individual. The most that can be expected, given the complexity of human existence, is that "rules of thumb" will be taken into consideration in particular decisions. Individual discretion is necessary in deciding whether the case at hand conforms to a general rule or is an exception to it. Expectations more fixed than that do injustice to the differences in life situations.

Finding a Middle Ground

At this point it may occur to some readers that a middle ground is possible between these two points of view. Surely no sensible person would deny either the utility of rules or the diversity of human situations. Therefore, in real life we are not likely to find pure act or rule utilitarians. Let us consider, then, what a moderate position would be. First of all, we will acknowledge that moral decisions should be influenced by rules, for various reasons:

1. Although situations are never totally alike, neither are they totally dissimilar. If every situation were unique, there would be nothing to learn from history, or from the example of others, or even from our own previous experience. So the real question concerns whether situations are similar in relevant respects. To the extent that they are, the same general rule can apply. The applicability of a rule derives, then, from the commonality of needs, experiences, and interests to which it addresses itself. Insofar as an act, in relevant respects, is like other acts to which a rule appropriately applies, consistency dictates acting according to the same rule.

2. Individuals lack sufficient time, experience, and wisdom to discover for themselves the tendencies of every kind of act, and more particularly all the consequences of each alternative they are contemplating. Rules provide a convenient and reliable summary of accumulated human experience. It would be foolhardy to disregard this wealth of evidence. Imagine someone who aspires to be a physician deciding to "start from scratch" in treating patients, rather than beginning with education in a medical school and training under those who are experts in the profession–all of which involves drawing upon the data of medical history.

3. Because rules address themselves to the majority of cases, their observance stimulates habit formation. A salutary effect of this is not having to deliberate each and every time we confront a particular kind of situation. This frees us to attend to the unusual or the unexpected in our experience. We would be exhausted if every act of every day were subjected to scrutiny. By responding in routine fashion to routine situations, we conserve our intellectual resources for coping with the unique.

4. Education of the young and inexperienced is facilitated by rules. However, the ideal is not rote memorization of rules, nor their mechanical and thoughtless application. Growth as a moral agent implies increasing reflection concerning the reasons for rules in general, and concerning the justification for specific rules. As individuals mature in their ability to evaluate the wisdom of each prescription, they can then appropriate it as their own or reject it. Only when rules are internalized in this fashion do individuals become moral agents in the full sense of taking responsibility and acting from personal conviction.

5. Rules impose considerateness upon the agent. That is, they compel us to take into account the effects of our acts upon other people, because it is those effects which have given rise to rules in the first place. In the absence of rules, many people would be tempted to make selfish decisions, not always deliberately, but often unwittingly because of inattentiveness to the impact on others of what they do. Rule observance builds into our acts a sensitivity to the well-being of the rest of the community.

Given these reasons for respecting rules in the process of decision making, what should be said about exceptions to rules in the moderate utilitarian view we are sketching?

1. Since rules apply only to general cases, they cannot cover every possible contingency. "[T]here are some things about which it is not possible to speak correctly in universal terms."[2] A rule so heavily qualified that it could accommodate every sort of situation is a practical impossibility. Therefore, the prudence of the mature individual, or of a guardian in the case of the immature, corrects this deficiency in the statement of rules. When exceptions to rules are in dispute, either before or after action was taken, people may appeal to judicial or other authority to resolve the dispute.

2. It is possible to identify the most frequent kinds of justified exceptions to rules. For example, we can qualify the rule about killing by saying, "Do not kill except in self-defense." What accounts for formation of rules—namely, the frequency of a type of occurrence—is also what makes it possible to identify major categories of exceptions to the rule. An important reason for incorporating many of these into our statement of the rule is that this mitigates a tendency to break the rule at will. In other words, by specifically authorizing exit through this door "in emergency only," we accommodate infrequent occurrences while not encouraging wholesale violation of the rule. In fact, such exceptional behavior, because it is provided for in the rule, is not a case of breaking the rule. There can be an important distinction between a *qualified rule*, for example, "Emergency Exit Only," and *exceptions to the rule*, for example, sneaking out an emergency exit merely for convenience.

3. Not all rules have exceptions. For example, rules forbidding murder, rape and torture are exceptionless. This is because the words themselves refer to acts which are unjustifiable. "Rape" does not name morally neutral sexual inter-

course, but a sexual act occurring in impermissible circumstances. "Murder" already contains in its definition the fact that the person's life does not deserve to be taken. Words like these already specify conditions which make the act immoral by definition. As a consequence, it is a contradiction in terms to talk about "justifiable murder" or "licit rape." If the killing is justified, then it is not murder. The same can be said for words which name morally right acts. Courage and temperance are virtues. We use those categories to describe acts that are appropriate in the circumstances. Thus, an act cannot be "too courageous." Other words, such as "rash" or "cowardly" describe acts motivated by too little or too much fear relative to the situation.

4. Exceptions often result from conflicts of rules. Once again, it is practically impossible to qualify each rule such that we specify what should be done when it conflicts with other rules. Let us suppose that I have promised to meet you at my office at 3 P.M. to go over the results of an exam. But just before three o'clock a colleague of mine down the corridor cries out in distress, and apparently should be rushed to the nearest hospital. What should I do? My promise to meet you is in conflict with assisting my colleague.

In such conflict situations, the utilitarian can determine the right act directly by application of the general principle of utility. That is, when two rules are in conflict, he must decide what rule to observe to produce the best consequences. Therefore, I must calculate not only the advantage to my colleague of assisting him, but also the disadvantage to you of breaking my appointment. This is why we initially defined the right act in terms of *net* consequences, since both good and bad effects must be considered.

One way to avoid functioning as an act utilitarian in conflict-of-rule situations is to rank the rules themselves. For example, the Supreme Court has said that, when a newsreporter's right to conceal the identity of his sources conflicts with a defendant's right to full disclosure in a criminal trial, then the latter takes priority. This ordering of rules cannot be complete, however. It is obvious that, at some point, direct appeal to the utilitarian principle is necessary in making decisions about individual acts.

5. In cases where rule violation is considered, among the effects which must be calculated is the impact of that exception both upon our own commitment to rule observance, and the effect upon others who are aware of the violation. One risk involved in breaking a rule is that it weakens general reliance upon the rule. For example, although we may have good reason to cut across the lawn on one occasion, our act may encourage others to do the same in less justifiable circumstances. Unless others clearly understand the exceptional nature of an act, we may be setting a bad example. In short, among the consequences of rule violation which we must weigh is the effect it will have upon general observance of the rule both by ourselves and by others.

As we summarize reasons for respecting rules and allowing exceptions, it becomes apparent that utilitarians involve themselves in no inconsistency by accepting reasons for both. Whichever way we state it, we seem to be able to collapse the act/rule distinction. A properly qualified act utilitarian view includes regard for the accumulated experience of consequences reflected in the rules. And a properly qualified rule utilitarian view acknowledges the possibility of legitimate exceptions to the rule, not all of which can be specified. Therefore, a reasonable and consistent position fully compatible with the utilitarian principle can incorporate aspects of both act and rule theory. Although some philosophers exaggerate this dichotomy, it has been argued here that a realistic utilitarian view can successfully achieve reconciliation.

THE HEDONIC CALCULUS

Earlier we noted that utilitarianism calls for the weighing of all consequences, both good and bad, in deciding which act to perform; it will be our duty to do the act whose *net* results are a greater good or a lesser evil than that produced by an alternative action. One philosopher prominent in the history of utilitarian theory, Jeremy Bentham (1748–1832), is noted for his attempt to make as precise as possible that sort of determination.[3] Just as today there is a tendency to quantify scientific evidence and to introduce rigor into various disciplines through the application of mathematics to their subject matter, so also Bentham wanted to put moral choice on a scientific footing by the introduction of his *calculus of pleasures*. Simply put, it amounted to assigning a value to each factor that can be analyzed; for example, to (1) the intensity of pleasure which the act tends to produce, (2) the duration of the pleasure, (3) its likelihood of occurring, (4) the immediacy or delay in experience of that pleasure, and (5) its tendency to be followed by pleasure. The tendency of an act (6) to produce the opposite effect, pain, will be similarly calculated, with the result that one can then compare acts in light of the net balance of good or evil they tend to produce. The calculus is completed with the multiplication of that balance by (7) the number of persons who experience it. This seventh circumstance reflects the utilitarian concern for promoting the general happiness. In measuring extent, an egalitarian norm is applied, that is, "each person is to count for one, and none for more than one."[4] In other words, each individual in the community is treated as equal to every other in the pursuit of happiness.

Issues Concerning Bentham's Theory

Bentham's calculus has been criticized on various counts, some of which he himself anticipated. While admitting the difficulty in assigning precise values to each circumstance of an act, Bentham simply pointed out that our judgment will be only as exact as circumstances permit. Even his use of the word "tendency" in discussing consequences of acts points to the possibility that an individual act cannot be certain to have the effects anticipated. But, as Bentham himself reminds us, his calculus introduces nothing really new into the practice of humanity. We already have a natural tendency to make at least some rough calculations about the effects of alternative acts whenever we are trying to decide what to do. We make these calculations even though our assignment of values is inexact, and even though we cannot be absolutely certain of the consequences. That these practical difficulties do not prevent us from both deliberating and then acting confirms Bentham's claim that in practice we unavoidably calculate and then act on the basis of what we anticipate will have the most desirable results. Also, we often find it sufficient to make *ordinal* rather than *cardinal* comparisons. That is, it is not necessary to assign a specific numerical value to each act. Rather, we can rank our different preferences as first or second or third in priority.

Some may protest that moral judgments should have something more than a degree of probability about them; however, we should not expect more from life than it is capable of offering us. How often can we be *certain* about the consequences of what we do? Were certitude the necessary condition for terminating deliberation and proceeding to act, we would never act. How often have we eaten a meal, crossed an intersection, or purchased an appliance with absolute certitude that this particular choice was the best possible? If nothing else, there are likely to be factors beyond our control which intervene when we act, and these will obviously affect the results as well. Since virtually every act is undertaken with some degree of uncertainty regarding its outcome, and only partial control over that outcome, practically we can hope only for a greater degree of probability regarding the correctness of our decision. "Although it is the best bet to wear seat belts always, it may be that a very few people have been burnt alive through wearing them when they might have survived without them."[5]

At this point some might object that what is of greater importance morally is the motive and disposition of the agent, however uncertain the consequences of the act. Utilitarians respond with an important distinction between judgment of the *act* and judgment of the *agent* who is performing the act. Whereas the act is judged to be right or wrong because of the good or bad consequences it produces, the agent will be judged praiseworthy or blameworthy because of the motives, extenuating circumstances or dispositions with which he acted.

The need for this distinction is revealed in practice, since we recognize that a right act may be performed by a person who is not praiseworthy, and a wrong act may be performed by a person whom we do not blame for the act. A cashier who is given a $10 bill by the customer who purchased $8.60 in groceries does the right act in returning $1.40 change. That is not sufficient evidence, however, to warrant a judgment that the cashier is a "just person" or a "morally praiseworthy human being." What if the clerk cheats whenever he can, but is cautious in this case because he knows this particular customer always counts his change, or because the manager happens to be standing nearby? The fact that on this occasion the customer obtained correct change can lead to no conclusion that the clerk is a "good person," since under other circumstances he may shortchange customers. There is even the possibility that the clerk intended to cheat the customer, but mistakenly gave the correct change. Although the act was right, there certainly was nothing praiseworthy about the agent.

By the same token, a cashier who innocently but inadvertently gives out the wrong change should not be immediately labelled a thief. Given that no one is infallible, it is to be expected that people may perform wrong acts on occasion through no fault of their own. Judgments concerning states of character take into account motivation, the regularity with which acts of a certain sort are performed and the responsibility that can be assigned for awareness of what is happening. For example, whether an agent is blameworthy in performing a wrong act can depend on whether his ignorance was culpable, in other words, whether he should have known what in fact he did not know. It should be clear that having a good motive is not sufficient for doing a right act, although some get confused on this point. The criterion of right and wrong in human action is not the quality of the motive. A person may be well intentioned and still not know *what* to do.

The foregoing discussion ought not suggest that there is no relation between judgments of acts and judgments of agents. In fact, the utilitarian will agree that a virtuous agent is one who is motivated to, and habitually performs, right acts. Nevertheless, the presence of good (or bad) character traits offers no guarantee that every act will be of comparable moral quality. Our realization that in particular cases we must distinguish between judgments of act or of agent is manifest in statements such as, "Well, as it turns out, that was the wrong thing to do. But, how were you to know?" When people confuse judging the act with judging the agent, indefensible conclusions are often drawn. For example, a person might unfairly be called "antisemitic" because he questions the wisdom of an Israeli foreign policy decision. Or a parent may instinctively defend his son's every deed on the grounds that he is a "good boy."

Another aspect of Bentham's theory that draws criticism is its *hedonism*, reflected in the opening line of his major work: "Nature has placed mankind under the governance of two sovereign masters, pain and pleasure."[6] Critics are less vocal when they find Aristotle saying, "As a matter of fact what we see is people avoiding pain as evil and choosing pleasure as good. Therefore it is as good and evil that they are opposed."[7] Earlier, in Book II, Aristotle had said, "Pleasure and pain are also the standards by which with greater or less strictness we regulate our considered actions."[8]

Critics have objected that quantity of pleasure is not the sole determinant of right action and that, in any case, pleasure and pain themselves are not objects that motivate our acts. We have already devoted some attention to this issue in Chapter 4. Without examining in detail the many questions which hedonism raises, let us identify a number of considerations that bear on the matter.

1. Utilitarianism is not necessarily linked with hedonism. The former simply maintains that the end of general happiness functions as moral norm. This imposes no obligation on any utilitarian to adopt one or another view regarding the specific nature of happiness. There are differences of opinion concerning what is *intrinsically good*, that is, valued for its own sake. (This contrasts with an *instrumental good*, for example, a job interview, which is something valued as a means.) Consequently, among utilitarians there are *monistic* as well as *pluralistic* conceptions of the good. The latter will be as varied, as there are different analyses of the "integral whole" that constitutes happiness. As one philosopher has put it, "Using the formal notion of utility does not commit one to monism in values. One can value many different things, and value them not for any state of mind they result in, but for themselves: leading a certain sort of life, having a certain sort of relation with people, being a certain kind of person."[9]

2. It was John Stuart Mill (1806–1873), a friend of Bentham, who pointed out in his classic essay, *Utilitarianism*, that we can distinguish *quality* as well as

quantity of pleasure. That is, we can discriminate between *kinds* of pleasure as well as *degrees* of pleasure. Mill's distinction of *higher* and *lower* pleasures ultimately rests upon a view of human nature, according to which powers proper to human beings, such that they transcend the capacities found elsewhere in nature, constitute higher potentialities. Accordingly, for Mill, human happiness most excellently but not exclusively consists of the exercise of intellect, of imagination, and of the moral and aesthetic sentiments. What Mill calls attention to is the fact that sources of pleasure are not the same for humans and other animals. This permits a distinction of kind as well as of intensity of pleasure.[10]

3. There is an obvious sense in which it is true of all of us to say, as Aristotle does, that "we choose what is pleasant and shun what causes us pain."[11] To this extent hedonism is hardly an objectionable theory. However, as was argued in Chapter 4, what distinguishes us morally is not the mere fact that we seek pleasure, but rather what gives us pleasure. Of course, Mill and later utilitarians were as well aware of this as anyone, insisting that all pleasures are not on an equal footing. A life that consists in the pursuit of pleasure is capable of moral evaluation only when the kinds of pleasure it contains have been specified. As Aristotle remarked, just actions are a source of pleasure to a just person, as unjust acts please an unjust person.

4. Although it appears trivial that we all seek pleasure, and fallacious to reason from the fact of a desire to a moral judgment of its desirability, there is an important insight contained in all this. Various philosophers from Aristotle to Mill have urged that our ethical theories be brought to the test of the facts of life. Ultimately, a theory of morality, they suggest, is to be rejected if it is inconsistent with what we all seek in life. A natural and empirical beginning for a science of morals is found in the fact that we have desires, which explains our acting in the first place. Moral reflection does not invalidate the quest for satisfaction of desire as such, but rather enables us to select those desires whose realization contributes to the fulfillment of our needs and interests adequately considered.

What is desirable cannot simply be equated with what is desired, since some desires do not survive the test. However, the desirable must ultimately be rooted in what is desired. Otherwise, the theory is literally incredible: it cannot be believed. In the present context, this suggests that there is little point in trying to erect a credible ethical theory on the condemnation of natural pleasures.[12]

PROBLEMS WITH UTILITARIANISM

A question has been raised concerning the means/ends distinction as it applies to utilitarianism. We have already explained that what has an instrumental value (value as means) is judged morally right because it is useful in achieving what is good or has intrinsic value (value as end). Does this suggest that the end justifies the means? Surely, it may be objected, it is possible to use immoral means to attain a worthy end.

A second question concerns the utilitarian claim that whatever is valued for its own sake must be a constituent of happiness, and that we approve rules and institutional structures only because they have utility in promoting happiness. However, is it correct to assume that morality necessarily is linked to happiness? Living a moral life carries with it no assurance of happiness, as the experience of many great persons in history attests. Moreover, we can certainly be happy in this world without being virtuous, as the opulent existence of some crooks and dictators suggests. That there are virtuous people who suffer and vicious people who prosper seems to threaten the connection between morality and happiness.

Not only that, a third objection maintains, utilitarianism tempts us to abandon moral duties when they do not contribute to our happiness. If being happy is the point of being moral, it seems absurd to persevere in right action when it produces suffering. Yet we have praised many persons in history who made just such sacrifices in the name of moral principle.

Finally, it is objected, the utilitarian justification of rules just does not hold up. Any number of responsibilities prescribed by moral rules bind us, quite apart from their utility in promoting happiness. For example, consider the obligation of parents to their offspring, or of a politician to serve the public interest. These duties derive from peoples' stations in life and should be faithfully executed simply because of prior commitments. Were it otherwise, parents would abandon their children and politicians the public service, whenever perseverance in those vocations proved frustrating. Can we seriously maintain that happiness is what justifies all the moral rules in our society? What about rules regulating various kinds of sexual behavior, or rules about truth-telling or promise keeping?

Utilitarian Responses

Let us consider how a utilitarian might respond to these objections, beginning with the last one first. A distinction between explanation and justification can be made here. It is not part of the utilitarian thesis that the theory explains every rule observed in every society. The theory is prescriptive, not descriptive. Utilitarians are prepared to admit that actual practices may be at variance with the utilitarian principle, but that simply leads them to the conclusion that these are not good practices. From this point of view, if there is no demonstrable connection between people's being required to act in a particular way and people's experiencing happiness in the long run, then there is no justification for the rule or practice. One advantage of the utilitarian theory is that it demystifies the process of justifying moral rules. We are asked to consider if we can agree on what is ultimately worth seeking in life. On the basis of what is a matter of consensus regarding the good, we fashion means to those ends. As the circumstances change, so may the rules.

This last observation helps to explain, incidentally, why some rules and practices continue to be observed, despite their present disutility. What previously served some useful purpose, and was therefore valued instrumentally, can become something valued for its own sake as a result of conditioning over a long period of time. Various hygienic rules described in the Old Testament, for example, survive as religious symbols long after they have lost their original utility. Similarly, sexual taboos that arose in the first instance because of the unavoidable link between sex and procreation may still be observed, even though scientific advances in contraceptive techniques enable us effectively to separate sex from procreation. Although science may have rendered needless a particular taboo, whether about hygiene or sex, the force of habit and tradition may preserve the practice.

The power of conditioning can even create a situation in which people claim to just intuit the moral quality of acts; that is, their response becomes conditioned to the point that acts are immediately apprehended as fitting or unfitting, quite apart from what might have originally justified such a response. We need not even assume that a present practice was ever justified, however clear may be the explanation of it. For example, superstitious practices of all sorts may have originated simply out of ignorance and fear, which is what warrants our calling them superstitious. (Of course, even superstitions may serve some useful purpose: they may give people some measure of security and sense of controlling events. However, as previously argued in Chapter 3, a subjective sense of well-being, if it is incompatible with the facts, cannot represent an ideal condition.)

In short, intuitions of intrinsic and instrumental values might only be relics of values whose utilitarian origins, real or fancied, are lost in time. The philosophical critique of existing practices forces us, the utilitarian contends, to evaluate each of them in the rigorously empirical fashion that utilitarianism prescribes. (We described this in Chapter 1 as the ongoing challenge of reflective morality.)

What of the third objection mentioned above? A particular duty, say that of a banker to transact business honestly, is binding despite the happiness he might experience with large sums of embezzled funds. Utilitarians make two responses to this question. First, a particular act of fulfilling a contract or keeping a promise is appropriate simply because it is consistent with commitment. It is redundant to argue that we have an obligation to do what we have undertaken an obligation to do. No utilitarian arguments are needed to explain that, nor are there any utilitarian arguments to deny it either. It is another question, however, whether we should have practices and rules of that sort. For example, whereas we may argue that Mr. and Mrs. Jones should remain together because they vowed to do so, this does not answer the question of whether it is wise to have an institution of marriage that binds partners to lifelong, irrevocable commitments. The utility of the practice, not of the particular act, is the issue at this level.

Secondly, whether the banker is made happier by embezzling depends on the kind of person he is. What sort of things does he value? As we mentioned earlier, doing the just thing is itself a source of pleasure to the just person, and for the just person the act of embezzling will produce pain rather than pleasure. Moral standards are not set by consulting the preference of the depraved. Indeed, the very possibility of distinguishing between virtuous and depraved persons rests upon the completion of a prior task, namely, to decide what practices are on the whole desirable. If the practice of embezzlement is unjustifiable, then persons can be judged according to whether their dispositions are in accord or in conflict with that prior judgment. The utilitarian thesis prevents appeal to what makes an individual banker happy regardless of its effect upon others. The case against egoism has already been argued.

What is to be said regarding the second objection, namely, that there is no necessary link between morality and happiness? Some of the same considerations we applied to the previous objection apply to this one as well. Since we can argue that doing the moral thing is itself a source of satisfaction to the moral person, we should recognize that this kind of happiness cannot be denied to a virtuous person. Other kinds of happiness might be sacrificed—for example, wealth or health—but what is arguably the most significant element in the good life remains. Secondly, utilitarians do not contend that each and every act prescribed by a useful moral rule promises happy consequences to the agent. If we keep issues distinct, we can see that the utilitarian argument might simply be that the justification of a moral system is its long-range utility in maximizing general well-being.[13] That humanity is better off in the long run if a particular rule is universally obeyed is a contention quite distinct from the claim that Mr. Jones here and now is going to get more satisfaction out of doing his duty as prescribed by that rule than out of not doing it. Of course, we should use every means to ensure that society offers sufficient rewards and punishments to provide an increased likelihood that "crime does not pay." But the assurance can never be complete nor, in the case of virtuous people, is it even needed. There is for them some meaning in the phrase "Virtue is its own reward."

The Means/End Distinction

Do utilitarians argue that "the end justifies the means," as was charged in the first objection we identified earlier? This issue deserves more than a cursory examination. In the final analysis it leads us to the most frequently voiced criticism of utilitarianism, which concerns justice. Let us address the problem through a series of considerations.

1. In one sense it seems obvious that the end *does* justify the means. If the end does not, what does? It is important not to rush past this question. Means are means precisely because they bring about an end. The very concept of means includes their relationship to an end. Not only does the end provide a rationale in practice for undertaking the means, but beyond that, reference to the end is itself what enables us to identify the means as means.

2. It is essential to distingiush between *subordinate* ends and the *ultimate* end. (We also speak of *intermediate* and *partial* ends, in contrast to the ultimate and all-inclusive end.) The moral point of view requires us to consider comprehensively human purposes in living. The end that functions as a moral criterion for judging acts, rules, and institutions must take into account not only the self but others; not merely immediate but also long-range consequences; not solely one or another interest of the agents, but all of the needs and interests of the agents. Consequently, when the end or ultimate purpose of human striving is described as "happiness," what is meant is the harmonious fulfillment in a social context of peoples' needs adequately considered. It is this end that justifies the means. Clearly, subordinate ends of particular individuals may be in conflict with this comprehensive goal of the moral life. For example, an individual may acquire a drug addiction that conflicts with the realization of most of the other purposes he could have in life. Or a community might pursue some objective that has an immediate pay-off but ultimately proves disastrous, as happened to the Nazis under Hitler. If we restrict

our consideration solely to a particular end, it is indeed possible to select means that are immoral. But the particular end itself may be immoral because it is in conflict with what we have defined as the ultimate end. Judged by reference to the ultimate end, no immoral means can be justified, since it is precisely that end which provides the standard for judging particular means and particular ends to be immoral.

3. Too often a compartmentalization of means and ends is assumed which is contrary to experience. The fact that impermissible means have been used has important consequences for the agent and for the results of his action. That is to say, the use of means which are in themselves corrupt tends to corrupt the user and to contaminate the result. It is myopic, for example, to think that enforcement of law and order permits unconstitutional abridgement of people's basic rights, such as presumption of innocence, protection against unreasonable search, and guarantee of public trial. If means are used that are incompatible with these values, what kind of order results? And law would only be selectively conceived and enforced. History has provided abundant evidence of the steady deterioration in the character of those persons who indiscriminately employed intolerable means for supposedly worthwhile purposes. The end result often is a lawless and terrorized society.

4. The previous consideration enables us to understand the view of John Dewey that there is a "continuum of means and ends."[14] That is to say, the distinction between means and ends depends upon perspective. From the standpoint of what has preceded X, we can view X as an end. From the standpoint of what follows X, we can view X as a means. For example, let us assume that my purpose is to obtain a degree in music history. To that end, I matriculate in a university, complete the required courses, and write a thesis. These are means to that end. Now, having obtained that degree, it in turn becomes a means for the realization of my future goals and purposes. No actualized end is insulated from its influence in determining the future; what has already transpired conditions the present and disposes the future. Note also that an end as yet not actualized but only intended itself functions as a means for its actualization. I use the goal that is before my mind as a yardstick for judging the worth of measures taken and for making appropriate selections of means to that end.

The reciprocal nature of means and ends is also manifest in the way that reflection on the availability and desirability of means often leads to abandoning or modifying ends. I may decide that I should forego my pursuit of a degree in music history, if I conclude that the cost in time, effort and financial resources is excessive, or if experience proves that I lack sufficient aptitude or willingness to sacrifice other goals that conflict with that degree. In short, not only does the end influence selection of means, but also the means influence the selection of ends. Dewey, in emphasizing the *continuity* of life experiences, helps us realize that it is only by focusing exclusively on a dissected segment in the flow of human activity that we can characterize something absolutely as means or end. Relative to what precedes or follows, its characterization can change.

5. Some may argue that it is unseemly to reduce moral reasoning to a kind of cost-benefit analysis. But why should this be thought objectionable? Consider the problem of deciding whether a critically ill patient should be sustained by extraordinary means. How do we go about this? What factors influence our moral judgment? The availability and cost of medicines, trained personnel, hospital space, the financial means of the family, the condition of the patient and his wishes, the emotional toll on the loved ones, the extent to

which others require similar treatment are all considerations that are relevant to a sober assessment of the situation. The argument that a patient should be kept alive "at all costs" may reflect insensitivity to the needs of others who might benefit more at lesser expense. Missionaries in times of disaster have frequently had to make hard choices about the distribution of limited food and medicine—in effect deciding life and death for those affected by the pattern of distribution. What is morally correct in a conflict-torn practical situation is hardly discernible without cost-benefit analysis. The alternative is capriciousness.

6. This example brings us finally to a question which for many constitutes the major objection to utilitarianism in any of its forms. They argue that justice and utility can conflict. What prevents the utilitarian from employing unjust means to achieve the end of general happiness? Is it not conceivable that a calculus of net consequences, good and evil, might justify the sacrifice of the legitimate claims of a minority in order to maximize the interests of a majority? After all, the utilitarian objective—bringing about "the greatest good of the greatest number of people"—is a consideration distinct from the moral issue of how that good is to be *distributed*. On balance, an unjust distribution of benefits and burdens may produce the greatest amount of good, but it is still morally wrong, because it is unjust. We will consider this objection, because it is so common and also because it introduces a host of complex problems, in a separate section.

JUSTICE AND UTILITY

Let us begin with an example to illustrate the difficulty. One that is frequently cited concerns *scapegoat punishment*. Suppose that a community has been the scene of a particularly brutal rape and murder. Intensive investigation by police fails to uncover the perpetrator. Townspeople grow increasingly restive as the investigation drags on without producing results. Finally, convinced that law enforcement officials are unequal to the task of protecting the citizenry, townspeople decide to take matters into their own hands. Confronted with a lynch mob that might wreak vengeance upon any suspected persons and spark a major racial conflict, the sheriff decides that serious breakdown in law and order can be prevented only if justice is swiftly done. A poor, half-witted person already held in jail on other minor charges could easily be framed, with the result that the community's desire for vengeance will be satisfied as the fellow is tried, convicted, and executed. In other words, the sacrifice of this one person may eliminate the threat of an ugly riot in the community. Let us assume, for sake of the example, that execution of this innocent dullard does restore peace to the area and reestablishes popular support for letting the police handle problems of crime. Although an injustice has been done, can utilitarians argue that it is impossible for greater good to result from it?

Two Meanings of "Just"

Before considering utilitarian reactions to this example, we should clarify the notion of justice itself. Two uses of the term "just" can be distinguished. In one sense it is synonymous with "virtuous" or "righteous." That is, it refers to someone who acts rightly in all kinds of situations because he possesses virtue in the complete sense. This meaning of justice is intended when the Bible tells us, "The expectation of the just is joy: but the hope of the wicked shall perish."[15] In the second sense, justice is not equivalent to complete virtue, but is one particular virtue contrasted with others. In this sense, justice was defined by Cicero as "rendering to each his due."[16] This means that what a person *deserves* is the criterion for just treatment. Aristotle expressed the requirement of justice as one of treating equals equally and unequals unequally. Unequals are to be treated in proportion to their relevant differences.[17] Unlike other virtues, then, justice concerns itself with the distribution of benefits and burdens to persons according to their deserts. Other terms, such as temperance or benevolence, describe other praiseworthy qualities in the good person.

We also speak of *social justice*, which is this virtue as predicated of a community. However, the essential element in the concept of justice remains the same, namely, concern to render to others what is properly theirs. When we speak of a society as just, once again we contrast that quality with others, such as the material prosperity, the efficiency, the military strength, or the literacy found in that society.

Because "just" in the narrow sense is not synonymous with "right" but is simply one right-making characteristic, it is possible that other right-making characteristics may justify action which is not, strictly speaking, just. We find in the Gospels an example of this, when Christ pays some workers what they had contracted for, thus fulfilling the requirements of justice. At the same time, Christ gives other workers the same pay for fewer hours of work, illustrating that benevolence can go beyond that to which people have a strict claim. What is distinctive of justice, then, is that it regards the rights or legitimate claims of those who are affected by the action. As a *moral* quality, of course, justice does not mean conformity to the rights of persons merely as defined by the positive law, or even by the prevailing moral rules in the community. It is possible to describe a prevailing rule or law as unjust, however much popular support it has. (We considered this question earlier in Chapter 2.)

What, then, are the valid moral principles that provide the criteria for what is just? As Aristotle's definition indicates, justice has always concerned itself with equality. The presumption has been that people should be treated equally unless there are relevant differences among them. To this extent, justice simply satisfies the general requirement that behavior be governed by rule. The universalizability of any rule implies that similar situations will be treated similarly and dissimilar ones dissimilarly. Accordingly, we might say that the *formal* criterion of justice is that the same thing be done in instances of the same kind or, in simple terms, that we act impartially. However, the requirement of impartiality, while necessary, is not sufficient to guarantee that an act is just. Someone might with complete even-handedness brutalize every member of the community or all members of a certain kind, for example, Hispanics or libertarians. For this reason, *which* rules should impartially govern distribution and retribution is a question regarding the *material* criteria for justice. To answer this question, we must determine the purpose of justice.

Presumably, people have a right to conditions that make the good life possible. Respecting the fact that all persons, precisely because they are persons, are capable of pursuing the good life, justice requires that there be equality in the treatment of those persons, unless the objective of promoting the good life itself justifies unequal treatment. In other words, what differences will be judged *relevant* depends upon how that difference bears upon the ability of the persons affected to lead the good life.

Equality: Arithmetic and Proportional

We might note, then, that two considerations support the view that justice implies equality of treatment. First, applying any rule requires impartiality. Rule-governed behavior simply is behavior that is consistent from case to case. Second, justice demands equality because its purpose is to respect the equal right of every person to pursue the happiness of which he or she is capable. Another way of putting this is to say that all persons should be treated as equals, because they are all equally human beings, that is, capable of enjoying a good life however varied may be their capacities for happiness. The just society will equally respect and protect its members in this pursuit.

Those rights that people possess simply because they are human beings are called *human* or *natural rights*. That is, they are rights the possession of which depends on one condition only—namely, that one be a human being. It is at this level that the presumption of equality is most essential to the concept of justice. With respect to *acquired rights*, which are distinguished from human rights, there will be inequalities among persons in the community. For example, it is an acquired right to park in a particular structure by reason of having paid a fee. As the word implies, one must acquire that right through possession of qualifications beyond that of simply being a human being.

At this point, it may appear paradoxical that justice, which emphasizes equal treatment, can justify unequal distribution. However, the confusion dissolves when we consider that there is such a thing as *proportional equality*. This means treating people equally in proportion to their relevant characteristics. For example, distribution which is proportionate to need will be unequal if different doses of medicine are required to remedy the illnesses of different individuals. A cough medicine bottle prescribes different doses based on the age or the weight of the patient. However, even when unequal treatment is justified, we might argue that the objective of unequal distribution is equality of benefit, in this case, effective relief from cough symptoms. Similarly, an equal degree of security requires an unequal allocation of police resources, when comparing the potential risks faced by the president to those faced by a grocer's file clerk. In contrast to proportional equality, there is *arithmetic equality*, which implies treating everyone exactly alike. When a professor distributes the identical exam to all members of the class, or a cook serves slices of cake of the same size to each guest, the treatment is arithmetically equal.

Whether persons are to be treated with arithmetic or proportional equality depends on whether or not there are relevant differences among them. It has been suggested that, in practice, one way to decide whether a difference is relevant is to invoke reciprocity.[18] Would I be willing to be treated differently if I possessed that characteristic? For example, let us suppose that I am a Nazi busy with the extermination of Gypsies. Now, what if the tables were turned, and I found myself in a cattle car, being shipped off to the ovens because I am a Gypsy. Would I now accept the notion that race is a relevant difference justifying a person's being incinerated at the hands of non-Gypsies? However, this is not a foolproof test for relevance, since a fanatic might be so concerned to preserve racial purity that he would permit himself to be incinerated if it could be proved that he too were a Gypsy. Once again, consistency is a necessary but not a sufficient condition for justice.

More precisely, differences will be relevant if they can be shown to have an intrinsic relation to the burden or benefit to be distributed. We must ask, "Is there a necessary connection between this characteristic and the pattern of distribution?" Whether there is such a connection, however, will depend upon the purpose of the distribution. Height is a relevant difference relative to distribution of basketball scholarships, and age is a relevant difference relative to voting privileges. But it is immaterial to the objectives of basketball whether players have hair of a certain color. And the amount of wealth a person has is not germane to his ability to discriminate between candidates in a voting booth. So these differences are irrelevant relative to those purposes. Obviously, for other purposes wealth may be treated as relevant, for example, to taxation; and height is irrelevant to admission to law school. We cannot decide in the abstract whether a difference is relevant or irrelevant, since this must be judged in context.

We have said that the distinguishing feature of justice is distribution that respects the rights of those who are affected. When there are relevant differences, that distribution will be unequal. However, given that the most fundamental characteristic of persons is their humanity itself, which is the basis for identification with all other persons, the presumption in a just society favors strict equality of treatment. That is to say, the burden of proof is on those who wish to justify unequal treatment. Since one way to express this is to say that "all persons have a *prima facie* right to equality of treatment," we should understand the key phrase here. Rights (or duties) may be either *prima facie* or *all things considered*. A *prima facie* right is based on one morally relevant consideration. That consideration justifies the claim, unless there are stronger counterclaims in the situation. Such counterclaims may themselves have the form of *prima facie* rights (or duties).

Recall an example used earlier in this chapter. My promise to meet you at the office at 3 P.M. immediately establishes a *prima facie* duty on my part to be there at 3 P.M., and a *prima facie* right on your part to expect me there. However, shortly before 3 P.M. I hear the cries of my colleague down the corridor, who suddenly finds himself in paroxyms of pain and obviously should be rushed to the nearest hospital. I now find myself with another *prima facie* duty, namely, to aid my colleague in distress. Clearly these two *prima facie* duties conflict, since I cannot simultaneously satisfy them both. What is my duty all things considered is what I decide after taking into account *all* the morally relevant aspects of the situation, employing some criterion to weigh the relative importance of conflicting claims. Of course, when there are no counterclaims, my *prima facie* right (duty) will also be automatically my overall right (or duty).

The cases that generate greatest concern about justice involve conflicting claims about rights and duties. Your right to smoke cigarettes (perhaps not a moral right at all) may conflict with my right to breathe clean air. In a case like this we must decide which is the weightier claim. A just society must be attentive to the legitimate claims of all its citizens. But where these claims conflict, priority will be given to those claims which tend more to promote the common good. The *prima facie* right peacefully to assemble might yield, for example, to a concern for preventing the spread of disease during an epidemic. For a time, a community might close down theatres and swimming pools, and ban all large gatherings. All things considered, we would not have the right to assemble. No injustice has been done, although a right has been suspended, because a greater good has been served. That greater good may itself be based on a justice claim, or it may be based on some other right-making characteristic which overrides a justice claim.

Utilitarianism Reconciled with Justice

This last point is central to the utilitarians' defense of their principle against the charge that it conflicts with the requirements of justice. We have sufficiently illuminated the nature of justice to be able to address that dispute. Let us begin with a return to the example of scapegoat punishment with which we began. What are possible utilitarian responses to that situation? We can identify nine.

1. It is a misnomer to call the execution of an innocent dullard "punishment" at all. The term properly applies only to the case of a person who has committed an offense. Although this appears to be merely a semantical point, it is important to try not to saddle an ethical theory with the intuitively objectionable view that punishing the innocent can be justified.

2. If we respect that *caveat* and describe the act instead as "doing injury to an innocent person" in order to promote a greater good, then utilitarians may ask why they are thought to judge that act so differently from other persons of moral sensitivity. Utilitarians are capable of judging that act to be unjust for precisely the same reasons as any other moralist. For a utilitarian, the injustice of an act can be the moral consideration that overrides all other considerations in a situation. It must not be unfairly assumed that, for the utilitarian, justice counts for nothing. In the words of John Stuart Mill, "Justice is a name for certain classes of moral rules which concern the essentials of well-being more nearly, and are therefore of more absolute obligation, than any other rules for the guidance of life."[19] For utilitarians such as Mill, the happiness that constitutes the end or purpose of action is a complex whole. That in which happiness consists is in fact a plurality of goods. Mill is explicit on this point. "The ingredients of happiness are very various, and each of them is desirable in itself. . ."[20]

   Sometimes it is alleged that for Mill (and Aristotle) the end is *monistic*, in other words, only one thing. This obscures the fact that, materially speaking, happiness is a *cluster* concept. Just as a university consists of many buildings and faculties, so happiness consists of many parts, which are not merely means, but themselves intrinsic goods. If we say, for example, that our end is happiness, does this mean that we seek only one thing? We may respond that a plurality of goods constitutes happiness, because of the diversity of needs and interests. Thus, we might say with Aristotle or Mill that happiness means, among other things, robust health, friends, a modicum of wealth, a clean environment, education, a good reputation, intellectual and moral excellence and good luck. Happiness, then, is an umbrella term for a whole host of goods that *mean* happiness as integrally and completely conceived.

Justice can just as readily be valued as part of the whole for a utilitarian as for anybody else. In fact, there is no standard set of intrinsic or instrumental goods that must be accepted by someone regarded as a utilitarian. Moreover, there is no fixed weight that a utilitarian must give to the justice of an act, any more than other right-making factors have a determinate value. Consequently, utilitarians do not necessarily assign lesser value to justice than to any other factor when considerations conflict. Indeed, it was Mill's contention, as cited above, that justice is given greater priority than any other moral rule. If this be so, it is not at all clear that utilitarians would be more disposed to execute innocent persons than other moralists who criticize them.[21]

John Dewey has noted that neglect of the consequences of acts in the moral standard has two unfortunate consequences. First, we are left with a merely formal principle. Second, we fail to recognize that means can be organically integrated with the end they serve. Justice is not merely an external means to human happiness. It is a means which is also a constituent part of the consequences it helps to bring about. "On this account," Dewey says, "the character, the self, which has adopted fair play and equity into its own attitude . . . will also be protected from any temptation to disregard the principle in order to obtain some short-term specific goods."[22]

3. Utilitarians, if their position is not caricatured, must be recognized to be concerned about the consequences, not merely of an individual act, but of an act as an instance of a certain kind of act. That is, the utility of rules is important. As applied to the example, utilitarians will immediately note that railroading an innocent person to the electric chair violates all sorts of rules that are essential to the long-term good of the community. Consider the importance to the community of preserving such standards as due process of law, the presumption of innocence, the rules of evidence, the integrity of the judicial system and the impartiality of law-enforcement officials. The general happiness so essentially depends on the maintenance of fair play that it becomes increasingly difficult to see how it can be useful to violate fairness criteria. Every deviation from justice serves to weaken the confidence that all must have in the fairness of the system. Mill says that

> we feel that the violation, for a present advantage, of a rule of such transcendent expediency is not expedient, and that he who, for the sake of convenience to himself or to some other individual, does what depends on him to deprive mankind of the good, and inflict upon them the evil, involved in the greater or less reliance which they can place in each other's word, acts the part of one of their worst enemies.[23]

Given that this is so, the utility of preserving inviolate rules for the administration of justice would surely lead utilitarians to oppose executing innocent persons.

4. "Each to count for one, none for more than one" has always been a cardinal tenet of utilitarianism. It expresses the view that every person counts equally in the calculus and has the same *prima facie* right to equality of treatment as any other theory of justice presupposes. If persons are presumed to be of equal worth or dignity, as utilitarians contend, and the implicit conditions of impartiality and reciprocity are considered, it is difficult to see how utilitarianism would readily lead to scapegoat punishment. First of all, utilitarianism requires us to recognize that the scapegoat is as much entitled to fair treatment as is every other person in the community. Furthermore, law-enforcement officials must treat him with the same degree of impartiality as morality requires in the application of any rule. And third, those who might be tempted to exploit the scapegoat's condition must ask themselves if they would be equally disposed to this method of restoring community tranquility if they were the victims of the injustice. Presumably, the reversibility criterion would be a powerful deterrent to any rationalization of the morality of railroading innocent persons. Given the unlikelihood that anybody welcomes suffering a "bum rap," it is as open to the utilitarian as to any other moralist to reject such a practice.

5. We have already pointed out that utilitarians can build the idea of equal and fair treatment into their concept of the end. Justice then becomes an integral part of happiness. If so, the utility of an unjust act can be clearly discounted by reason of its incompatibility with the end. But equal distribution is usually a means of achieving the greatest total happiness. Throughout history, one of the most powerful arguments for equality of consideration is that in the long run the common good is maximized. Equal access to such advantages as education, medical treatment, the ballot box and job opportunity have been thought to be the soundest long-term means to community well-being. If so, then it can be argued that the utility of justice gives it unique importance in our calculations. "The necessity of justice to the support of society," the utilitarian David Hume said, is such that "no moral excellence is more highly esteemed."[24] As applied to our example once again, it is doubtful that executing innocent persons in order to calm community passions can be called a useful practice.

6. That unequal treatment is fair has been established in those cases where there are relevant differences between individuals. But even when individuals are relevantly similar, unequal distribution can still be justified if the process itself is fair by which some must be selected for favored treatment. For example, if a person has only one extra ticket to a game that two friends wish to attend, he might propose that the ticket go to the one who wins a toss of the coin. Neither can claim that this solution is unjust, if there is no basis in relevant differences for deciding between them. The relevance of this to inflicting or permitting injury to innocent persons is simply this: there are circumstances in which we recognize an important common good to justify an otherwise unacceptable distribution. The example of missionaries denying food and medicine to the weakest in order that the strongest might survive, sometimes called *triage*, is one of this sort.

Another example illustrates the propriety of sacrificing some so that others may be helped, even when there is no relevant difference. Imagine that a lifeboat that can safely accommodate only twenty persons instead has thirty persons scrambling into it. If thirty persons remaining onboard means that the lifeboat will capsize and everyone will drown, it is not obviously wrong to draw straws to decide who goes overboard. While the process is impartial, it surely results in the sacrifice of a minority in order to promote the greatest happiness of a majority. It may even be that the losers, once they discover themselves to be such, have to be forcibly thrown overboard. But is this unjust?

7. Opponents of utilitarianism have often assumed that, whereas the morality of utilitarian calculations is suspect, the determination of what is just is crystal clear. However, both Hume and Mill have shown at length that what is just often is a matter of considerable dispute. It is, for example, far from intuitively clear what method of taxation or property distribution is fair. History manifests how uncertain nations can be about just rules of warfare, or restrictions on trade, or justifications of punishment. It is naive to think that clarity about what is just is the good fortune of all non-utilitarians. On the contrary, Hume and Mill argue that controversies about different theories of punishment, taxation, and the like manifest that it cannot be by instinct or by simple introspection that we know what is unjust. Rather, we can make a case for employing the principle of utility to mediate opposing justice claims.

For example, some argue that affirmative action programs are unjust because they amount to reverse discrimination and thus violate the principle of equality. Others reply that such programs are just because they help to correct an imbalance caused by historic denial of equal rights. This principle of *compensatory justice* is invoked to justify what others employing the principle of strict equality would deny. Since there are conflicting views about what is just here, it may be possible to decide which policy is, on the whole, right by deciding which of the opposing just distributions is productive of the greatest amount of good in the long run.

8. This same invocation of the principle of utility is appropriate not only to decide between opposing theories of what is just, but also to justify exceptions to rules in general. It is a practical impossibility to specify every condition which qualifies rules such as truth telling or respect for life. We would have little difficulty imagining a case that justifies telling an untruth to prevent harm to an innocent person. This exception to the rule might be justified, says the utilitarian, because of the greater good resulting from the untruth. Consider also the quandary faced by Allied bombers in World War II. Should they have bombed Nazi concentration camps, in the process killing many innocent persons, but achieving thereby a great reduction in the number of persons who could be exterminated? Would such bombings have been morally wrong? The testimony of survivors of concentration camps indicates that they themselves in many cases hoped the allies would destroy the camps.

However we decide what is, on balance, the best course of action, it is clear that no simplistic solution is available through the invocation of justice, either when there are conflicting justice claims or when justice conflicts with other right-making considerations. In such cases, it is not utterly implausible to look to consequences for the general happiness in order to resolve the issue. As Mill puts it, "If utility is the ultimate source of moral obligations, utility may be invoked to decide between them when their demands are incompatible."[25]

9. Some critics charge that, if two acts have equal value, for example, fifty net units of good, but one is unjust, the utilitarian cannot say the unjust act should be avoided.[26] The reply to this is that the injustice has already been calculated when it is said that the act has fifty *net* units of good. Therefore, the act which includes an unjust aspect is of equal moral value with the other act. Were the critic to claim that the unjust act still is of less value morally,

then he cannot claim that it possesses the same number of units of good. Saying that the acts have an equal net value, and yet contending that one of them should be avoided because it is unjust is counting the injustice twice. Recall that, as utilitarians, we can give the (in)justice of the act as much weight as we wish, but other virtues besides justice have their value, too. Whatever totals one concludes with *do* indicate what is right, all things considered.

We have concluded this chapter on utilitarianism with consideration of a major difficulty posed by its opponents. In summary, it has been alleged that the principle of justice is distinct from that of utility, and that the latter can often be invoked to deny fair treatment. In reply, utilitarians have argued that nothing in their theory opposes the inclusion of just distribution among intrinsic goods, or even that a top priority be given to that value. Moreover, exceptions to rules and cases of conflict between rules reveal how helpful the utilitarian principle can be in determining hard cases. The reader must decide whether these defenses are effective against objections to utilitarianism. Another set of theories, offered as an alternative to consequentialism, awaits us in Chapter 6.

REVIEW QUESTIONS

1. Define utilitarianism, and distinguish between the act and rule versions of that theory.
2. Summarize arguments offered by both act and rule utilitarians in support of their positions.
3. In the moderate position, what reasons support respect for rules?
4. In the moderate position, what are five considerations with regard to exceptions?
5. Describe a utilitarian theory that collapses the distinction between act and rule theories.
6. Explain Bentham's hedonic calculus.
7. What are utilitarian responses to the following objections?
   a. Precise values cannot be assigned to each effect.
   b. Rarely do we possess certitude regarding consequences.
   c. Motive and disposition are more significant morally than consequences.
8. What are four considerations bearing on the issue of pleasure and pain in relation to utilitarianism?
9. How might a utilitarian react to these charges?
   a. Not all moral rules are ordered to happiness.
   b. Duties have binding force regardless of consequences.
   c. Happiness is not an inevitable effect of acting morally.
   d. The end does not justify the means.
   e. Cost-benefit analysis is inappropriate to moral reasoning.
10. What is the objection of those who oppose justice to utility?
11. Distinguish between formal and material criteria of justice.

12. For what two reasons does justice demand equality? How is unequal treatment justified?

13. Distinguish arithmetic and proportional equality, natural and acquired rights.

14. What criteria can be invoked to decide if differences are relevant?

15. Distinguish between rights which are *prima facie* and those which are all things considered.

16. What does it mean for justice to be considered an "integral part" of happiness?

17. How do the following considerations serve the utilitarian case regarding justice?
    a. The utility of rule observance.
    b. Each to count for one.
    c. The utility of equal consideration.
    d. Impartial procedures in unequal distribution.
    e. Utility as a principle to mediate opposing justice claims and decide exceptions to a rule.

NOTES

1. See, for example, Warnock, *The Object of Morality*, Chapter 2.

2. Aristotle, *Nicomachean Ethics*, trans. Martin Ostwald (Indianapolis: The Bobbs-Merrill Co., Inc., 1962), 1137b13.

3. Jeremy Bentham, *An Introduction to the Principles of Morals and Legislation* (New York: Hafner Publishing Co., 1948). See Chapter IV.

4. ". . . Bentham's dictum, 'everybody to count for one, nobody for more than one,' might be written under the principle of utility as an explanatory commentary." Mill, *Utilitarianism*, Chap. 5, p. 76.

5. Hare, *Moral Thinking*, p. 204.

6. Bentham, *Principles of Morals and Legislation*, p. 1.

7. Aristotle, *The Ethics of Aristotle* (Thomson), Bk. X, Ch; 2.

8. Ibid., Bk. II, Ch. 3.

9. James Griffin, "Towards a Substantive Theory of Rights," *Utility and Rights*, R. G. Frey, ed. (Minneapolis: University of Minneapolis Press, 1984), p. 150.

10. Contrary to misrepresentation by some of his critics, Mill explicitly appeals to human nature in distinguishing qualities of pleasure, as well as what is desirable. See *Utilitarianism*, Chapters 2, 3, and 4. Mill's appeal, in Chapter 2, to the preference of a majority reflects Artistotle's appeal in his *Rhetoric* to what "must be so" because it is so judged by all, or by a majority, or by the ablest. (1363a8 and 1364b12-1365a3). Again, Mill's argument from each person's happiness to the general happiness, the sum of goods being a good, is also found in Aristotle's *Rhetoric*, 1363b17-20. A fine article showing that the "characteristic features of Mill's utilitarianism including his 'proof' of the principle of utility are doctrines from Aristotle's *Rhetoric*" can be found in Micheal Bayles, "Mill's Utilitarianism and Aristotle's Rhetoric," *The Modern Schoolman*, LI (January, 1974), 159-70.

11. Aristotle, *The Ethics of Aristotle* (Thomson), Bk. X, Ch. 1.

12. See Ashmore, "Deriving the Desirable from the Desired," *Proceedings of the American Catholic Philosophical Association*, XLIV (1970), 152-60.

13. John Rawls, "Two Concepts of Rules," *Philosophical Review*, 64 (1955), 16, has pointed out that there are good utilitarian reasons for not allowing easy appeal from a sound moral rule:
    Indeed, the point of the practice [of promising] is to abdicate one's title to act in accor-

dance with utilitarian and prudential considerations in order that the future may be tied down and plans coordinated in advance. There are obvious utilitarian advantages in having a practice which denies to the promisor, as a defense, any general appeal to the utilitarian principle in accordance with which the practice itself may be justified . . . It is a mistake to think that if the practice is justified on utilitarian gounds then the promisor must have complete liberty to use utilitarian arguments to decide whether or not to keep his promise.

14. John Dewey, *Theory of Valuation*, pp. 40–50; also *Human Nature and Conduct*, pp. 34–36.

15. *Proverbs* 10:28.

16. Cicero, *De Officiis/On Duties*, Harry G. Edinger, trans. (Indianapolis: The Bobbs-Merrill Company, Inc., 1974), Bk. I, Sect. 15, p. 10. Also of interest are the opening words of Book I in the Emperor Justinian's codification of Roman law, "Justice is the constant and perpetual wish to render every one his due." *The Institutes of Justinian*, Thomas Collette Sandars, trans. (Westport, Conn.: Greenwood Press, 1970), p. 5.

17. Aristotle, *Nicomachean Ethics*, Bk. V, Chap. 3.

18. See, for example, R. M. Hare, *Freedom and Reason* (New York: Oxford University Press, 1965), pp. 217–221. In *Moral Thinking*, p. 63, Hare makes another point about the concept of relevance: "In general, to treat a feature of a situation as morally relevant is to apply to that situation a moral principle which mentions the feature . . . It is the principles which determine what is relevant."

19. Mill, *Utilitarianism*, p. 73.

20. Ibid, p. 46.

21. Illustrative of such criticism is Alan Donagan, *The Theory of Morality* (Chicago: University of Chicago Press, 1977), Chap. 6; also H. J. McCloskey, "A Non-Utilitarian Approach to Punishment," *Inquiry*, VIII (1965), 249–263; and H. J. McCloskey, "An Examination of Restricted Utilitarianism," *The Philosophical Review*, LXVI (1957), 466–485.

22. Dewey, *Theory of the Moral Life*, p. 105.

23. Mill, *Utilitarianism*, p. 29.

24. David Hume, *An Inquiry Concerning the Principles of Morals*, Charles W. Hendel, ed. (New York: The Liberal Arts Press, Inc., 1957), p. 34.

25. Mill, *Utilitarianism*, p. 33.

26. William Frankena, *Ethics*, 2nd ed. (Englewood Cliffs, N.J.: Prentice-Hall, 1963), p. 36.

CHAPTER SIX

Deontological Ethics

Nonconsequentialist (sometimes called *deontological*) theories offer a contrast to the reasoning of the last chapter. They maintain either that consequences do not count at all in deciding what is morally right, or at least that rightness is a function of many considerations, only some of which are the consequences of the act. Like utilitarian theories, a distinction is often made between *act* and *rule* deontology. The latter holds that moral judgments are determined by reference to something general, a rule or principle. Act deontology sees no necessity for appealing to principles, maintaining that it is straightforwardly a matter of perception whether an act is right or wrong. *Intuitionism* is a name sometimes given to such an act theory. We shall find it necessary to discuss carefully the role of intuition a bit later. It functions in a more modest way in rule deontology, as well as in consequentialist theories.

OBJECTIONS TO CONSEQUENTIALISM

Many kinds of reasons have been brought forth historically in opposition to consequentialism. One very general consideration has been that it seems simply irrelevant to the morality of an act whether it has this or that consequence. Fulfilling a promise, caring for our offspring, and paying back a debt are examples of acts that are intrinsically right. The appropriateness of doing them derives from their own nature and not from whatever effects they produce. That is, the fact that we have made a promise or are parents is sufficient to create an obligation. The consequences of meeting our obligations do not determine whether we have those obligations. Secondly, an act that is right because it fulfills a commitment may have both good and bad consequences. If so, how is the act to be judged? Moreover, these consequences are not always due to the agent who performs the act, nor even foreseeable to those who act or are affected by the act. Consequently, it seems unreasonable to decide the morality of an act by reference to what either accidentally or unforseeably follows upon its commission.

It has also been argued that the attempt to ground moral rules in the pursuit of happiness or the fulfillment of interests cannot yield universal ethical principles. The inclinations and interests of people are too varied to permit any consensus about moral principles. Moreover, deontologists argue, the concept of happiness is surely subjective. What individuals perceive as constituting their happiness is peculiar to their experiences, tastes, and environment. Given people's idiosyncratic needs and desires and also the changeability of any given individual's perception of what will make her happy, it seems that no foundation for ethics can be constructed on such shifting sand.

Another argument against consequentialism maintains that our duty must not be confused with what satisfies our interests or makes us happy, since the fulfillment of duty often requires the sacrifice of interest and happiness. Moral obligations do not come into being merely as means for the attainment of some purpose, whatever that might be. Were moral imperatives conditional, in the sense of being required only if we desired the attainment of a given end, then we could relieve ourselves of those duties by choosing not to pursue the end. For example, what if the justification for dealing honestly with our customers is that this is the best way to encourage them to continue doing business with us? If so, our indifference to keeping them as customers or our decision to get out of this business altogether would allow us to cheat them. Also, if we're clever enough to cheat them and still keep their business, we're even better off!

KANT'S CATEGORICAL IMPERATIVE

Considerations such as these have led nonconsequentialists such as Immanuel Kant (1724–1804) to distinguish between two kinds of imperatives, *hypothetical* and *categorical*. Only the latter are moral, for they oblige us unconditionally, that is, regardless of our subjective and vacillating purposes or objectives. Hypothetical imperatives of the form "If we want X, then we ought to do Y," clearly commit us only if we have the desire in question. Moral "oughts," however, are not this conditional. What we have a duty to do, for example, because of our role as parent, plant manager, or judge, is determined by our station in life. Such duties are absolute, not at the mercy of whimsical desires or limited by ifs, ands, or buts.

Because Kant has had such great influence in the development of deontological theory, it will be helpful to consider his views in greater detail. Moral law, for

Kant, is characterized by universality and necessity. This follows from the very concept of law, which is general, not particular, and which binds all those who are moral agents. However, it is as free agents that we accept the necessity of the moral law. We give ourselves the laws we obey, although the law commands us absolutely and unconditionally. This is because the law derives from our reason, which is universal among human beings, rather than from our feelings or inclinations, which vary from individual to individual.

Since reason tells us that the form of the law must be universal and necessary, we can formulate a standard for testing the morality of any rule or policy that we propose to guide our actions. "Act only according to that maxim by which you can at the same time will that it should become a universal law."[1] This formulation of the *categorical imperative* enables us immediately to detect a possible source of immorality in our behavior. For we often make exceptions for ourselves to rules that we expect others to obey. And we would be most unhappy if others behaved toward us as we do towards them. Consequently, we can recognize as immoral any rule of action we might set for ourselves that we could not will to be universalized, binding upon everyone alike.

Failure of a maxim to pass this universalizability condition can be of two kinds, either *objective* or *subjective*. The former may be defined as the internal impossibility of a maxim's being thought of as a universal law. For example, it is impossible to universalize the maxim, "Never buy a newspaper before boarding the bus; always read over someone else's shoulder." It is obvious that, were everyone to attempt to observe such a maxim, the act it prescribes would be impossible.

What I have called the subjective kind of non-universalizability refers to maxims that it is possible to universalize, but which we judge it undesirable to universalize. We find ourselves disinclined to will such maxims, because they would conflict with our other desires. For example, it is possible to conceive of a world in which all adopt the maxim, "Every person for herself; don't help others in time of need." But as a matter of fact, we have only to discover ourselves in need to realize that universal observance of this maxim is undesirable, since we now want the assistance of others.

What Kant provided with the categorical imperative was a criterion for elimination of immoral maxims, those which cannot become part of the moral law. He also provided other formulations of the categorical imperative, one of them being "Act so that you treat humanity, whether in your own person or in that of another, always as an end, and never as a means only."[2] With this formulation, Kant emphasized respect for the personhood of other moral agents. The word "only" should be noted, however, for the imperative does not prohibit the many permissible ways in which persons serve us as means, for example, as taxi drivers, telephone operators or mail clerks. What is prohibited by the imperative is treatment of persons as mere instruments for our own purpose; that is, in a manner which violates their dignity as ends in themselves.

According to Kant, our acts do not have moral worth simply because they are consistent with what our duty requires. What must also be present is a moral motive, namely, that we acted from duty. This motive contrasts with action done from self-interest or from inclination which, although it might be materially right action, was not done for a moral reason. We can schematize the alternatives as follows, and then clarify them with an example.

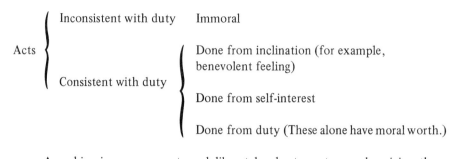

A cashier in a grocery store deliberately cheats customers by giving them incorrect change. This is an act inconsistent with duty and is immoral. What is consistent with duty is to give customers the change that is due them. However, if the cashier does that only when the customer is her friend, the act has no moral worth. Similarly, if the cashier gives correct change only because it is in her self-interest to do so because the manager is standing nearby, or because she knows the customer to be one who carefully counts her change, then the act has no moral worth. The only proper motive is doing the right act *because* it is the right act; that is, doing it from duty.

What Kant wishes to avoid is any attempt to locate morality on subjective grounds like feelings or self-interest. Not only do these vacillate, but they lack the universality necessary to establish a moral law for all rational beings. Consider our example once more. It is a merely contingent fact that the customer is a friend or that the manager is standing nearby, as a consequence of which the cashier gives correct change. Were the customer a stranger or were it to the cashier's advantage to cheat, the cashier would no longer have a motive for doing the good deed. What the moral law requires, Kant insists, is that we fulfill our duty even when it conflicts with self-interest and inclination. They cannot be trusted as sources of morality. If motives of self-interest or inclination exist alongside the disposition to act from duty, well and good. But it is reason alone that provides the universal basis for moral judgment.

Reflecting back on the distinction between categorical and hypothetical imperatives, Kant would say that treating customers justly in the matter of making change is the cashier's duty, period. Whether or not it makes the cashier happy or advances her career is irrelevant. A moral imperative is not of the conditional form, "If it feels good, do it." A sadist could have a field day with that guideline.

Problems with Kant's Theory

Before proceeding further with the discussion of deontological theories, we will look at some of the objections that consequentialists have raised to Kant's theory.

1. Kant has tried to rely exclusively upon reason to derive the moral law, but *a priori* reasoning (not based on experience or empirical evidence) cannot alone establish morality. The point of moral rules is to guide our choices in pursuit of happiness or human well-being. Rules are not observed for their own sake. Ultimately, then, the test of a rule is how well its general observance promotes human happiness, and we know that only through experience in living.

2. Human beings act as a result of felt needs and wants. That is, we act because of inclination or desire for something. Ethics, which proposes to discover appropriate guidelines for actions, must, therefore, take as its starting point those appetites, inclinations, and drives which set us in motion. Reason alone doesn't move us to anything. Rather, reason assists our inclinations by discovering what objects will best satisfy our needs or inclinations, and also by discovering the most effective means for the attainment of those objects. In effect, needs and inclinations provide the starting point for determining the ends of action. Without wants and desires we have nothing to aim for; our reason has no reason to function.

3. Kant argued that morality based on inclinations or the pursuit of happiness could not have the requisite universality. However, as was discussed in a previous chapter, there is empirical evidence that basic needs and drives do provide a common denominator of human striving in all parts of the world. Practically speaking, what does draw people together in cooperative endeavor, whether in units as small as a family or as large as the United Nations, is shared perception of what is needed or valued.

4. Kant's insistence upon the universality of the moral law led him to the extreme view that exceptions were never morally permissible. For example, he would say it is never permissible to tell a lie, or commit suicide, or have sex outside marriage. However, this rigorous view of moral rules fails to take account of certain features of our moral experience. For example, in some circumstances, rules may present us with conflicting duties. If we are asked by an assassin for directions to an innocent victim, the rule of truth telling can clearly put us in conflict with our duty to protect the innocent. The moral duties that Kant would defend are not absolute, but *prima facie*. That is, each is based on a morally relevant consideration, which establishes an actual duty unless overridden by a weightier consideration. Our duty, everything considered, is decided after taking into account all the morally relevant factors in the situation and, in a conflict situation, may involve violating one *prima facie* duty in order to fulfill another. Kant is unable to engage in such practical reasoning, because he fails to recognize the basis for resolving conflicts: the greatest net good over evil, all things considered.

5. A distinction should be made between *exceptions* to a rule and *qualifications* of a rule. It is possible to have a universal moral rule which contains qualification; for example, we may not kill except in self-defense. In this case, an exception is built into the rule, and we could say that there are no exceptions to that rule as thus qualified. However, it is impossible to spell out all the conditions under which rules such as truth telling or promise keeping may be overridden. The list of qualifications would make the rule unteachable and unlearnable. There is no legislatable substitute for the prudent judgment of the individual who must apply the rules to the situation.

6. The fact that we would not want to universalize a maxim does not necessarily establish that our behavior is immoral. For example, we may choose to remain celibate for any of a number of good reasons, but to universalize this

maxim would mean extermination of the species. Also, the mere fact that we consider a maxim universalizable does not qualify it as moral. What the sado-masochist would universalize is abhorrent to most people.

7. Kant's emphasis upon the motive of an action alone as giving it moral worth blurs an important distinction between judging the *act* and judging the *agent* who performs the act. A right action might be performed by an evil person, and a praiseworthy person might perform a wrong act. Motives are certainly relevant factors in deciding whether the agent is praiseworthy or blameworthy. But this does not justify disregarding the consequences when deciding whether the act itself was right or wrong. A caring mother may give her baby the wrong medicine, as a horrible consequence of which it dies. Assuming no negligence on her part, it makes sense to say, "She did the wrong thing, although she can't be blamed. It wasn't her fault . . ." To put it another way, a good will is neither a necessary nor a sufficient condition for producing right action.

8. A final objection is perhaps most telling. Does not Kant himself appeal to con-sequences in deciding whether a maxim can be universalized? His argument against a policy of not helping others in distress is that, if it were universalized, we might find ourselves denied of assistance when we need it. In other words, if the result of everyone's doing a particular act is undesirable, then the maxim must be rejected. Although Kant has identified the form of law through an *a priori* analysis of the concept of law, he cannot give content to the moral law except by considering the consequences of the universalization of a rule of conduct. What Kant threw out the front door has returned through the back door.

ACT DEONTOLOGY

At the beginning of this chapter we pointed out that a distinction can be made between rule and act nonconsequentialism. The latter maintains that we do not need to appeal to principles or rules to decide whether an act is right or wrong. Rather, values are capable of being directly or immediately apprehended. What this means is that moral judgments are not proved by inference or argument from other knowledge. They are *intuited*, that is, seen to be true in a manner analogous to the perception of colors and sounds. Act deontologists offer various reasons for claim-ing that moral knowledge is not a case of drawing conclusions about particular acts or objects from a knowledge of moral principles or from other kinds of knowledge.

In the first place, whatever principles would supposedly be the premises of a moral argument must themselves have been derived from many particular percep-tions, as inductions. The *inductive method* begins with direct experience of first one particular and then another, with the eventual formulation of a generalization based upon what all these particulars have in common. If there is any progression, then, it is from the intuition of individual acts that general principles are derived, not the other way around.

Second, although we can try to develop general moral principles that capture the moral truth in our immediate experience, this effort can never be completely successful. Each particular act, situation, or person is unique. Therefore, we must approach each case of moral decision making individually, and in the presence of the peculiar circumstances which that case presents, make a specific judgment.

Third, it is true of any kind of knowledge, whether moral, scientific, or aesthetic, that not everything can be known as a conclusion from something else. There is no infinite regress in offering proofs. Ultimately, we are pushed back to some things known without proof. This is a point of logic, that the starting points of inferred knowledge cannot themselves be inferred. A chain of reasoning must have its beginning in what is not itself a conclusion of reasoning. The question arises, then, concerning how we know these undemonstrable truths. The answer must be that they are self-evident. In other words, the moral quality of a particular act or person or situation is a matter of direct inspection. Just as we immediately perceive sensory qualities of objects—for example, this flower is red—so we directly intuit non-natural qualities like moral goodness or rightness.

Act nonconsequentialists reject the necessity of relying upon moral principles in making particular moral judgments. They also reject the view that moral knowledge is derived from any other kind of knowledge, such as that of scientific facts. On this latter point, act nonconsequentialists remind us of the gap between *is* and *ought*. Ethical judgments are not to be confused with factual judgments; how things are and how things should be are distinct questions. It is not possible to provide answers to the one by recourse to the other.

However, having said this, many act nonconsequentialists go on to explain that various conditions must be present for us accurately to apprehend the truth of a particular.[3] In order to appreciate the rightness or wrongness of an act, for example, we must be aware of what effects that act will produce (for example, it will boost someone's feelings), and what relationships exist in the situation (for example, this is an act of returning a favor). The possibility of error in an intuition can arise from the fact that the nature of the act is not completely understood. Moreover, our perceptions may be clouded by prejudice, fear, or overstimulated desire. Or, we may lack sufficient experience to appreciate the value of certain aspects of the act, or even lack the maturity to understand what is and will be occurring.

In view of all of this, the claim that moral judgments are direct or immediate perceptions of what is self-evidently true must be tempered by the realization that these judgments are fallible and corrigible. We can err if the preliminaries of a moral intuition are incompletely or distortedly presented. We also can err if we lack the mature powers of discernment found in a developed moral being. Although the judgment that "X is right" is immediate and underived, there is much that conditions that judgment. Disagreements in moral perceptions can be explained in terms of the different degrees of moral development and of the completeness with which the relevant conditions are comprehended.

Criticisms of Act Deontology

Critics of intuitionism have pointed out a number of difficulties with the theory. First of all, is there some special faculty that enables us to perceive moral qualities? And, what exactly is the nature of these moral objects of perception?

G. E. Moore was led to say that good is like yellow.[4] In other words, we apprehend the so-called non-natural qualities of an object as immediately as we perceive its sensible qualities. However, if this is the case, why should it be necessary to know anything else about the object in order to know that it is good? I certainly can know that a thing is yellow without knowing anything else about it.

If we accept the claim of other intuitionists that apprehending the goodness of a thing is a function of our knowing the preliminaries and circumstances discussed above, how is it possible to say that our judgment is not really inferred? It would seem that if good or right is directly intuited, then other knowledge about the object is superfluous. If other knowledge is relevant, then the intuitionist must explain the linkage between facts and moral qualities.

The distinctiveness of the intuitionist position seems to dissipate with the admission that intuitions are fallible and corrigible. The door is then opened to all the standard philosophical efforts to justify moral judgments. It is our common-sense experience that we seek and we give reasons for our moral judgments. "Reducing Helen Smith's insurance benefits would be unfair" is clearly unlike "This beach ball is yellow" in many ways. One difference is that it doesn't make sense to ask "Why?" in reaction to the latter statement; it does make sense with respect to the former. In short, ordinary moral discourse is replete with reasoning, with the examination of evidence, and with the attempt to resolve conflicts of moral judgment by appeal to facts and principles considered relevant to the argument.

Critics have charged that the appearance of self-evidence in intuitionist examples of moral judgments derives from the fact that the chosen examples are either obvious or trivial. The real test of the adequacy of a moral theory is in the hard, disputed cases; for example, should the United States try to overthrow the government of Nicaragua? It is in questions like this that most of us see the necessity for logical consistency, for careful examination of facts, and for judicious appeal to principles. The intuitionist, however, seems to rely on familiar conventions and a moral consensus that might reflect nothing more than training and habituation. Were that generally accepted framework of moral assumptions to be challenged, to what could the intuitionist appeal?

THE STATUS OF FIRST PRINCIPLES

Although these objections make it clear that there are serious difficulties with some versions of intuitionism, have we established that there is no role at all for intuition in ethics? Philosophers as far back as Aristotle have found it necessary to allow for some kind of intuitive knowledge. They maintain that this is true not only in ethics but also in all sciences and systematic inquiries. Every area of inquiry must have its starting points, those beliefs that are presupposed as a basis for any other knowledge. The foundation of any scientific inquiry such as physics or psychology is *first principles*, which, precisely because they are first, are not proved but must be assumed. Unless they are accepted, nothing else can be demonstrated, and the inquiry cannot proceed.

Mathematics is sometimes given as the clearest example of a discipline that demonstrates from axioms and postulates which themselves are not demonstrated. But other sciences have their presuppositions as well. A standard textbook in abnormal psychology contains the following in its early pages:

> Some degree of social conformity is clearly essential to group life, and some kinds of deviance are clearly harmful not only to society but to the individual. *However, the present text maintains that the best criterion for determining the normality of behavior is not whether society accepts it but rather whether it fosters the well-being of the individual and, ultimately, of the group.* By *well-being* is meant not simply maintenance or survival but also growth and fulfillment—the actualization of potentialities. According to this criterion, even conforming behavior is abnormal if it is *maladaptive*, that is if it interferes with functioning and growth.[5]

Now it is possible that what one discipline takes as presuppositions may be proven by another discipline. But, the argument goes, there cannot be any infinite regress. All knowledge is found ultimately to rest upon some basic truths, such as "A thing cannot both be and not be at the same time in the same respect."

Aristotle on Intuition

It was Aristotle's contention that the origin of scientific knowledge is intuition of first principles.[6] However, since awareness of these principles is not innate, he had to explain how they are acquired. Aristotle argued that this knowledge begins with sensory experience. A universal is the product of a process by which first one sense impression then another is formed. With the aid of memory, we have the power of systematizing these impressions, as a consequence of which we are said to develop experience. In recognizing that which is common to all these particulars, we form universal concepts. The principles that develop from this induction are what Aristotle calls the *primary premises* of scientific argument.

It is not only in theoretical knowledge that we develop first principles. In the area of action with which ethics is concerned, we also need to develop understanding of the sources of action. Since we act for the sake of some end, it is the end which functions as ultimate major premise in practical reasoning. Once again, experience of particulars is what enables us to develop our concepts of the ends or purposes of human striving. This is one reason why Aristotle believes it difficult for a young person to have the virtue of prudence or practical wisdom. It takes time to develop the experience out of which emerges an intellectual grasp of how life ought to be lived. In order to make correct choices in our day-to-day existence, we must not only have an understanding of the major premise—the end; we must also possess awareness of particular facts so that we can intelligently apply ultimate practical principles. The conclusion of a practical reasoning process is an action that deliberation has led us to choose after consideration of the facts of the situation together with an awareness of the goals we seek.

The ability to perceive the ultimate particular fact, that this action rather than that should be undertaken here and now, is an ability perfected through experience. A person who has been well brought up will have an advantage here, since habits of right action will have been encouraged from a very early age. Young people can develop a sense of the appropriate action under the guiding hand of those who have already acquired a large store of practical wisdom. Although the earliest beginnings of education occur when children's reasoning powers are undeveloped, the moral ideal is to stimulate development of the critical powers of understanding and reflection as they mature. Ideally, they will grow from a stage in which the example of others simply indicates the *fact* that this is how they should behave, to a later appreciation of the *reason* for the fact. Mature people take full responsibility for judgments concerning both the ends and the means, which in earliest years could only be set for them. (The question of whether freedom of choice at a later stage is possible, given the conditioning process of youth, will be dealt with in Chapter 8.)

The perception (or intuition) of a particular act as right, then, is a function of training at a prereflective stage in a person's development. With experience and the maturation of intellectual powers, individuals form general principles of action from which they eventually deduce for themselves the rightness of particular acts of the same sort. According to Aristotle, we intuit ultimates in both directions, since we directly grasp, not only the first principles, but also the variable facts that are the actions to which the principle is appropriately applied. For example, it is one thing to understand the principle that "We should not drink alcoholic beverages to excess, especially before driving." It is another thing to recognize when that prudent limit has been reached. Clearly, it is not sufficient merely to assent to correct principles, especially since the principle cannot specify what is moderate in each individual case. For this reason, Aristotle would say that the decision rests with *perception*, a sizing up of the situation which depends upon the particular facts and which is more likely to be handled appropriately by a person of sound habits and experience.

Hume and Mill on First Principles

Although this discussion has focused exclusively upon Aristotle's explanation of the proper role of intuition in the moral life, any number of other philosophers have expressed similar ideas about the necessity to posit ultimate principles of practical living. The English philosopher, David Hume (1711-1776), had this to say:

> Ask a man why he uses exercise; he will answer, because he desires to keep his health. If you then inquire why he desires health, he will readily reply, because sickness is painful. If you push your inquiries further and desire a reason why he hates pain, it is impossible he can ever give any. This is an ultimate end; it is never referred to any other object.
> Perhaps to your second question, why he desires health, he may also reply that it is necessary for the exercise of his calling. If you ask why he is anxious on that head, he will answer, because he desires to get money. If you demand, Why? It is the instrument of pleasure, says he. And beyond this, it is an absurdity to ask for a reason. It is impossible there can be a progression in infinitum, and that one thing can always be a reason why another is desired. Something must be desirable on its own account, and because of its immediate accord or agreement with human sentiment and affection.[7]

Hume's claim that it is our sentiments or passions which should determine the ends of human action flies in the face of Kant's contention that reason alone can determine the moral. And, like Kant, many deontologists would see in an appeal to sentiments no basis for universalizable moral rules. In fact, morality based on inclination seems to make choice an essentially arbitrary thing. If the ultimate ends cannot be accounted for by reason, but must be specified by reference to our inclinations, deontologists fear that we will reach the height of irrationality and arbitrariness. However, Hume, like Aristotle, did not see this to be a consequence of the claim that reason alone can move us to nothing. ("Thought wedded to desire" was Aristotle's way of expressing the need to begin with appetites or inclinations.) Hume and Aristotle shared the view that there is enough similarity among people regarding basic requirements for happiness or well-being to derive moral principles from those empirical necessities.

John Stuart Mill, whom we considered earlier in the context of utilitarianism, explained how the inability to prove first principles of human action cannot lead to the conclusion that they must be arbitrarily chosen. Mill draws an important distinction between *proof* and *evidence*.[8] Questions of ultimate ends are not amenable to direct proof, Mill agreed with Aristotle and Hume. However, evidence can be presented that is the equivalent of proof in establishing the credibility of a claim concerning what is intrinsically valuable. That evidence consists in examining the actual desires of people or, in other words, what people really seek in life. Since they desire what is either a constituent of happiness or a means thereto, Mill argued that no ethical theory could be acceptable which does not square with this reality.

Mill's critics claim that he was here ignoring a distinction between "desired" and "desirable," since what people in fact desire is not necessarily what should be desired or deserves to be desired. Mill, it is charged, made an illicit inference from facts to values. However, it can be said in Mill's defense that he was not trying to say that human beings only desire that which is morally desirable. Obviously, there are bad desires. Rather, he was suggesting that we cannot seriously propose as a purpose in life something that people do not in fact desire.[9] This is similar to Aristotle's claim that the test of the truth of an ethical theory is the facts of life. The starting point of a theory of what is desirable must begin with facts concerning our desires. But this is only the starting point. Those desires, multiple and often conflicting, must be reconciled with one another within the same individual, and must also be harmonized with those of other people in society. This means that we must reflect upon the phenomenon of desiring, so that long-run satisfaction is not imperiled for the sake of immediate gratification. The process of moral valuation begins as we establish priorities among desires, consider the consequence of alternative acts, and restrain some impulses in order to give fuller expression to others. Although some desires will not survive this kind of scrutiny, there is no departure from the initial claim that the desirable is derived from the desired. The standard by which individual desires are judged is the greatest happiness, that is, maximum fulfillment of human desires, all persons considered. Mill's point was, simply, that to propose any other end as the object of moral striving would be to advance a theory that lacks credibility—precisely because it is experience that has the last word.

If we think carefully about it, then, the appeal to the facts of life concerning what in the long run maximizes happiness in no way supports arbitrariness in human choice. This standard is what *de facto* operates to prohibit acts of cruelty and deprivation, as well as to mandate acts of cooperation and considerateness in supplying the basic goods of survival and prosperity. Although people may differ with regard to some specifics, there can be no doubting the general consensus about the principal sources of happiness and misery in human existence. This, of course, is a point that we discussed earlier in considering natural law theory.

What conclusions can we draw, then, concerning intuition and the differences between deontological and consequential approaches to morality? First of all, there seems to be little reason to deny that *basic* moral judgments are intuited. First principles, because they are first, cannot be proved. However, intuitionists go too far in claiming that *all* moral judgments, basic and nonbasic alike, are intuited. There is abundant evidence of reasoning and of a process of justification in ethics which cannot be explained by intuitionists. We may see a certain conclusion as appropriate at the end of a complex investigation, but that perception is only as good as the reasoning process that produced it and the principles and facts upon which it rests.

For their part, rule nonconsequentialists also appeal to intuition, in that the rules, *prima facie* or absolute, are taken as starting points. However, as we have seen, rule theorists have great difficulty in giving a satisfactory account of how we decide between conflicting duties. And, as consequentialists would argue, there is no rationale for including or excluding any particular duty from the list, unless some criterion such as human happiness is invoked.

This brings us to a view held by some, that a reconciliation of deontological and utilitarian theories is possible. The deontologist is correct in identifying the formal conditions of a moral norm. Universality and prescriptivity are necessary features of moral rules. However, the utilitarian is correct in claiming that we cannot decide what rules should be universally prescribed without consulting experience, that is, without a consideration of the consequences of general observance of proposed rules. Whereas the deontologist suggests the form of moral law, the utilitarian provides a method for giving content to that law. Moreover, the utilitarian suggests that it is by appeal to the happiness principle that we can decide between particular moral rules when they conflict. For example, when a duty to tell the truth is in conflict with a duty to aid someone in distress, reflection must determine which act on balance will be productive of the greatest net good. The happiness principle, then, becomes a standard for deciding priority among *prima facie* moral requirements.

WHAT IS CONSCIENCE?

Before concluding this chapter, some reflection on the meaning of *conscience* is appropriate, in view of what we have already said about intuition, the appeal to principles, and the importance of education and habituation. Often, we hear conscience invoked as though it provides a special sort of justification for moral deci-sions, or is even a unique faculty for making such judgments. To the question "Why didn't you do that?" or "Why did you think it was wrong?" people reply, "My conscience told me . . ." This type of response is even thought to be unassailable. That is, it is assumed that no argument is possible once we have invoked conscience. This is supposedly the conversation stopper, the appeal to the individual's ultimate moral authority.

In fact, as we have seen in discussing intuitionist theory, it is difficult to defend the claim that we possess a distinct power or faculty which illuminates us concerning unique, moral qualities of acts, persons and situations. Evidence suggests that we are born with the ability to acquire experience. As a consequence of this ability, we formulate general criteria for conduct and apply to each specific situa-tion the norms we accept either on the basis of our own reflection or that of others who have taught and guided us. Certainly it cannot be established that innate in human beings is knowledge of the moral quality of myriad specific acts and rules, especially since such judgments must be tailored to each situation and must vary with the culture and experience of each individual.

It is much more plausible to view conscience as a product of experience, not independent of it. Many of our moral judgments are immediate or intuitive, but this characteristic is a result of education and experience, much of which has become a matter of habit. To the extent that our training and habituation have been misdi-rected, our spontaneous evaluations will not be trustworthy. Consequently, there can be no assurance that the dictates of conscience are correct. As a reflection of what has preceded in the experience of the individual, conscience may be well-formed or ill-formed. Of course, its insights are capable of being modified by the critical and constructive work of thought, together with enlarged acquaintance with the facts about which it expresses judgment. The limits of intuition are based on the experience that gives birth to those insights. Consequently, conscience can only operate with regard to the familiar, not the novel. For this reason, there is always the danger that reliance upon intuition will lead to dogmatic conservatism, a com-fortable assumption of the unchallengeability of well-entrenched convictions.

Conscience can be viewed as merely another way of talking about the ordinary process of making value judgments in the light of personal experience, the accumu-lated wisdom of others, and direct assessment of the facts of the situation. Accord-ing to this definition "my conscience tells me . . ." simply means "my reasoned conclusion is . . . ." In other words, moral judgments are not mysterious and unique sorts of evaluations. They are part and parcel of a quite ordinary reflective proce-dure that operates in all kinds of contexts where the value of something needs to be determined or priorities weighed. In our daily lives we constantly make value judg-ments about important and trivial matters, moral and nonmoral. We decide questions about where we shall eat supper, what is appropriate to wear to the concert, which automobile is most likely to give good service—all of which are value judgments.

The development of conscience claims about right and good in a moral con-text is not utterly different in kind from the way we go about acquiring and applying evaluative criteria for other sorts of things. If this is the case, the appeal to conscience in a moral argument is far from constituting a conversation stopper. Rather, it should naturally invite the followup question, "But, *why* does your conscience tell you that?" In short, it is appropriate to seek and give *reasons* for judgments of conscience. It may be that we should always act in accordance with what conscience dictates. However, this means nothing more than that we should act the way we have decided we should act. The interesting moral issue concerns the validity of the reasoning and the accuracy of the factual claims that support that judgment of conscience. The best intuitions come *after* reasoned investigation, rather than existing apart from it. Thus, intuitions are subject to correction by the same process that gave birth to them in the first place. Growth in moral insight means growth in experience of the consequences of living according to those norms which custom and personal reflection have previously dictated. Frequent adjustments in valuations are the necessary accompaniment of opening our consciences to the trial and error experience of living with our convictions. Making those continual reassessments is a sign of a thinking life.

REVIEW QUESTIONS

1. Distinguish act and rule deontology.
2. Identify five deontological arguments against consequentialism.
3. Distinguish categorical and hypothetical imperatives.
4. What are two formal characteristics of law, according to Kant, and what is the formulation of the categorical imperative which expresses them?
5. Explain the difference between objective and subjective impediments to universalizability of a maxim.
6. Explain that formulation of the categorical imperative that expresses respect for persons.
7. Explain the division of acts into those which are immoral, moral, or lacking moral worth.
8. Summarize eight objections to Kant's theory, explaining distinctions found in several of those objections.
9. What are three arguments of act nonconsequentialists in support of the non-inferential character of moral judgments?
10. How is error in intuitions possible?
11. Identify four criticisms of intuitionism.
12. What is the role of experience in the formation of theoretical and practical principles, according to Aristotle?
13. What are objects of intuition in Aristotle's philosophy?
14. What are areas of agreement between Hume and Aristotle on the question of ends?
15. Explain the significance of Mill's distinction between proof and evidence.
16. How is the desirable derived from, but not equivalent to, the desired?
17. What is proposed as a way of reconciling deontological and utilitarian theories?

18. Why is appeal to conscience not an ultimate criterion of action?

19. What characteristics do moral judgments share with all other value judgments?

NOTES

1. Immanuel Kant, *Foundations of the Metaphysics of Morals*, trans. Lewis White Beck (New York: The Liberal Arts Press, 1959), p. 39.

2. Ibid., p. 47.

3. Cf. H. A. Prichard, "Does Moral Philosophy Rest on a Mistake?," *Mind*, XXI (1912), 487–499.

4. G. E. Moore, *Principia Ethica*, Chap. 1, Sect. 7, p. 7.

5. James C. Coleman et al., *Abnormal Psychology and Modern Life*, 7th ed. (Glenview, IL: Scott, Foresman & Company, 1984), p. 15.

6. In what follows I rely upon Aristotle's *Posterior Analytics*, Bk II, Chap. 19; *Nicomachean Ethics*, Bk. II, Ch. 9; Bk. IV, Ch. 5; Bk VI, Chs. 3, 6, 7, 8, 11.

7. Hume, *Inquiry Concerning Morals*, p. 111.

8. Mill, *Utilitarianism*, pp. 7 and 44.

9. Everett Hall, in a fine article dealing with Mill's argument, refers to this as the "test of psychological realism." "The 'Proof' of Utility in Bentham and Mill," *Ethics*, LX (1949), p. 9.

CHAPTER SEVEN

The Life
of Virtue

One kind of conceptual framework for discussing morality emphasizes the observance of rules. The central question then is, "What should I do?" Bound up with this approach to the moral life is a preoccupation with such issues as duty or obligation, the characteristics of a code of conduct, the justification of exceptions to rules, the determination of priorities among imperatives, and the sanctions reinforcing observance of rules. In preceding chapters we have examined these concepts and have looked at how utilitarians and deontologists, for example, build a moral system. Their emphasis was upon establishment of criteria for right action. The criteria were thought about in terms of a hierarchical structure of principles and rules which a moral agent was duty-bound to obey.

CRITIQUE OF RULE THEORIES

A criticism of this emphasis on rules takes the form of claiming that the prior question does not so much concern what I should *do*, but rather "What kind of person should I *be*?" From this point of view, the initial concern is to identify the good of human beings and establish that as a norm for self-actualization. The target to be aimed at requires a certain conception of what is ultimately worth seeking in life. This end or purpose then becomes standard for the sort of person we want to become. Of course, when we set about becoming a certain kind of person, we do not discard rules or the concept of duty altogether. But the emphasis does shift to a concern with character development, the role played by virtues and vices, and the components in our biological and psychological nature that are affected by and influence moral growth.

Several contemporary philosophers (among them Elizabeth Anscombe, Alasdair MacIntyre, and Philippa Foot) have criticized the modern tendency to emphasize rule theory and have called for a return to the classical approach represented by ancient Greek and Roman philosophers. The moderns have it backwards, they say, because the question of virtue should come first, then the discussion of rules. Rules are derived from and justified in terms of a conception of the good. Thus, the construction of an overall plan of life presupposes some clear ideas about what an ideal human being is like. Facts about human potentialities are obviously relevant, since what we are capable of sets limits to what we can become. The wholesome actualization and integration of those potentialities becomes a goal of continuous striving.

Virtue is a key concept in this approach, because the habits or dispositions that are formed in the process of moral development constitute the character of the individual. They determine the pattern of behavior and of responses to life situations. The basic insight here is that as a person *is*, so that person *acts*. Since death is the only thing that stops the process of becoming, a practical question faces us at every turn in life: what person *shall* we be?

Things behave the way they are constituted, and human beings have options regarding their own constitution. MacIntyre argues that many moderns have surrendered to the view that any choices on this matter are arbitrary, because they do not accept the concept of human nature or of any objective basis for deciding what is good or bad.[1] Also, these modern thinkers have gone too far in maintaining a distinction between facts and values. We have investigated these issues in Chapters 2 and 3, and need only point out here that the classical approach to be examined in this chapter assumes that facts about what we are and what we can become are essential to the task of deciding what is good and right. There is a sufficient homogeneity of basic needs and interests to warrant generalized claims about ideals and limits in human striving.

Anscombe has suggested that between the time of the Greeks and modern times Judaeo-Christianity intervened with its *law* concept of ethics.[2] What we are permitted or required to do, or excused from doing, comes from God, who is a lawgiver. An absolute verdict, like that of sin or guilt, follows upon behavior that is unlawful. If, after many centuries, belief in God as the source of such moral law is given up, the notion of being obligated in certain ways remains—but without its roots. That is, we continue to feel psychologically compelled in certain ways, but we no longer possess the intellectual framework necessary to make those obligations intelligible. This causes people to be at a loss when challenged to justify their moral norms. Anscombe's suggestion is that we can once again study ethics in a nonlegalistic fashion if we pursue a methodology that investigates the requirements for human flourishing and that bases the analysis of virtues and vices on what humans need in order to flourish. Such a procedure will not enable us to infer moral oughts having the "mesmeric force" of divine commands, but we will be able to make the transition from what human beings are, to what they need, to what is good for them to acquire. That kind of analysis will be examined and critiqued in this chapter.

Human Flourishing as the Goal

A naturalistic justification of the virtues is based on their usefulness in achieving the good for human beings. That good is discovered through an analysis of what human beings have the potential to become. Obviously, people have the potential to develop opposite values—that is, both good and bad. If an important conceptual link is made between what is good and what enables people to survive and prosper, the way is open to characterizing the end or goal as one of *human flourishing.* (The term *happiness* is frequently employed as a synonym, but some philosophers think it has too many subjective connotations.) Even while allowing that we should pursue what makes human beings flourish as our end, there is still the possibility that humans may flourish in many different ways. Variety is not inconsistent, however, with sameness, as we have already seen in Chapter 3. Thus, a general framework for evaluating achievement is appropriate to the extent that it reflects the common denominator of human needs and aspirations. Morality respects diversity by not dictating one particular lifestyle. Rather, it prescribes conditions within which lives are to be lived and ends pursued. Those conditions are specified as experience in living reveals what is necessary to enable humans to prosper in community.

The injunction to "Become what you are" captures the sense of life's course as one of developing potentialities. Human excellence, according to this way of thinking, means the greatest possible actualization of those powers which are a given of our nature. Just as health, in a physical sense, is promoted or impeded by individual and social measures of various sorts, so also the well-being of a human being, in a moral sense, is affected by behavior that advances or retards self-fulfillment.

What is the nature of the self whose full development gives meaning and purpose to virtues, principles, and rules? In the most general sense, we can say that humans are able both to know and to desire. Knowledge for us is made possible by two kinds of powers—sensory and intellectual. We discover ourselves and the world around us through sensations such as touch, taste, and vision. And we leap beyond the rest of the animal world in the forms of knowing associated with reasoning and reflection. In parallel fashion, humans have desires or appetites of a sensory and of an intellectual sort.

HABITS AS THE HALLMARK OF CHARACTER

It is clear that, if we are going to talk about an ideal human being, then we must include excellence in both knowing and desiring. This gives rise to the distinction between *intellectual* and *moral virtues.* Intellectual virtue is the perfection of our ability to know, and moral virtue is the perfection of our ability to desire or feel inclined. Before discussing each of these kinds of virtue in detail, however, let us clarify what we mean by a virtue in general. A *virtue* is a good habit, that is, a relatively fixed disposition to be and to act in an excellent way. Bad habits, called *vices*, impede the full development of human beings and worsen the human predicament. To say that virtues and vices are *habits* is to point out that they are stable tendencies we have somehow acquired. We are not born with these habits; what is innate is the ability to feel and to know in the various ways that are perfected by virtues.

Habits are not necessary in order for an individual to be able to act. It is obviously possible to experience a sensation, feel an emotion, or generate a thought without having a habit of it. In fact, it is through repetition of the same kinds of acts that we form habits, at least when we are talking about moral dispositions, and it is through repetition of opposing acts that we break habits.

There are several advantages to cultivating habits. Consider an analogy with learning to use a typewriter. Before a person has developed the skill, it is possible to type a term paper, but only with great difficulty. A "hunt and peck" attack on the keyboard involves an enormous amount of time, exhausting expenditure of energy and concentration, frequent errors, and a great deal of frustration because the whole process is so imperfect. Given the desirability of possessing the skill because it is such a useful means of communication, a student may set himself to acquiring facility in typing. Through a series of exercises involving practice, repetition, and perhaps some instruction, the skill develops. Fingers, typewriter, paper, and even elements like posture and appropriate lighting all become organized into an efficient operation. With sufficient experience, an admixture of trial and error, the habit grows. At some point it may even be possible to say that a real talent for typing has developed, an excellence in performance that was hardly imaginable in the old days when the student first confronted that foreign object, the typewriter. Now the activity proceeds with facility, promptness, and even delight. Pain and uncertainty are past, because typing has become second nature. A certain justifiable pride attaches to having mastered the technique and having overcome a number of obstacles in so doing. Even when the student is not actually typing, that habit remains as a characteristic part of the self, ready to function smoothly and efficiently when required.

In somewhat similar fashion, we can talk about the origins, the nature, and the purposes of virtues in the moral life. Our capacities for knowing, for feeling emotion, and for acting to satisfy desires are all capable of being perfected through the formation of habits. Virtues organize the resources of the self in a way that produces internal harmony and effective interaction with the environment. If a certain kind of activity or mode of reaction is judged desirable, then the cultivation of a habit secures that behavior in an enduring form. Thinking about the complexity of human impulses and capacities makes us realize the absolute necessity of introducing discipline, cooperation, and understanding if this diversity of energies is to be harnessed for worthwhile objectives. The utility of the virtues is that they accomplish precisely this. The raw material of emotions and inclinations is shaped into serviceable dispositions. Then a person can express in a controlled, consistent, and enduring way what otherwise would manifest itself chaotically, sporadically, and even blindly.

Both intellectual and moral virtues are necessary for human flourishing simply because the formation of ideas as well as their execution depend on habits. In order to be equipped so that we can operate as we *choose*, we must improve our mental and physical resources so that we are in command of their operation, and our energies are expended efficaciously in coping with the environment. Our character can be defined in terms of our network of habits, because the sum total of acquired predispositions constitutes the self. Who we are is contained and manifested in the typical way we think, act and react.

It is of practical importance to realize that habits are responsible for unity of character and conduct. Of course there is no exact equation of disposition and outcome, because no set of habits establishes complete control of an environment that may have its own independent impact on actual results. Desirable traits do not always produce desirable results, and good things often happen by accident. Nevertheless, habits are tendencies that create *probabilities* about how the self will function and what the self will accomplish. Given all the contingencies in life, many often unforeseeable, we simply try to perfect what is under our control.

Preeminently, then, we are responsible for our character. Other things being equal, right disposition will produce right deed. Consequently, over time we find it possible to form an estimate of character from a judgment of conduct. Although we cannot judge character from a single deed, the fact that dispositions are persistent in their expression makes it possible to infer what kind of person someone is from the *pattern* of his behavior. Reflecting back to the discussion in previous chapters about the utilitarian emphasis on consequences and the Kantian emphasis on motive, we can locate in habit the link between what is inner and what is outer. Motive or will is not opposed to consequences, but is a cause of them. Our characteristic deeds are made possible and predictable by the abiding organization of ideas and affections called habits.

The subtle influence of habits is such that, even when they are not on display in some overt act that impinges on the world, their operation is continuous upon the self. Because habits so intimately constitute our character, it is impossible for any moment of existence, conscious or unconscious, to remain unaffected by the standing predilections which are our virtues or vices. All experience, whether moving inward from the environment or outward from the self, is filtered through our acquired tendencies. It is for this reason that we might justifiably attribute an act to habit, even if it occurs only once.

Let us consider an example. A homicidal act at first might be considered an aberration, an uncharacteristic or atypical occurrence, or even a manifestation of temporary insanity. It may indeed be all of these things, but we cannot conclude that simply from the fact that the person never previously committed a murder. Careful investigation might reveal that the act was consistent with a set of attitudes that provided the natural breeding ground for what superficially appeared to be involuntary. Suppose that a person has grown up in a neighborhood that took pride in its "WASP-ish" homogeneity and that disliked and distrusted different people, such as Asians. Suppose further that this individual reinforced customary prejudices by selectively reading literature that caricatured the history and characteristics of Asian peoples, all the while neglecting to confirm the reliability of his sources. He further avoided any opportunity for personal contact with Asians which might be a direct way of confirming or falsifying the stereotypic images he had. Moreover, this person enjoyed association with others who favored exclusivity, thought themselves superior to nonwhites, and entertained one another with crude jokes about the appearance or personality of Asians. More ominously, let us assume that this individual and his buddies were known to participate in demonstrations against the location of Asians in the area and even organized to protest the purchase of imports from far-eastern countries.

If it is a fair conclusion that we have here described someone who can be termed a racist, then it follows that specific sorts of feelings and activities would be in character. Having become, by so many acts and omissions, a kind of person who considers Asians non-persons, this racist has acquired a special sensitivity to certain classes of stimuli. In thought and attitude, he is poised for discriminatory action. Given this carefully cultivated personality as context, what is now to be said about the racist's "sudden" clubbing to death of an Asian trying to get through a picket line on his way home from work one afternoon? Although the judge is told that the racist has no previous record of such acts, is this really a "first offense"? Indeed, why should anyone, least of all the racist, not expect the eventual eruption of violent behavior from such long-festering inclinations? In short, the particular act may be unique in the history of the individual, while at the same time be a natural offspring of habit or training.

We can summarize much of this section by quoting a passage from John Dewey's *Human Nature and Conduct* in which he identifies four characteristics of habits. This is a word used

> to express that kind of human activity which is influenced by prior activity and in that sense acquired; which contains within itself a certain ordering or systematization of minor elements of action; which is projective, dynamic in quality, ready for overt manifestation; and which is operative in some subdued subordinate form even when not obviously dominating activity.[3]

Intelligent and Routine Habits

Dewey makes an important distinction between *intelligent* and *routine* habits. This distinction calls attention to the fact that conduct can be under the continual influence of reflection or can be purely mechanical. There are several good reasons why habits should never become fossilized. To the extent that individuals face the same situations and find that the same response provides a satisfactory outcome, habits are a convenient and efficient organization of past experience. However, new experiences are also possible. Our environment often confronts us with the unexpected. The ability to incorporate what is new into patterns of response requires that our habits be flexible. Recognizing that adjustments are warranted is a function of intelligence. In its absence, the tendency is to shun what is new and to be fearful of change. We can become uneasy if old habits are questioned, and irritable when familiar ways of acting do not meet the need or solve the problem any longer. Refusal to employ intelligence to reassess habitual responses means that routine behavior is not invigorated by the stimulus of the new and, hence, fails to cope appropriately with the new. Lack of sensitivity to changes in the environment blocks changes in the way the self interacts with the environment. The result can be disastrous. In reactionary fashion we might condemn and attack the unfamiliar simply because it is such. We may refuse to consider whether it actually threatens what is of value in our prevous habits. Or we might simply withdraw from active engagement with the changing world, finding security by ignoring transformations of reality. Needless to say, "hardening of the categories" poorly disposes us to comprehend and to respond to varying kinds of life situations.

Merely routine habits are not only dysfunctional in accommodating a changing environment and, hence, in allowing correspondingly appropriate changes in the self who must cope. The routineness of habits is also ill-suited to the character of past transactions. No one kind of response is ever suitable for a diversity of situations. Even something like driving an automobile, which would seem to be a simple example of routine behavior, requires an ability to act differently in differing circumstances, for example, on whether it is day or night, on the open road or a city street, in clear visibility or fog, up a winding hill or an easy terrain, or in a school zone. Imagine how much more subtle and complicated is the exercise of a moral virtue like patience or generosity. The point is that just one particular kind of act is no match for the enormous variety of contexts in which we must act. The ability to act repetitiously must be combined with *thought* about how each situation may be relevantly different from the next. Flexible habits tailor our responses to the requirements of individual circumstances.

The advantages of flexible rather than fossilized habits remind us once more of the cooperation that must exist between reason and desire, intelligence and impulse. We shall see this reflected again in our discussion of the *unity of the virtues*, by which we mean the fact that in their perfection the moral virtues require intellectual virtue, and vice versa. Acquiring the virtues can be seen as a "package deal." We cannot obtain one without the other. This essential link will become progressively clearer as we discuss the moral and intellectual virtues in detail. At this stage it is sufficient to point out that habits of correct *feeling* and of correct *action* are a necessary component of the good life for human beings. Having characterized happiness or human flourishing as full development of our potentialities as social beings, the classical view is that this self-fulfillment consists, at least in part, in the proper exercise of our rational and appetitive powers. Knowing what we should and desiring what we should are integral parts of an ideal life. However, is that the whole story? Has *complete* happiness thus been described? Clearly not, for the needs and interests of human beings are numerous. Let us consider once again the concept of human flourishing.

A PLURALISTIC CONCEPT OF HAPPINESS

Perhaps the best way to understand the classical concept of happiness is to ask, "In what does the best life consist?" That is, what might we say when attempting to describe an ideal existence? Rather obviously, we would not claim that there is only one ingredient in the completely desirable life. Therefore, the concept of happiness is not *monistic*, consisting of just one element, but is *pluralistic*. This means that the human good is adequately described only in terms of many components. We get some idea of how Aristotle thought about our question from his statement:

> It may be said that every individual man and all men in common aim at a certain end which determines what they choose and what they avoid. This end, to sum it up briefly, is happiness and its constituents. Let us, then, by way of illustration only, ascertain what is in general the nature of happiness, and what are the elements of its constituent parts. . . We may define happiness as prosperity combined with virtue; or as independence of life; or as the secure enjoyment of the maximum of pleasure. . . From this definition of happiness it follows that its constituent parts are: —good birth, plenty of friends, good friends, wealth, good children, plenty of children, a happy old age, also such bodily excellences as health, beauty, strength, large stature, athletic powers, together with fame, honour, good luck, and virtue.[4]

Whatever we think of Aristotle's own list of the goods that constitute happiness, it is safe to say that anyone else's concept would also be pluralistic. While there are many ingredients in a life of complete fulfillment, this need not suggest that all components are of equal value or importance. It may well be that some goods are more essential than others. Also, a ranking of these goods might place at the top of the list those which are most characteristic of us as human beings, that is, those which distinguish us from all other creatures. Aristotle himself described the noblest part of the happy life in terms of contemplation, an activity of the intellect. He reasoned that of all the goods in which happiness consists, the best will be an activity of that part of us which is uniquely human, namely, our rationality. What he meant by contemplation, then, was an activity of our highest power when focused on the finest objects that humans can think about. Once again, we get some clue to Aristotle's reasoning if we ask ourselves, "What is the noblest sort of activity in which a human can engage, and what are the most important things that can function as objects of that activity?"

Within a conprehensive plan of life, then, we can distinguish, in terms of priority, between *paramount* and *subordinate* goods. At the same time, we can think of these as part of the one ultimate end, which is happiness or human flourishing. Clearly, to talk of human flourishing as an ultimate end does not mean something acquired at the termination of a person's life. Rather, it is that greatest good which, as every moment of our existence, we should endeavor to possess. Our concept of the ideal life, whatever it is, functions as a target to aim at, a purpose that gives direction to our life. Any intelligent action requires a clear idea about its objective. With regard to the larger picture, we need even more to be convinced about our overall purpose in living. "What are our goals?" is the *first* question asked, precisely because it is the controlling question. It is in view of what is worth pursuing as a goal that all questions are decided about means. What is ultimate provides the rationale for what is proximate or intermediate.

Intrinsic and Instrumental Goods

A helpful distinction is made between *intrinsic* and *instrumental* goods. What is valued for its own sake, as an end of action, is called an intrinsic good. Such goods are desirable in themselves. Other things are valued as means to these intrinsic goods. What is desired for the sake of something else, because it helps to make that other good attainable, is called an instrumental good. Clearly, the point of choosing a means is that, by its definition, it is instrumental in the achievement of an end. In this sense, it is the end which justifies the means, as we explained in Chapter 5. What happiness or human flourishing provides is a possible answer to the question concerning that ultimate end which constitutes the target and the justification for all of life's decisions. This end, as an object of striving, is called good. Because the human good consists of many things, we can consider it an inclusive whole. That is, the unified concept of happiness includes, or contains within itself, many component parts which are called intrinsic goods. Together they constitute complete happiness.

Although at first it may sound puzzling, something can be valued both for its own sake and also because it is useful for the attainment of something else. We considered an example of this in the earlier chapter when friendships were discussed. We may choose people as friends merely because they have utility value. But the noblest kind of friendship exists between persons who value each other for their own sake. Such a friend, loved because that person is good, is nevertheless going to possess the other desirable qualities of friendship; that is, noble friends whose good we will for their own sake will also be a source of pleasure and will be useful to us.

Many kinds of things can have both intrinsic and instrumental value. Knowledge can be pursued for its own sake, because it satisfies our curiosity to know, and also for its value as a means, for example, making a living as a teacher. The career of a poet or painter or composer can be understood as creating means-end values. And the customer who purchases a painting may value it both as an end and also as a means. "I bought that picture because it is such a beautiful landscape scene, but also because I needed something to cover the big bare spot in my living room." What is said of objects can also be said of activities. Sailing or cooking can be an intrinsically satisfying experience, while at the same time be useful to other ends. Indeed, the most fortunately employed individuals are those who can make a living doing what they find rewarding in itself.

The sad reality is that, for many people, work has no intrinsically redeeming feature. Such persons work only because it has instrumental value—and barely that, if their wages are low. A Marxist critique of labor highlights the fact that, in all too many instances, people's long hours of work over many years are spent in dull, repetitive operations that neither enable the worker to grow as a person, nor produce a product of any lasting value. "Humanizing the workplace" does not make welding door joints more fulfilling labor. But what is lacking in intrinsic satisfaction may be partially offset by attention to other needs of the worker valued as a person, for example, better provisions for safety, privacy, recreation, medical care, participation in decision making, and retirement. It's little wonder that people who find nothing meaningful in their line of work are often tempted to "call in sick." Others are preoccupied with thoughts of what to do after work, and they agitate for more vacation time and a shorter work week.

What contributes to this flight from work is its intrinsic frustrations. Even worse is the labor expended in producing products that are positively harmful to people, such as making cigarettes, working in a chemical weapons factory, or marketing sugar-laced cereal to children. Confronted with this moral dilemma, workers sometimes take refuge in such defenses as "We are only giving the public what it wants," or "My job isn't to ask questions," or "If I don't do it, someone else will." (The last excuse could justify *any* crime. From the moral point of view, would it not be better to dig ditches than to peddle lung-rot?) A course in business ethics would be required to address these issues adequately.

What is important for our immediate purpose is to realize that virtue itself is a *means-end value*. It is possible to say both that virtue is a means to happiness, and that happiness consists (in part) in virtuous activity. The instrumental value of virtues is evident in the way they dispose their possessor to act in ways that are beneficial both to the agent and to others. Not only is the community's well-being advanced by sympathetic and cooperative dispositions in each of its members, but individuals themselves find it useful that they have habits of careful deliberation, control of emotions, and moderation in their sensual desires. Mitigating human suffering and enhancing the prospects of human happiness provide justification enough for cultivation of virtuous dispositions.

The end, then, explains the *point* of the virtues: they are means to happiness. At the same time, we describe the happy life as consisting in activity as well as in the possession of certain kinds of desirable objects. Activity according to virtue is an integral part of ideal living and not just a means to it. That is, happiness need not be thought of as something beyond acts of generosity, courage, temperance, and reflection. Rather, it is possible to say that we flourish in the very act of eating moderately, or learning astronomy, or visiting with friends. If the end is living well, and living well means activity, then we can say that the human good or happiness is (in part) *identical* with virtuous activity.

Philosophers have employed various terms to explain this special relation that virtues bear to the human good. Some describe virtues as "means internal to the end," signifying that the end itself cannot be characterized independently of the means. "For what constitutes the good for man is a complete human life lived at its best, and the exercise of the virtues is a necessary and central part of such a life, not a mere preparatory exercise to secure such a life."[5] That virtuous acts can have instrumental value as means while at the same time have intrinsic value as constituent parts would seem to be Aristotle's point when he says, "Honor, pleasure, intelligence, and all virtue we choose partly for themselves—for we would choose each of them even if no further advantage would accrue from them—but we also choose them partly for the sake of happiness, because we assume that it is through them that we will be happy" (1097b1-4. Ostwald).

Before moving on, we should again emphasize the folly of not organizing our lives in view of some end or goals. What can be said about a life in which we do not plan sensibly or get our priorities straight? It is difficult to imagine a more fundamental difference between one person and another than in the objects which they seek. Some engage in "ardent pursuit of the trivial."[6] For example, some people clutter their minds with gossip of the entertainment world, or talk about nothing except the weather, or are prepared to kill over a soccer game. Others parasitically preoccupy themselves with immediate and momentary pleasures at the expense of society. According to the *Milwaukee Journal* of June 18, 1985, city sanitation workers were paid to pick up trash that was thoughtlessly discarded along the beachfront, despite empty litter cans in the vicinity.[7] There is a powerful contrast between such people and what in the classical tradition is called a *highminded* person—one who possesses the virtue of magnanimity (1123b). The highminded are those who can distinguish between what is important and what is unimportant, can avoid pettiness, and can keep things in perspective. The ability accurately to assess the real worth of ends and means, together with the strength to act on that knowledge, comes close to encapsulating the moral ideal.

VIRTUES IN GENERAL

When the subject of virtue was introduced earlier in this chapter, several characteristics were noted. First of all, the virtues are *acquired*. We are not born with them, but we come to possess them either through instruction and learning or through practice. The virtues are *habits*, which means that they are relatively fixed dispositions. Once habits are formed, stable tendencies exist in the individual that can be called characteristic of that person. What is manifested by habit, then, is not accidental or irregular; it is an expression of the kind of person someone is. The virtues are *operational*. They dispose us both to be and to act in certain ways. These operations can be merely internal, such as the activity of thinking about a mathematical problem. Or the activity can proceed externally, as when we bandage the wounds of an injured person. Virtues are *good*. This distinguishes them from vices, which are bad habits. Virtues are perfective, enabling us to act in an excellent way. In the acquisition of virtues we develop as human beings, fulfilling and actualizing ourselves. Vices have an opposite effect, disposing us to behave in a manner that undermines our real good. In this way, they are destructive rather than perfective of our capacities.

Skills and Virtues

In the complete sense, virtue perfects both the agent and the operations of the agent. Not only the possessor, but also his works are excellent. People who have virtue without restriction possess an aptness for certain kinds of activity and also make right use of that aptitude. The significance of this distinction is made clear when we consider something like the art of medicine. The knowledge and the techniques of operation acquired by a medical student are goods. They are perfections of a human being's natural capacities. They confer skills of a particular sort. But it is possible not to make proper use of those skills. A physician may neglect to exercise his talents when they are called for; he may lazily refuse to respond to an emergency call. Or the physician may actually put his medical skills to malicious use, employing knowledge of drugs and deftness at surgical procedures to kill rather than save a life. It goes without saying that virtue, from the moral point of view, means a disposition to act well in the complete sense. This implies both the ability and the exercise of that ability for the proper ends. We have already seen that the ultimate end is happiness or human flourishing in a social context. This purpose is what justifies activity, and virtue is recognized by its expression in acts ordered to that end.

A person who possesses talents and puts them to bad use causes greater harm than one who lacks ability. "Corruption of the best is the worst." An evil genius or a perfect liar illustrates the difference between having a skill and having a virtue. Virtues, in the complete sense to which we are referring, enable a person to live righteously. Both the agent and his works are good. The individual possesses correct knowledge of the general end of human existence and desires that end. Such a person employs the means necessary to achieve the correct end. Consequently, we cannot make evil use of a virtue. Activity, however skillful, which is directed to a bad end is not virtuous. Remember that virtue perfects both knowledge and desire with regard to the end and the means to the end. An artful liar acts for improper ends, and so his skill is no virtue. Similarly, boldness in committing murder is not courage.

Although we shall see more of this later in analyzing specific virtues, it should be emphasized here that unqualified virtue is not a mere capacity. It engages the will. And the will is thereby directed to proper ends. In the moral life, then, to fail deliberately is worse than to fail accidentally. This is because our inclination and purpose is perfected by virtue; the intention to do evil reveals a basic lack of virtue. By contrast, voluntary error is preferable to involuntary error in the exercise of an art or skill. Someone who by design misspells a word is not faulted the way one is who errs through lack of knowledge. "I did it deliberately" gets the novelist off the hook. Similarly, drops of paint on a canvas are a matter of reproach if accidentally spilled, but not if purposefully applied (*à la* Jackson Pollock).

There are other differences between virtues and skills.[8] (1) Virtues are character traits that are important for everyone to have. Some skills, for example, being able to wiggle your ears or work crossword puzzles, lack such importance. Although a skill may not even be worth having, that cannot be said of any of the virtues. Skills, but not virtues, may be exercised in trivial pursuits. (2) Virtues are qualities enabling us to succeed in life generally. The excellence which virtues confer is appropriate in whatever we do. This contrasts with skills, such as wood-carving and skiing, each of which is an excellence for just one specific kind of activity. (3) Skills involve a mastery of technique. Instruction, followed by practice, leads to proficiency in glass blowing. There are no tricks of the trade, however, in acting virtuously. Telling the truth may be difficult, but this is not due to problems that are overcome by special techniques. Difficulties in being virtuous are due to contrary inclinations. (4) Skills can be forgotten, for example, how to play gin rummy. But, can we "forget" the difference between right and wrong? When a spouse asks why the partner is no longer faithful, it will not do to reply, "I forgot how." This is a question of will, not of skill. For that reason, we do not censure someone who loses a skill like card playing, but we blame someone for a loss of virtue. People cease to be patient or honest, not by accident, but by ceasing to care. What we deplore in moral decline is a change of heart, not a loss of information or technique. (5) It is perfectly allowable to "take a break" from exercising a skill. For example, an auto mechanic may decide to go away for a weekend, and this is not considered a failing. But, what of someone who decided to take a "moral holiday" and cheat customers one weekend a month? In the case of a skill, such as playing the piano, it is permissible even to decide never to play again. However, we exhibit no similar tolerance toward a person who abandons telling the truth. (6) Finally, and perhaps most importantly, a virtue is not merely a capacity to perform acts that have certain characteristics. In addition, the agent must be in a certain condition when performing those acts. This difference is captured in the distinction between a *right act* and a *virtuous agent*. Aristotle identifies three conditions that must exist if the agent is to be considered virtuous in performance of right acts.

> In the arts, excellence lies in the result itself, so that it is sufficient if it is of a certain kind. But in the case of the virtues an act is not performed justly or with self-control if the act itself is of a certain kind, but only if in addition the agent has certain characteristics as he performs it: first of all, he must know what he is doing; secondly, he must choose to act the way he does, and he must choose it for its own sake; and in the third place, the act must spring from a firm and unchangeable character . . . In other words, acts are called just and self-controlled when they are the kinds of acts which a just or self-controlled man would perform; but the just or self-controlled man is not he who performs these acts, but he who also performs them in the way just and self-controlled men do (1105a28-b9. Ostwald).

Earlier, in Chapter 5, the difference between judging the act and judging the agent who performed the act was seen to be useful for utilitarians. Some explanation of Aristotle's three conditions might be helpful. An act can be just. For example, a cashier may give correct change to the customer. However, the *just act* may not be an *act done justly*. The latter implies exercise of a virtue, wheras even a vicious person can perform a just act. For example, a thieving cashier may give correct change unknowingly. Although he intended to cheat, by mistake he gave the customer his due. Also, the cashier may do the just act unwillingly, even if knowingly. Perhaps the customer was given correct change only because in this instance the vigilant manager was standing nearby. In a sense, the cashier was compelled to do the right act and did not act by choice. To act justly means to perform the act voluntarily, and to choose the act for its own sake, in other words, because it is right.

The question of *motive* enters here. For the cashier to be honest only because the customer is his buddy or because he fears detection is not characteristic of a virtuous person. The *reason* for a just person's act is precisely the fact that this is the appropriate act to perform. Finally, the cashier who only gives correct change now and then, or as the mood strikes him is hardly described as a praiseworthy person. It is the consistently honest individual who is called virtuous. Acting justly means that this kind of behavior is characteristic, that a firm disposition exists to behave in that manner. The three conditions can be summed up by saying that when Aristotle talks about performing acts "in the way just and self-controlled men do," he means (1) knowingly, (2) willingly, and (3) consistently.

INVOLUNTARINESS

If virtuous action means action undertaken knowingly and willingly, then we can immediately identify two ways in which an action becomes involuntary. Both *ignorance* and *compulsion* are causes of unfree acts. And, as we shall see in Chapter 8, when freedom is lacking it makes no sense to praise or blame the agent who performs the act. A person can be held responsible only for voluntary acts, not for acts due to ignorance or force.

The matter becomes more complicated, however, when we look carefully at these circumstances. Not all ignorance is an acceptable excuse. In some cases we can be held responsible for the fact that we do not know. Thus, we must distinguish between *culpable* and *inculpable* ignorance.

Acting in ignorance does not diminish our blameworthiness when: (1) the ignorance is of things that any reasonable person can be expected to know; or (2) if the ignorance is due to negligence; or (3) if the ignorance is caused by our own voluntary acts. For example, students who miss a final exam because they do not know the exam schedule are hardly deserving of sympathy. That information is readily available to everyone. Or, what can be said of hunters who are so negligent that they immediately fire into rustling bushes, not pausing to determine the source of the movement? In ignorance they may have killed a hunting companion. But are they without blame? Not every "accidental" homicide is beyond moral criticism.

An illustration of the third kind of situation is provided by a person who becomes mean when he drinks too much. Mean and drunk, he then beats the children, smashes the china, and terrorizes the family pet. Can we take seriously the regrets expressed next day by the sobering derelict, especially if this is a repeat performance? Not knowing what he is doing is culpable ignorance when he is responsible for the drunkenness that caused it.

Some people may even set out to get drunk, reasoning that they can feel less responsible or guilty for acts like illicit sex or vandalism, on the grounds that they were in a drugged condition. However, since they really did want the sex or the violence, we certainly cannot call the act involuntary. In fact, Aristotle argues that the penalty should be twice as high, since the agent is responsible for two wrongs: drunkenness and the act committed in drunken ignorance (1113b31).

When we turn to the factor of compulsion, similar complications arise. An act is most clearly forced when the person acted upon contributes nothing to it. If someone's hand is bumped as he signs a contract, the scrawl he makes on the paper is obviously involuntary. If a person's buddies throw him into a pool, he is not responsible for getting his friend's borrowed wristwatch soaked. However, in many acts the source of motion is not entirely external. When a person *chooses* to perform an act out of fear of the alternative, for example, paying "protection" money to a gang of thugs, the act is of a mixed nature. It is involuntary in the sense that the person acted under the constraint exercised by the gang's threats. He surely would not have given money were it not for the possibility of great harm. Nevertheless, this payment was the result of a decision, a choice made concerning the more desirable act at the moment. In situations of this sort, what we can perhaps call *mixed voluntary* acts occur. The act is chosen, but only under duress.

What can be said about the responsibility of the agent in such circumstances? It seems sensible to recognize that there are degrees of responsibility, just as there are of compulsion. In general, we can maintain that blameworthiness is in proportion to (1) the gravity of the act committed, (2) the amount of force applied, and (3) the extent of the agent's own contribution to the act. Certainly our moral assessment in particular situations is affected by whether someone is asked to part with his wallet or betray his country, whether pressure takes the form of mild teasing or of a revolver to the forehead, and whether he is constrained merely to join the hostages or asked to help cut their throats. The extent to which an act is voluntary or involuntary cannot be determined in the abstract, but must be judged in each circumstance by reference to each of these factors.

Pleasure/Pain Reactions

A special case of self-deception can enter into the discussion of compulsion, just as earlier in the case of ignorance. We argued that we cannot be excused for not knowing when the ignorance is due to negligence or drunkenness for which we are responsible. In the case of compulsion, people sometimes claim that their acts are involuntary because they are "overcome by passion" or are "victims of habit." However, we should think more about the presumption that pleasure and pain can rob us of our freedom in action. Putting in quotation marks the words and phrases people sometimes use when describing acts of passion calls attention to the special pleading associated with those words. An effort is made to argue that pleasure and pain are independent of us, that we cannot be held responsible for our emotions, and that choices influenced by passion are involuntary.

When discussing egoism in Chapter 4, we noted that "what one finds pleasurable or painful will depend on the dispositions he has formed." Everybody seeks pleasure and avoids pain. The moral difference depends on the *kinds* of pleasure or pain. Just about anything can be a source of pleasure, depending upon the sort of person someone is. Similarly, whether a situation is painful or not is a function of the character formed by our virtues or vices. One person is angered at the passage of gun control laws, while another is overjoyed. The promise of free tickets to a rock concert prompts frantic action in some and leaves others unmoved. These examples suggest that psychological reactions of pleasure or pain take the form they do from the disposition of the person experiencing those reactions. Each person will find pleasurable what corresponds to his character. Since we are responsible for our habits and preferences, and since it is in our power to change those qualities if we so decide, we cannot easily deny our own control over the acts affected by them. After all, our emotions are as much a part of us as our reason, and both are capable of being disciplined and directed. Hence, what is said about our will or intellect is also true about our emotions. Whether they function properly is due to our own decisions and efforts. Admittedly, the environment can have its influence here. But influence is not the same thing as control. Moreover, personal choices help to determine precisely what elements in the environment are going to be influences in our lives. That is, our choices of friends, of hobbies, of schools, of what we read, and of where we go are in effect decisions about how we want to be influenced.

Although psychological pleasure and pain appear to be greatly influenced by our discretionary decisions, we might argue that physical pleasure or pain is a different thing. Techniques of persuasion and of coercion the world over are based on the power of physical pleasures or pains to motivate us. Human beings everywhere possess the same biological equipment, meaning they experience basically the same physical attractions and aversions. While this may be true to some extent, we may still ask how significant that fact is for the discussion of voluntariness in human behavior. Even with regard to physical pleasures and pains, there is enormous elasticity in individual response. One person may insist that the heat of a factory work area is utterly intolerable, while another works steadily each day without complaint. One roommate has an insatiable appetite for salty junk food, whereas another has cultivated a distaste for salty food based on an awareness of negative health effects. The point is that our response even to physical stimuli is a largely conditioned response. Both what we seek or avoid and the degree to which we are committed to the process of pursuit or avoidance is a matter of malleable human capabilities.

As with most issues of moral concern, extremes in this case cannot be defended. Ordinary human beings find deprivation of food and water to be effective means of forcing compliance. No reasonable person is tempted to consider a confession voluntary when it follows the pain of prolonged physical torture. Sufficient for our purposes is the easily established fact that in normal circumstances, the actions that spring from our appetites or passions are simply a reflection of the people we have made of ourselves. Whether and to what extent a physical pleasure or pain will motivate us is something that largely remains with us to determine. As a consequence, in the case of compulsion, the mere fact of feeling compelled is not enough to establish involuntariness. A relevant question is "Need I feel so compelled?" That is, "Could I become a person different from the one who reacts in this way?" To the extent that we discover within ourselves the causes of action, to that extent we establish voluntariness and personal responsibility.

A summary statement about virtues, then, is that they perfect (1) agents, (2) their emotions, and (3) their actions. When these are voluntary we deserve praise or blame, as the case may be. Since an action is involuntary when it is performed under constraint or through ignorance, a voluntary act can be defined as one in which the initiative lies with the agent who knows the particular circumstances in which the action is performed (1111a22).

THE MORAL VIRTUES

Action requires the interaction of reason and desire. This becomes the basis for distinguishing between two kinds of virtue, intellectual and moral. Although we differentiate the intellectual from the moral virtues on the basis of what powers they perfect, there is a unity among the virtues. As we proceed, this point will become clearer, namely, that virtues constitute a "package deal." When we acquire one, we acquire them all. This is because in their perfect state the virtues depend on one another. We will see that perfection of the moral virtues requires intellectual virtue, and that intellectual virtue needed for right conduct is not possible without moral virtues. Since success in living the good life demands excellence in both knowledge and desire, the interdependence of the virtues serves us well.

Having discussed the virtues in general, it is time to investigate them in particular. Let us consider first the moral virtues. Our procedure will be to take one of the many moral virtues and examine it in detail. Through this analysis, we shall discover characteristics common to all the moral virtues. As a consequence, we will be able to develop a framework for understanding any of the other virtues.

Courage

Courage, sometimes called fortitude, will serve for our purposes. When we call someone courageous (as opposed to cowardly), we are referring to a praiseworthy quality in that individual. Specifically that person is thought to have mastery over feelings of confidence and fear. A virtue does not imply the elimination of emotions, since they are a natural and necessary part of us. According to this theory of the virtues, goodness does not lie in some puritanical suppression of our passions. The legacy of philosophers such as Plato and Kant is not a sound one in this regard. They viewed with suspicion the influence of emotions and encouraged the disengagement of reason from "physical contamination." Against that view, the theory we propose here suggests that the objective is not to act against inclination, but rather to act from well-ordered inclinations. A moral virtue, then, is a disposition to feel.

With regard to the emotion of fear, it is clear that in some circumstances it is appropriate to be afraid, and in other circumstances it is not. Fear itself is morally neutral. Only in context can we decide if it is reasonable to be fearful and, if so, how much. We recognize situations in which people manifest too much fear, as when someone hides under the bed during every thunderstorm. Cowardice is the vice opposed in this way to the virtue of courage. There are also circumstances in which someone might be possessed of too little fear; for example, a tipsy person who cavorts on a high, narrow ledge. Such persons are called reckless or foolhardy. Some things should be feared, such as dishonor, rattlesnakes, and herpes. In sum, acting because of an excess or a deficiency of fear is possible, and these opposites are contrasted with the virtue of courage.

Notice that courage implies excellence not merely with regard to an emotion, but also with regard to actions. The external behavior of people is called courageous, as well as their inner feelings. Courage perfects both the possessors and their works. In calling courage an *action-state*, we draw attention to this complex nature of the virtue. People who possess courage have fear under control; and the passion is manifested to an appropriate degree in actions that involve danger. Ethics is practical, meaning that the purpose of ethical inquiry is to live well. And living consists in activity. Consequently, courage names a virtue enabling us to act well in specific kinds of situations. To call it a state implies that courage names not just this or that individual action, but rather that it stands for a certain ordering of character. The agent possesses a mastery of the passion of fear that is stable and abiding. Courageous people do not act bravely merely on one particular occasion, but have a *disposition* to confront dangerous situations appropriately. It is readiness to act courageously that the virtue names, and that quality exists whether or not there is a suitable occasion for its exercise.

Since both too much and too little fear or confidence constitute vices opposed to the virtue, courage is said to be *in the mean*, occupying an intermediate position between extremes of excess or deficiency. Courageous people possess a state of character located in a mean between two other kinds of character: one which shies away from any danger, great or small and real or imaginary, and the other which brashly plunges into every peril, treating caution as a symptom of being "chicken." This tripartite analysis locates the *golden mean* of courage intermediate between the vices of cowardice and rashness.

It is tempting to understand these relationships in purely quantitative terms, as if the virtue were a case of splitting the difference between extremes—in the same way that six pounds of meat is midway between two and ten pounds. It is true that sometimes the issue of what is right turns on quantitative variables, for example, how much to eat. The glutton takes too much, and the anorexic takes too little. The doctrine of *moderation* is a theory about where the mean lies, namely, in a moderate amount of fear, or pity, or recreation, or whatever else the virtue regulates. However, the doctrine of moderation is not the same as the doctrine of the mean, if moderation is understood in this simply quantitative sense. For example, in most circumstances zero amounts of fear are called for; for example, there is nothing to fear in stepping on the cracks in the sidewalk. On other occasions a moderate amount of confidence may be irrational, as when members of a cult are led into battle believing that bullets will not hurt them. A doctrine of moderation is correct in claiming that we are rarely required to exhibit extreme emotion or action, but circumstances can justify that rare display.

There is still another reason for avoiding a simplistic quantitative understanding of the mean. Any act can be right or wrong in a variety of respects that are not quantitative at all. Factors that are relevant in deciding an appropriate response are: (1) who the agent is; (2) what the agent is doing; (3) what person or thing is affected by the act; (4) what means are used; (5) what result is intended; and (6) the manner in which the act is undertaken (1111a3). The act of attempting to rescue someone in the water is not in the mean. In other words, it is not courageous if the agent cannot swim (factor 1), or if the life preserver is stolen from someone else in danger of drowning (factor 4), or if the agent acted only for the sake of a monetary reward (factor 5). Evaluating the circumstances which affect our judgment concerning what is virtuous obviously entails something more than mathematical analyses. A doctrine of the mean, then, must appreciate the non-quantitative aspects of aiming at the intermediate.

> . . . both fear and confidence and appetite and anger and pity and in general pleasure and pain may be felt both too much and too little, and in both cases not well; but to feel them at the right times, with reference to the right objects, toward the right people, with the right motive, and in the right way, is what is intermediate and best, and this is characteristic of virtue (1106b17-20. Ross)

In the quotation above Aristotle refers to the "right motive" as a relevant factor in judging whether one is virtuous. In our example, we suggested that the agent is not courageous if he attempted a rescue only for the sake of a financial reward. What motive, then, is characteristic of a virtuous person? The answer must be that a good person does the right act *because* it is right. In other words, a courageous person attempts the rescue because that is the noble thing to do. Our commonsense judgment is that an agent is not praiseworthy for acts performed with ulterior motives. A person may be fearless for all sorts of reasons that have nothing to do with the virtue of courage. For example, someone may be motivated to bold action by lust or greed or by fear itself. He may be so cowardly in the face of danger that he will try anything to avoid it.

This brings us to another important point about courage. Other qualities and actions may resemble courage, but they are not the real thing. As we have seen, courage names a state of character, not merely an individual act or momentary feeling. And according to that stable disposition, a virtuous person acts for the sake of real and true goods. The courage which is a virtue, then, *perfects* its possessor. Such perfection implies that people of courage have a true perception of the facts, have the proper values, and are ready to act accordingly. Courageous people exercise intelligence in judging the nature of the dangers, deciding if it is rational to take the risks in proportion to the real good that is to be achieved. Because they have become certain kinds of people, they will act as they do because courage requires it. Even when fearing what is truly fearful, courageous people will endure it in the right way, that is, nobly.[9]

Contrast this description of courageous people with one of people who bear only a misleading resemblance to those possessing the virtue. We do not mistake a bold bank robber or a fearless mercenary soldier or a daring rapist for a person of courage. Fearlessness and courage are not the same thing. Someone may act fear-lessly under compulsion, or because of ignorance, or due to drugs, or because of base motivations. In contrast, we identify an act done virtuously with (1) aware-ness, (2) choice, and (3) nobility of purpose. When any of these is lacking, the act that remains can have only the appearance of being courageous. For these reasons, it is impossible for a virtue to produce bad acts. Bear in mind that virtues perfect both their possessors and their works. Courage confers right use, as well as aptness for doing good. If the characteristic that brave people exhibit is a virtue, then it is part of an overall orientation of those individuals to a good life. We can appreciate even more at this point the importance attached earlier to deciding in what consists the ultimate end. That is the standard by which acts, rules, and states of character are judged. Measured by that criterion, the fearless rapist and safecracker fail the test of courage.

The Mean as Relative

A fact of fundamental importance concerning the golden mean is that it is not found at the same point for everyone. What is intermediate will vary from person to person. What is too little food for a pro football linebacker is too much for a ballerina. What are normal flying conditions for an experienced pilot may be hazardous for a beginner. One way of expressing this is to say that virtue consists in a *relative* mean. What is moderate or reasonable must be judged relative to the circumstances. The rescue attempt that we would expect of an accomplished swimmer would be foolhardy rather than courageous if undertaken by an invalid.

In saying that the mean is relative, however, we learned in Chapter 3 not to confuse this with the untenable theory of relativism. In prescribing medication, a physician will tailor the recommended dosage to the age or size of the patient, or the seriousness of the person's condition; these are facts which have an objective relation to the correct prescription. That the mean must be *relational* to the rele-vant facts about individuals and their situation is distinct from the murky thesis of the relativist. Imagine someone standing atop a tall building. That person suddenly says, "I want to take off from here and fly to the next building. I think I can do it." No one in his right mind would respond, "It's all a matter of how you feel about it. People have nothing to fear but fear itself. If you feel it's right for you, then it is right." That kind of encouragement would be followed by funeral arrange-ments. (We might object that this example is too easy. In that case, take a question involving temperance or generosity or patience. What people drink, or how much money they give away, or how long they endure mistreatment can be irrational, despite how they happen to feel about it.)

In determining the relative mean for each situation, it is clear that intelligence must be employed. Not only is desire needed, but also a knowledge of appropriate facts and applicable norms. We identified above factors that must be assessed in making a prudent decision. Clearly the path of virtue is not completely laid out in advance. Each significant circumstance must be weighed in reaching that conclusion which is a desirable action or an appropriate attitude. In other words, clear thinking is indispensible for virtuous living. That translates into correct reasoning both about the end and about the means to the end. It implies not only an understanding of the relevant principles, but also a correct application of those principles. Even when virtuously disposed, we must still ask ourselves, "What does courage require of me in this situation?" Infinitely variable circumstances make the answer no foregone conclusion. Because we are virtuous, we are already committed to doing the right thing. But, precisely what is right here and now? This requires a judgment of reason. Specific moral precepts like "Aid others in distress when you are able" condition the thinking of a courageous person standing on shore. But, whether that principle is applicable to this situation and, if so, how it should be carried out are practical problems that demand intelligence. The point we are working up to is that exercise of moral virtue requires intellectual virtue. Whether fear should be overcome, whether confidence in attempting a rescue is well-founded, and what means are most appropriate to fulfillment of our duty in this context must be established by reflection.

Experienced people have an advantage when deliberation is called for. Individuals who have confronted similar types of situations time and again develop a knack for making the correct choice. The tyro defers to the pro because with experience people acquire habits of sound judgment that no set of rules can adequately cover. Earlier we established that habits are unequal to the task of judging the truly unusual. But habits condition attitudes and create patterns of behavior that are indispensable for sound living. There is truth in the claim that what we do spontaneously is more a sign of our character than what we do after much deliberation. The person who unhesitatingly gives correct change is more obviously an honest cashier than one who must ponder the choice. In fact, the importance of good habits is once more made clear in that, when there is no time to deliberate, we are still acting from choice—namely, the choice to be that kind of person.

In thinking about this, we are made aware of two very different kinds of difficulty that we may experience in acting as we should. Doing what is right may be difficult due to *external factors* or due to *defect of character*. Decision and execution may be complicated by circumstances that we did not originate, but that we must consider. For example, deciding what is our responsibility in the care of an aging parent may entail complex deliberations about such factors as the parent's own wishes, the real status of his health, our duty to our spouse and children, the proportionate burdens of other relatives, and our financial capability. We cannot be blamed for the fact that doing what is morally right in this situation is such a dilemma. However, the other kind of difficulty is one for which we can be held responsible. This occurs when a lack of virtue increases our resistance to acting as we should. We may know that someone is truly in danger, and that rescue is not beyond our capability. However, our fear overcomes our reason, and we fail to act according to our knowledge. Having the virtue of courage would have meant passion under the control of reason, rather than the reverse. Hence, the difficulty experienced here is something for which we are blameworthy.

Deficiency of virtue may also create culpable difficulty of another sort. In this case, the problem is not an opposition between what fear inclines us to do and what is the dictate of our reason. Rather, the shortcoming is that, because someone is a coward, he gives too much weight to dangers, and hence his reasoning is defective. An individual, because of excessive fear, exaggerates the potential perils in a course of action and thereby rationalizes a failure to act. A child in swimming lessons may be afraid as he is prodded to take that first plunge from the diving board. Nervously he offers all sorts of reasons why he really shouldn't dive in: the water is too cold; he hasn't had enough lessons; other people are in his way; no one can reach him if he falters; and on and on. Adult fears can be equally paralyzing. One might dwell on the potential pitfalls of married life to the extent of never being willing to take the vows of matrimony. The point to be made is that a deficiency of courage not merely creates resistance in the appetites to the judgment of reason, but can even corrupt the reasoning process itself. Fear can drive us to do or avoid what we know we shouldn't. Or fear can distort intellectual activity so that we come to think we should not do something we should.

The upshot of these observations is that we must exercise caution in assuming that the virtuous life is difficult and painful. Sometimes the pain and difficulty is merely a sign that virtue is incomplete. That is quite different from those other kinds of difficulties which simply provide the occasion for much virtue.[10] When the problem is an inclination or tendency not sufficiently under the control of reason, then the fault lies with ourselves. Overcoming the limitations of sympathy and rationality is precisely the achievement of virtues. People of courage do not experience resistance in their passions to what their reason prescribes. Nor is their intellect clouded by fear so that they fail to read the facts correctly and draw the appropriate conclusion. Moreover, because the whole orientation of their character is to act nobly, doing what is courageous will be a source of pleasure, not of pain. People find pleasant what fits with their nature. Occasionally we hear, "If it doesn't hurt, it isn't good for you." That is on a fallacious par with "If you enjoy it, it isn't work."

Virtues enable us to perform acts with ease and with delight, because we take pleasure in doing what is right. However, virtue is not merely something mechanical. Being a courageous person means doing appropriately different things in different circumstances. This means that we must act attentively. Although some situations can be handled routinely, in other cases we are challenged to use every resource at our disposal.

In concluding this section on courage, we emphasize again that the moral virtues require more than routine habit. This is because the intellect has to judge where the path of virtue goes in each particular case. We shall discuss later, in a more detailed examination of the intellectual virtues, precisely what kind of knowledge is required both with regard to the end and the means to the end of moral life. However, a word should be added here concerning the yardstick by which we should measure what is excessive, deficient, or reasonable in emotions and actions. An analogy with physical well-being may prove helpful.[11]

People are recognized as being ill or injured when they are incapacitated for normal human activity. What is normal assumes a standard of physical health that is no mystery to medical science. Being healthy involves a certain condition of the body that has become our medical model through an empirical investigation of structure and properly functioning physical systems. People who are neither ill nor injured have the capacity to act normally. In analogous fashion, people are recognized to be morally deficient when they are incapacitated for normal human activity by the presence of vices. Here the standard for normal activity is what contributes either instrumentally or intrinsically to the ultimate end. Bear in mind that the end is not understood as the termination of life, but as life itself—that is, a certain quality of life. People who are excessively afraid either suffer distorted judgment or experience disharmony between the judgment of reason and the pull of passion, or both. In any case, too much or too little fear means that they are hampered from acting well. By contrast, people of courage are able to behave in the manner of a well-ordered human being.

What we see, then, is that the moral ideal, expressed in terms of courage and related moral and intellectual virtues, both originates and later functions in a mode similar to the ideal of physical health. The perfectly healthy human being exists only in a medical manual. But, for all that, it is an empirical model and provides the norm for clinical practice. In like fashion, the completely virtuous human being exists only as a concept in an ethics textbook. But it too is derived from experience in living and gives us the target to aim at in our moral life.

Moral Virtue in General

Having chosen courage as our example, and after examining that virtue in some detail, we should now find it easier to grasp the concepts associated in general with moral virtue. Aristotle's own definition of moral virtue is intelligible in light of what we have already seen in the case of courage. "Virtue then, is a state of character concerned with choice, lying in a mean, i.e., the mean relative to us, this being determined by a rational principle. . ." (1106b36. Ross). The various elements of that definition can be clearly identified:

1. Moral virtue is a habit or state of character. As such it must be acquired. Moral virtue is not merely a potentiality or capacity to feel emotions of various sorts; we are born with that. Nor is virtue the emotion itself. Fear, anger, pity and the like are in themselves morally neutral, as are acts like giving money or having sex. They become good or bad only in context. Also, emotions can be expressed erratically and inconsistently. And the same can be said with regard to the performance of acts. But virtue implies a steady disposition. The habit is developed by a process of learning and repeated actions. Once formed, the disposition confers a readiness to act with consistency, the quality of that behavior now having become characteristic of the individual.

2. Moral virtue is concerned with choice. Ethics is practical knowledge, not simply knowledge for its own sake. Aristotle put it that "we are inquiring not in order to know what virtue is, but in order to become good. . ." (1103b28. Ross). The purpose or end of ethical knowledge is action, and action implies choices. That humans possess alternatives and can freely select from among

those alternatives is a necessary condition for holding them responsible. Moral virtue can exist only in those whose behavior is voluntary. As we have seen, ignorance and force oppose that voluntariness in human beings.

3. Moral virtue is a good habit. It exists in the mean, avoiding the extremes of excess and deficiency. Excellence of character is an intermediate disposition with respect to emotions and also actions. Both the agent and his works are perfected. Their usefulness in achieving the good is so fundamental that a fulfilling human life would be impossible without virtues. Imagine a world in which vices, rather than the moral mean, predominated in our attitudes and in our behavior.

4. The mean is not located at a similar point for all individuals, nor is it even identical in acts of one and the same person—if there are relevant differences in the circumstances of those acts. What is moderate must be judged in relation to all factors that have moral significance. That the mean is relative to the agent and the particular situation implies limitations in the usefulness of principles and rules. General norms require intelligent application, and the agent must consider on each different occasion what is required. Relative to one set of circumstances a feeling or an action may be appropriate, and relative to another it may be far off the mark. Nevertheless, the relative mean is determined by reference to facts. Objective reality rather than whim limits the choice.

5. The relative mean in the moral virtues is "determined by a rational principle." Discovering truth is a function of our intellectual powers. With regard to living the good life, we must have correct knowledge concerning both the end and the means. Insofar as the moral virtues perfect our emotions and our actions with a view to the correct end, they must be guided by intelligence. The relative mean in the moral virtues must be decided in light of facts concerning the individual agent and the particular circumstances of each situation. That determination of the facts, and the subsequent judgment about what feeling and action is appropriate in light of those facts, constitutes the role of practical intellectual virtue. What is sometimes called *prudence* or *practical wisdom* is a virtue perfecting our capacity to discover the truth about the means to the end of moral living. Correct reasoning about things to be done is characteristic of the prudent or practically wise person. We need to acquire excellence in our ability to deliberate and judge what is intermediate between excess and deficiency in emotions and actions. Deliberation and judgment are rational activities which obviously can go wrong. Hence, the need for intellectual virtue.

Proper Upbringing

In general, the moral virtues correct tendencies in our nature. We find ourselves tempted to overindulgence, impatience, selfishness, dishonesty, and wastefulness. These and similar inclinations in our appetites must be brought under rational control; otherwise, the propensity to act in a way that is detrimental both to ourselves and to others will go unchecked. When our appetites are in good order, such that we desire and seek what is truly beneficial, we are said to have moral virtue. But weighing the evidence and deciding what is truly beneficial requires excellence in intellectual operations. Clearly, it takes a long time to develop this maturity of our rational powers. Experience in living is indispensable to making our own sound practical judgments. That being the case, can we really say that children possess the fullness of virtue?

Since the human ideal is coming to correct decisions ourselves and then voluntarily doing desirable things, children can possess only inferior kinds of virtue. The young and inexperienced must be guided by others in moral matters, for the same reasons as others must decide for them regarding the right food to eat and the proper clothing to wear out in the cold. With time the child's capacity for self-directed behavior matures. However, that growth process presupposes the development of good habits early on. In other words, training in moral virtue must begin long before individuals have acquired their own independent intellectual proficiency. If there is a sound beginning in our moral training, it will be much easier to understand and accept the reasoning that supports that way of behaving when the stage has been reached where we can judge for ourselves. On the other hand, if bad habits are given an early start, it will be much harder to think properly at a later stage.

We often hear how critical are the first years of life. This is as true for moral as it is for physical growth. Malnutrition and improper exercise in infancy and early childhood have long-term effects upon the individual. Why should we expect it to be otherwise with regard to value formation? In early years our attitudes and preferences are shaped by parents, teachers, relatives, and the peers and prestige figures to whom we are exposed. If we are unfortunate enough to have poor role models, the effect upon personality and character can be lasting. It defies all evidence from psychology to suggest that the newly born are immune to the formative influence of their immediate environment.

Since we lack, in the beginning, an ability to discriminate for ourselves between what is good and bad, this judgment is supplied by others. If these others are deficient exemplars, the bad habits we develop will handicap our ability later on to exercise the intelligence and self-control necessary to take charge of our own lives. This is an important point in reply to a possible criticism. Someone may suggest that the young should be left free from the direction of their elders. Children should not be "brainwashed," but rather should discover for themselves how they want to live. It is wrong, the criticism runs, to prejudice youth by the taste and bias of older people.

This criticism is inspired by a naive assumption, namely, that there can be such a thing as a value-neutral early environment. In reality, we are exposed willy-nilly to all kinds of positive and negative reinforcements. Children do not grow in vacuum chambers. Therefore, the practical question is not *whether* there should be external influences, but of *what quality* they should be. Moreover, if the early training is a sound one, individuals do not acquire what can properly be called prejudices or biases. Virtues dispose us to act rationally when we might be inclined otherwise by inferior motives. The moral virtues prevent intelligent choice from being disrupted by irrational desires or aversions. And intellectual virtue habituates us in the exercise of the recollection, circumspection, and anticipation needed for the prudent self-control of our lives. In other words, proper upbringing is a necessary condition for later possession of the means to manage our affairs intelligently.

Since external influences on children are inescapable, imagine how unfortunate is an environment which encourages an anti-intellectual attitude in the young. When the popular culture denigrates reflection and extols the explosion of raw emotion, how likely is it that impressionable youth will cultivate respect for thoughtful inquiry and disciplined passions? Yet without them we are never truly free. As a consequence, no one concerned about quality of life can avoid serious criticism of the legal and social climate which creates the initial facts for children. What children take to be facts, both about how the world is and what is desirable or undesirable, will be relentlessly communicated long before the child can understand the reasons for claims and evaluate them.

In the moral life we begin with the facts, that is, with value judgments and rules inculcated by society. Only later are we in a position to evaluate those norms, and even then only if we have acquired the intellectual and emotional controls that make possible that examination. How helpful is it when moral facts are decided for the young by vulgar rock music performers, by immature sports figures, or by beguiling preachers like the Reverend Jim Jones? A virtue ethic posits persons as valid ideals of the moral life because of their maturity, expertise, and demonstrated grasp of what is important. Can we be confident about the moral message broadcast by many figures today, whether in entertainment, or sports, or politics? They are inevitably educative forces, for better or for worse. From a list of the culture's heroes, it is possible to draw conclusions about its value system. That value system, propagated by those who are admired and emulated, forecasts the future direction of a society's youth. Moral education in the hands of marketing executives, movie producers, and the National Rifle Association produces a distinctive product.

This exposition helps to make clear what Aristotle meant when he said that, "to be a competent student of what is right and just, and of politics generally, one must first have received a proper upbringing in moral conduct. The acceptance of a fact as a fact is the starting point. . ." (1095b4. Ostwald). Particular moral rules are the facts with which we begin, and later we can understand and evaluate the alleged reason for those facts, namely, that they are necessary for achieving the good. "Hence," Aristotle says, "it is no small matter whether one habit or another is inculcated in us from early childhood; on the contrary, it makes a considerable difference, or, rather, all the difference" (1103b24. Ostwald). If individuals have been well brought up, they possess a mastery of the intellectual and appetitive powers needed to function as effective, autonomous moral agents. It is a different story, Aristotle warns, for those who live "under the sway of emotion" and who "do not even have a notion of what is noble and truly pleasant, since they have never tasted it. What argument indeed can transform people like that? To change by argument what has been ingrained in a character is impossible or, at least, not easy" (1179b13-18. Ostwald).

The moral virtues include not only courage (discussed earlier in this chapter) and justice (discussed in Chapter 5). There are others: for example, temperance, generosity, truthfulness, patience, and sociability. While each is concerned with a specific emotion or kind of action, they all possess the general characteristics of moral virtue enumerated at the beginning of this section. When these virtues are fully operative, the individual not only performs the right act, but also understands *why* it is right, and does it *because* it is right. This distinguishes virtue in the complete sense from that possessed by children or those immature for other reasons. The latter may act in accord with what moral principles require. But they may do so only because of a system of coercion. In the beginning, of course, it is sufficient if we are made to act rightly. But, as we have seen, progress in virtue means growth in ability to act consciously and voluntarily.

Upbringing under sound laws is an indispensable part of the moral landscape. A perverse legal system rewards and penalizes the wrong kind of behavior, contributing to the development of vices rather than virtues. However, even in a praiseworthy legal system, there are some individuals who will never be motivated to right action except from fear of punishment. Although it falls far short of the ideal, at least a minimum good is achieved through coercive enforcement of good laws. The community's well-being is safeguarded by the performance and avoidance of some legislated behavior. Morality and politics, thought to make strange bedfellows, are in reality interdependent in promoting the good life.

INTELLECTUAL VIRTUE

Appropriate choices in human action require that "the reasoning must be true and the desire correct" (1139a24. Ostwald). Desiring as we should is the function of moral virtues, to which we have devoted earlier sections of this chapter. Now we must consider in some detail the intellectual virtues which perfect rational operations involved in moral activity. It was evident throughout the discussion of moral virtue that reason and desire must cooperate to produce right action. Identifying the correct end to be pursued, establishing priorities among competing goals, and determining the relative mean in each moral virtue are, all of them, tasks assigned to intelligence. Desire for the end and also for the means to the end presupposes accurate judgment concerning both end and means. It is for this reason that moral virtue cannot exist without intellectual virtue. In what follows, we shall not be concerned with every kind of knowledge, since some is not relevant to ethics—for example, physical science or artistic know-how. Rather, we shall focus on the intellectual operations essential for purposes of living the moral life. We can call the object of those operations *practical truth*.

Practical truth comprises two kinds of correct knowing. First, there must be apprehension of the proper ends of human action. That has to do with choosing the right values to guide our decisions. A person who has *false values* pursues ends which are not in fact productive of happiness, as previously defined. This knowledge, however, does not require special expertise. Every person of normal intelligence should be able to discover what in life is worth seeking. Here there is no need to consult an intellectual elite, because common sense, combined with experience in living, is sufficient to reveal how we ought to live. Consequently, ignorance at this level is culpable. That is, people who act on wrong moral principles should know better. Such people are capable of knowing the general criteria of correct behavior. Accordingly, ignorance of universal moral standards is blameworthy.

The kind of ignorance that is not blameworthy is innocent ignorance of particular facts. For example, a well-intentioned person who mistakenly takes someone else's umbrella rather than his own is not judged to be a thief. Similarly, a conscientious jury that convicts a defendant who is really innocent cannot be held responsible for knowing facts not presented to the jury. Innocent ignorance of particular facts is morally distinct from the culpable ignorance of someone claiming not to know general moral principles such as "Theft is wrong" or "Only guilty persons should be punished."

A second kind of correct knowing characteristic of practical wisdom is knowledge of the means to good ends. Once again, the requirement here is within the reach of any ordinary adult. How to act well in order to achieve goals belonging to human life in general does not demand unique skills. Truth telling, patience, and fellow feeling do not necessitate intellectual brilliance or special talents. The most fundamental matters of human existence can be grasped by any properly motivated individual.

Note that the intellectual virtue concerns means to *good* ends. This distinguishes practical wisdom from mere cleverness. A clever person is skillful at devising efficient means to ends, irrespective of whether they are good or bad. We condemn the inventor of fail-safe torture instruments because the goal is base. By contrast, the practically wise person calculates appropriate means to praiseworthy ends.

Knowledge of the End

To be virtuous in the complete sense, it is not enough that we do the right act. In addition, we must possess certain characteristics. ". . . people may perform just acts without actually being just men, as in the case of people who do what has been laid down by the laws but do so involuntarily or through ignorance or for an ulterior motive, and not for the sake of performing just acts" (1144a13. Ostwald). Knowing what we are doing and choosing an act because we know it to be right are essential conditions for acting virtuously. The knowledge that a particular deed, here and now, is the appropriate one presupposes a standard in the light of which such judgments are made. Since all action is for the sake of some end, the norm which will encompass all decisions is our conception of the good life in general. Our unified picture of the best possible life influences choices in a conscious way when we deliberately reflect. But even when there is no time for reflection, the ideal is operative in habits that are part of our character, and in that sense are chosen as well. A virtuous person need not take time to think about whether to pay for groceries selected from the shelves or whether to act swiftly to save a friend in peril. The choice to be a certain kind of person whose life is organized by reference to selected goals controls individual acts of a spontaneous as well as of a pondered nature.

How do we come to have this knowledge of the end? The order of discovery, that is, the step-by-step process by which we acquire our concept of the end, differs from the order of reasoning once we have knowledge of the end. After general principles are possessed and fully assented to, the process is one of applying principles to the situation at hand. Our immediate concern, however, is how we come to have those principles in the first place.

What is first in our knowing, as we look back to the earliest stages of childhood development, is the set of beliefs communicated to us by parents and teachers and other prestige figures in our environment. We are taught moral lessons at a very early age in various ways. Proverbs and sayings, stories of heroes and villains, admonitions to follow the example of our elders—all these are ways that ethical principles are inculcated long before we are mature enough to evaluate for ourselves that conception of the good life expressed in these maxims and examples.

Although rules of morality are often taught in formula fashion, another method by which they are acquired is inductive. In first one situation and then another we are told to show respect, or to share our playthings, or to exercise caution in approaching strangers. Slowly we build up, from an accumulation of repeated experiences, the recognition of a rule or principle. We develop a value orientation that conditions future choices of a similar sort. If our training is sound, not only will we have acquired a set of prescriptions, but we will also learn the value of reflection. Attentiveness to the different requirements of each situation becomes part of the perception that here it is appropriate to behave one way, and there it is appropriate to behave another way. In the beginning, our virtue is imperfect, built up by training and induction controlled by others. However, the habits and particular perceptions so acquired are able to become transformed into our own consciously adopted and justified moral system as time and circumstance foster the development of critical powers.

It should be noted that early habituation affects our desires as well as our thinking process. We come to like reacting in accord with the intuitive perceptions taught by our elders and, as our general concepts develop, we develop a feeling of identification with that ideal of the good life to which we have grown accustomed. The beginnings of both intellectual and moral virtue are seen here. Not only do we *learn* a certain way of life, but we also begin to *like* that perspective. The contribution of moral virtue to the development of intellectual virtue is enormous. In our earliest years, if there is a lack of moral virtue, it can prevent our learning correct concepts of the end, precisely because we are not properly disposed in appetite and inclination to accept such lessons. Later on in life, the moral virtues preserve our conception of the end from the corrupting influence of vice. Desires color perceptions; what we assent to intellectually can be governed by our wants. Virtue in its entirety, then, involves not only a *conception* of the good life, but also a *desire* for it, and the desire preserves the conception.[12]

Someone might ask at this point, "How do we defend the basic principles and the moral ideal we have adopted as our way of life?" In Chapter 6 the word *intuition* was used to describe our knowledge of ultimate principles. We pointed out that what is first cannot be proved, that is, derived from something else. Otherwise, it would not be first. Our conception of the end functions as a first in the moral life, since rules and individual actions are justified by reference to that end. Consequently, the end is not proven in any strict sense. But, as we saw in Chapter 6, it is possible to offer *evidence* in support of an intuited end. That evidence takes the form of people's carefully considered preferences when they try as impartially as possible to describe the best life for human beings. The fact that this species, out of its need and its experiences, fashions a roughly similar concept of the good life provides the evidence for its intuition of basic values. A person might reject that conception, challenging such values as truth telling, caring for the young, and fidelity to promises. In that case the challenger is invited to suggest how human beings, with the needs and limitations they in fact possess, *can* live happily and cooperatively. The test of any alternative intuition, in short, is experience in living.

Knowledge of the Means

The end, as we have seen, is an object of intuition rather than proof because it is the ultimate source of proofs. That end, happiness or human flourishing, constitutes the standard that reason employs in making decisions about particular actions. Just as a target gives direction to the sharpshooter, so the ultimate end of happiness provides the focus for human activity. The justification or rational basis for an action, then, is its compatibility with the goal to which all action is directed. Our choice is proved to be right because the act decided upon does in fact contribute to the end. Whatever conflicts with the ultimate end is, morally speaking, demonstrated to be evil or wrong.

Practical wisdom (sometimes called prudence) is the intellectual virtue perfecting our deliberations about the means to happiness. It is characteristic of a prudent person to judge well about what contributes to the good life in general. To call this habit a virtue presupposes correctness in our thinking about the end and also correctness in our desires for that end. Deliberating about the means to an evil end is obviously not virtuous. Consequently, moral virtue that causes us to want and seek the proper end is a prerequisite for practical wisdom.

Making sound judgments about the means to happiness requires an appreciation of the full complexity of the human situation. Clearly, individuals have an immediate moral responsibility for their own character and conduct. First of all, then, practical wisdom concerns the good of the self. However, humans are *social* beings. This is a fact of fundamental importance for the moral life. What it means is that the good of the self and the good of the community are inextricably bound together. Since individuals achieve fulfillment only in and through community, there is merely a difference of perspective when distinguishing between kinds of practical wisdom. What must be done in order to achieve one and the same good for human beings can be analyzed either from the standpoint of personal decision making or from the standpoint of group decisions.

Because we are members of many social units, some of them limited and others of them more inclusive, prudential judgments are required in a wide range of human activity. We can speak of practical wisdom involved in the relations between husband and wife, between parents and offspring, between employer and employee, and so on. On a wider level, the human good becomes a subject for political decisions. Practical wisdom then concerns itself with the legislative, executive, and judicial functions of government, whether of a local, a national, or an international scope. The good of community, at whatever level, is ultimately the good of the individuals who comprise the community. It is for this reason that, from the classical point of view, there is no fundamental distinction between ethics and politics, or between prudence and practical wisdom. The good of self and the good of society are linked in the very nature of human beings.

Excellence in deliberating about means to the ultimate end (which is the work of practical wisdom) presupposes desire for that end (the work of moral virtue). Yet there is another respect in which moral virtue itself presupposes practical wisdom. Recall the discussion of courage and of the moral virtues in general. We pointed out that finding the correct intermediate point between excess and deficiency in our emotions and actions requires intelligence and experience. Moral virtue consists "in observing the mean relative to us, a mean which is defined by a rational principle, such as a man of practical wisdom would use to determine it" (1106b37. Ostwald). With the mind's eye clearly fixed upon the ultimate end, a prudent person judges what it is that virtue requires here and now. For example, if the question is one of giving money, the aim will be to avoid both extravagance and miserliness. Generosity names the intermediate between too much and too little. However, to decide what is generous in a particular situation demands deliberation and choice relative to a number of variables such as our own financial circumstances, the worthiness of the object of our generosity, our responsibilities to other persons, and the motive for this action.

Clearly it is an advantage in decisions of this nature to have mature intelligence and experience. Knowing just what to do in a particular case in order to achieve the mean is characteristic of practical wisdom. This intellectual virtue presupposes knowledge of and commitment to the highest good. Of course, it is possible for a person of imperfect virtue to perform the right act. A child may be told by his parent, for example, "Here is how much you should give that blind begger." However, it is when the agent is himself able to perceive what generosity requires in this particular situation, in view of his own knowledge of the good life, that we can speak of virtue in the full sense.

In using the word "perception" to name the judgment made here and now, we recall a point discussed in Chapter 6. There we explained that it is not sufficient for right action merely that one assent to correct principles, especially since the principle cannot specify what is "moderate" in each individual's case. For this reason, Aristotle will say that the decision rests with "perception," a sizing up of the situation which depends upon the particular facts, and which is more likely to be handled appropriately by a person of sound habits and experience.

The perception (or intuition) of a particular act as right constitutes that determination of the mean in the moral virtues which is the function of practical wisdom. Regarding what contributes to achieving the final end, then, it is intellectual virtue that makes possible the moral virtues. In practical wisdom we find the unity of all virtues concerned with ethical life. To have practical wisdom is to have all the moral virtues, since it is practical wisdom which discovers the midpoint in each of the moral virtues. Also, right choice concerning, say, what is generous depends in part on the legitimate claims of other virtues in this situation. To decide what should be done, all things considered, involves weighing all competing claims and reaching a verdict in light of a unified picture of the best life. Because of the key role played by intellect in every question of choice, we can say that when we have one virtue (practical wisdom), we have them all.

The Practical Syllogism

The chain of reasoning that we go through in making moral decisions can be represented in a logical form called the *practical syllogism*. We are not suggesting that people actually think in such rigorously structured fashion. But the syllogism provides a clear reconstruction of the process by which particular actions are justified, making explicit the considerations that bear upon the conclusion we reach. An argument in syllogistic form has a major premise, a minor premise, and a conclusion that is derived from those premises. It is possible for an extended argument to contain many syllogisms, the conclusion of one becoming the major premise of the next syllogism. This reflects the fact that often in our deliberations we work out a plan of action only through a long series of reflections, with one decision becoming the basis for figuring out another.

In a syllogism the major premise states a universal proposition. If we try to represent the reasoning process of the entire moral life, it is clear that what functions as the supreme practical principle is the ultimate end. Since happiness or human flourishing is the target at which all action is aimed, a statement of that end provides the first and most universal premise in the sequence of reasoning which eventuates in concrete acts. "The syllogisms which express the principles initiating action run: 'Since the end, or the highest good, is such-and-such. . .' " (1144a32. Ostwald). Rarely in our actual reflections do we make explicit reference to this most general principle, our overall concept of the good life. Instead, it influences our day-to-day thinking and behavior implicitly, as a basic determinant of our character and, hence, of our perspective on life.

Assuming an orientation to some ultimate end, the form that a specific argument might take would be as follows. The major premise would express a rule of conduct, the minor premise would state a particular fact that makes that rule applicable to the present situation, and then a conclusion is drawn about what should be done here and now. A simplified way of representing the explanation of these two paragraphs is the following sequence of syllogisms.

Major: The ultimate purpose of human striving is happiness or self-fulfillment.
Minor: Happiness requires cooperation between persons in time of need.
Conclusion: Humans have a duty to assist one another when in need.

Major: Humans have a duty to assist one another when in need.
Minor: My neighbor next door is ill and laid up in bed.
Conclusion: I must help my neighbor take care of his chores.

Major: I must help my neighbor take care of his chores.
Minor: My neighbor's lawn needs cutting.
Conclusion: Action.

What we see in this chain of reasoning, greatly oversimplified, is a movement from the universal statement of life's ultimate purpose right down to a specific action undertaken at this moment. The final conclusion is an action that we have judged to be both good and possible. Of course, the action may not immediately follow the termination of the thought process. (Our resolution to cut the neighbor's grass may wait until tomorrow to be carried out, since it rained today.) In any case, the nature of practical reasoning is that it is designed to produce *action.* That action is justified by general rules combined with a perception (or intuition) that we now find ourselves in a situation where the rule applies. The general rules are themselves justified by a derivation from the ultimate principle, which in practical affairs is the end.

We can summarize all of this in the following way. The starting point of practical thinking is the end. The ultimate conclusion is action justified by reference to that end. Drawing the conclusion that we should act in this or that specific way can be the result of our own intellectual understanding of the good life. Or, it can be the product of experience obtained under the tutelage of another. In either case, the choice of action results from combining (1) a normative premise with (2) factual awareness that the present circumstance provides an appropriate occasion for implementation. In a morally weak person, action may not follow from realization of what is required. But for a person of moral virtue, the perception that something can and should be done here and now produces immediate action. The integrity of character and conduct manifests itself in the spontaneity with which desire responds to the dictates of reason.

REVIEW QUESTIONS

1. What is the criticism of rule theories expressed by those who favor a return to virtue-centered ethics?
2. What problem arises from a law ethic such as that of Judaeo-Christianity?
3. Explain the maxim, "Become what you are."
4. Define the following: habit, virtue, vice, intellectual virtue, moral virtue.
5. Why are habits useful for the moral life?
6. Explain the connection between character and conduct.
7. Identify the elements in John Dewey's definition of habit.
8. Distinguish between intelligent and routine habits.
9. Explain: "The concept of happiness is *pluralistic*; it is an *inclusive* whole."

10. What is the difference between intrinsic and instrumental goods, and how can something be both?
11. Explain four characteristics of virtues.
12. What are six differences between virtues and skills?
13. What three characteristics must an agent have in order to act virtuously?
14. When is ignorance culpable?
15. Define the following kinds of acts: voluntary, involuntary, and mixed voluntary.
16. Why is it that psychological and physical pleasure or pain reactions do not make acts involuntary?
17. What is the significance of calling courage an *action-state*?
18. Distinguish between the theory of the *mean* and the doctrine of *moderation*.
19. Explain: "Fearlessness and courage are not the same thing."
20. Distinguish relativism from the view that "virtue consists in the relative mean."
21. How does the source of difficulty in living virtuously affect culpability?
22. Explain five elements in the definition of moral virtue.
23. Discuss the impact of early upbringing on the exercise of virtues.
24. What kinds of knowledge are associated with practical truth?
25. Explain the origin of our knowledge of the ultimate end. How can knowledge of that sort be given intellectual defense?
26. Define practical wisdom and explain its presuppositions.
27. Interpret this statement: "Possessing practical wisdom means possessing all the moral virtues."
28. Explain the structure of the practical syllogism.

NOTES

1. Alasdair MacIntyre, *After Virtue* (Notre Dame, IN: University of Notre Dame Press, 1981).

2. G. E. M. Anscombe, "Modern Moral Philosophy," *Philosophy*, 33 (1958), 1–19.

3. Dewey, *Human Nature and Conduct*, p. 39.

4. Aristotle, *Ethica Nicomachea*, trans. Ross, 1360b4-26. Hereafter, all references to Aristotle will be identified in the body of the text by Bekker number, together with name of the translator in the case of direct quotation.

5. MacIntyre, *After Virtue*, p. 140.

6. Philippa Foot, *Virtues and Vices and Other Essays in Moral Philosophy* (Berkeley and Los Angeles: University of California Press, 1978), p. 6.

7. *Milwaukee Journal*, June 18, 1985, Metro section, p. 1.

8. James D. Wallace, *Virtues and Vices*, (Ithaca, N.Y.: Cornell University Press, 1978), p. 43.

9. Janet Smith, "Can Virtue Be in the Service of Bad Acts? A Response to Philippa Foot," *The New Scholasticism*, LVIII (Summer, 1984), 366.

10. Foot, *Virtues and Vices and Other Essays*, p. 11.

11. Cf. Wallace, *Virtues and Vices*, p. 69.

12. An excellent discussion of this issue is found in Richard Sorabji, "Aristotle on the Role of Intellect in Virtue," *Proceedings of the Aristotelian Society*, n.s. 74 (1973-74), 107-129.

CHAPTER EIGHT

Presuppositions of a Moral System

Having come this far in the examination of alternative theories of right and good, along with other related issues of concern to people attempting to construct a moral system, we must address this question: What assumptions are basic to a viable moral system? Is it possible to isolate features of a system which would be common to all effective ethical theories? In view of what has been previously discussed, the following are proposed as basic presuppositions for any workable system:

1. Action requires the interaction of reason and desire.
2. Freedom is a necessary condition of moral agency, although environment and culture must be reckoned with as influences in the shaping of behavior.
3. A system must be coherent or internally consistent, providing moral guidance without contradictory messages, and specifying some method for resolving conflicts.
4. Moral judgments must be universalizable. At the same time, the system recognizes the legitimacy of exceptions or qualifications of rules.
5. The system must be compatible with the facts, yet not merely descriptive.

The remainder of this chapter will be devoted to an examination of each of these presuppositions.

REASON AND DESIRE

An age-old controversy among moral philosophers has concerned the respective roles of reason and desire in determining right action. Some philosophers have extolled reason at the expense of appetite or desire, on the ground that our intellectual powers constitute what is distinctive in human beings. Reason not only makes possible the universal quality of moral legislation; it also restrains those impulses or inclinations that war against the primacy of intellect. This *rationalism* is contrasted with an opposing theory that emphasizes the centrality of emotion or desire in our behavior. The impetus to action is given by impulse, and reason is merely instrumental to its success in achieving satisfaction. At the extreme, *emotivism* translates moral judgments into expressions of feelings and interprets moral arguments to be simply techniques of persuasion.

As with so many other long-standing controversies, it appears that a false dichotomy is presented by these opposing theories. Common sense suggests that the most plausible account of our experience must recognize the complementary roles of reason and desire. Rather than viewing them in opposition to one another, the most unforced interpretation of moral action suggests their interaction. That is, knowledge and desire do not exist in separate compartments. It is not possible to explain behavior without understanding their mutual contribution.

Reason of itself does not move us. The impetus to action is provided by want or desire. Therefore, the explanation of human behavior must take as its starting point the fact of desiring. It is because we experience ourselves as drawn to some object or state of affairs that we are inclined to act. Another way of putting this is to say that knowledge alone cannot initiate action, because it may be knowledge to which we are indifferent. Knowledge which influences action must bear some relation to what we desire because of our interests or needs. As we saw earlier, the mere fact of desire does not establish that something is desirable, but only desires can provide an empirical starting point for inquiry into what is desirable.

What we quickly realize, however, is that desires are not rigidly fixed. On the contrary, they are malleable—shaped by education, example, culture, and personal experience. What can perhaps be called the impulses of our human nature give, of themselves, only a very general direction to activity. The specific form that those impulses will take depends upon their interaction with an environment. Impulses set limits to the range of ends which human beings can seek with satisfaction. Whatever we pursue as intrinsically valuable, or desirable for its own sake, must therefore be traced to its connection with appetite.

Although we begin with desires and interests, it requires much more to say that we have established an articulated and defensible set of goals for the moral life. Impulses and desires, precisely because of their plasticity, can be shaped well or ill. The movement of impulse may be toward an object that will not in fact satisfy that impulse. Or, the satisfaction of an impulse in one way puts the agent in conflict with other impulses that also clamor for attention. Long-term and immediate satisfactions may work against one another; if the goal is deficiently perceived, acts may lead to unexpected and undesired consequences. In short, intelligence must give direction to what otherwise is blind.

The tasks of reason become clearer. Impulse as it first manifests itself may have to be restrained, to allow reflection its opportunity to determine the nature of that impulse, its connection with other impulses, and what would follow upon the satisfaction of that impulse in this way or that. The ancient injunction to "Know thyself" requires, first, that we undertake a careful discovery process that reveals our basic needs or inclinations. Second, we must determine what objects or states of affairs will satisfy these needs. Finally, intelligence must calculate what means will be efficacious in the attainment of those ends of inclination.

Discovery of a whole range of facts is essential to the three tasks of reason just identified. Possession of facts concerning our needs, what will satisfy them, and the means to those satisfactions will enable us to distinguish between *informed* and *blind* desires. "Thought wedded to desire" (to use Aristotle's phrase once again) doesn't merely enhance the prospects that a particular desire can be efficiently satisfied, but contributes to elimination of "traffic congestion" created by diverse desires that in the selfsame individual can be a source of inner conflict. *Personal integration* is another name for the harmony that intelligence can engineer by analyzing the demands of impulse in the light of their long-term effects upon the agent as a unity.

Also, given the further fact that we are willy-nilly social beings whose integral fulfillment is within community, harmony must be achieved between our desires and those of our fellow citizens, to the end that moderated interaction in society can maximize the good which is achievable for all. Social as well as personal integration makes great demands upon our intellectual resources. The organization of our inner and our social life to produce a smoothly functioning system of acts and responses entails that priorities be established, that we make accurate calculations of long-range as well as immediate effects of alternative acts, and that we work vigilantly to obtain accurate and adequate information.

One way of putting it is that the moral life must be pursued with a *scientific* attitude. By that is meant a disposition to employ methods of observation, reflection, and testing which have as their objective the continual reshaping of impulses and desires in the light of on-going experience with the environment. The scientific attitude is as appropriate to moral inquiry as to any other domain of human knowing. Moral beliefs—if they are to be something other than castles in the sky—must be guided by evidence. If morality is concerned with action, and if the point of action is the realization of certain ends, then only a belief in magic could tempt us to assume that success is possible without control of impulses and control of external conditions. Intelligence brought to bear upon inclination is the surest way of achieving the objective.

In summary, rationality is not a force to invoke against impulse, but rather is a force for achieving a working harmony among diverse desires. Ideas condition desires, and desires give ideas momentum. This is the significance of describing the relation between knowing and desiring as *interactional*. Judgments concerning the morally desirable are the end product of a complex process, which begins with the surge of impulses and proceeds through the sifting and shaping operations of intelligence. The desired, as thus enhanced and integrated, becomes the desirable.

FREEDOM AND DETERMINISM

One question that affects morality in a very important way concerns whether human beings can properly be held responsible for their actions. It makes no sense to attribute praiseworthiness or blameworthiness to those who are not, at least in some sense, free agents. Talk of obligations and of acting from rules which are self-legislated is incompatible with the belief that the causes of human behavior lie outside the agent. If the explanation of behavior is ultimately traceable to factors beyond the control or influence of those performing the acts, then it appears futile to exhort, threaten, encourage, and reason with those whose behavior is an automatic response to external causes. Consequently, the very possiblity of ethics depends upon a supposition of freedom in some sense.

Opponents of the freedom hypothesis, for example, B. F. Skinner, argue that to say behavior is free is equivalent to saying it is spontaneous, miraculous, or uncaused. The mere fact that we might be ignorant of the causes of an event in a particular case does not justify our assumption that it has no causes. Every event has antecedents which are sufficient to account for its occurrence. The progress of science reveals the success with which causal explanations in first one domain and then another have been proven correct. There is no reason to assume that human behavior is exempt from similar law-like statements, or that a science of human behavior is not possible with advances in the study of anatomy and physiology.

The defenders of freedom, in contrast, maintain that we must assume it exists in order to account for our commonsense experience. In day-to-day existence, we constantly act in a manner that can only suggest our freedom: we ponder alternatives; we commend and we reprimand; we reason and argue. Virtually all of our practical living is predicated upon the assumption that we can influence the course of events by our own reflections and decisions, that our responses can be strengthened or weakened by choices that we make, and that the future course of events is affected by our projects and ideals.

In trying to sort out the complexities of this issue, philosophers attempt a number of distinctions. Let us see how helpful these can be. First, a distinction is made between *determinism* and *indeterminism*. Determinism maintains that every event has a cause, whereas indeterminism maintains that at least some events are uncaused. A more precise way of stating this is to say that, according to determinism, for every event there is an event or set of events that precedes it and is causally sufficient for it. That is, every event is necessitated by its antecedents. The indeterminist denies this.

One source of difficulties here concerns the use of the term *cause*. Does it refer only to antecedents that are external and beyond human control? Or can it be said that reasons and sentiments, too, are causes? In the latter case, although we might admit that all events are caused, nevertheless we can say of some events, namely, human acts, that they have their origin in inner causes proper to human beings and that are consistent with the predication of freedom. This is precisely the claim of so-called *soft determinists*. According to soft determinism, every event is caused, but some causes are inner and subject to the control of the agent. Feelings, intentions, and purposes would be examples of inner causes. In contrast, *hard determinists* maintain that all causes are outside human control, and therefore causality is incompatible with freedom. Hard determinists are inclined to say that all so-called "inner" causes are themselves sufficiently accounted for by antecedents not controlled by the agent and, hence, are not required in order to explain human behavior. Otherwise, hard determinists argue, we must assume that inner causes are themselves uncaused, and that is nothing other than the mysterious thesis of the indeterminist.

Freedom in Jean-Paul Sartre

In our own time two thinkers have drawn considerable notice for their arguments in support of, or in opposition to, human freedom. Jean-Paul Sartre, the French existentialist philosopher (1905–1980), maintains that only a human being is a *being-for-itself*: a being that defines itself through its own actions. Existence precedes essence in the sense that peoples' free choices direct what they are to become. Granted that our past is a fact about us which we cannot deny, it is possible for us at any moment of our existence to transcend that past and to move off in a new direction. Although we are finite, determinate selves, we have the power to transcend any self we have been. So we are not identical with our *facticity* (our past). In affirming the radical freedom of human beings, Sartre denies that the past determines the future. Indeed, it would be an instance of *bad faith* to seek to deny our freedom and responsibility by embracing some form of determinism—by claiming, for example, that God, heredity, or the environment causes our acts. Unable to make excuses, a being-for-itself must face up, perhaps with anguish, to the reality that it is radically free and can spontaneously determine what it is to become.

Sartre acknowledges that much of human behavior can be predicted. However, the opponent of freedom cannot assume that behavior is determined because it is predictable. All of us are guided in day-to-day decisions by our choice of projects, and the most fundamental projects of our lives, such as the choice of marriage or of a profession, establish patterns of behavior in their wake which enable us to predict behavior, as long as it is consistent with those fundamental choices. But there is no fixity of human projects that can withstand our ability, at any moment, to overthrow any project. What we can become is never identical with what we have been, and our freedom is precisely this power to transcend as well as to reaffirm any project at a particular stage of our existence. It is a mistake if a being-for-itself identifies with an achieved possibility. Our *essence* (what we have become) is always that beyond which we are projecting ourselves.

A dramatic illustration of Sartre's refusal to permit any escape from freedom is in his discussion of our responsibility for our passions. Feelings such as sadness or fear are not something that happen to us, Sartre says. Rather, we choose them. A situation presents itself. Our response to it is a matter of our decision. We can choose to be sad or not to be sad, and that selected reaction cannot be attributed to the situation but to our own free act. Rather than pretending that passion is causally determined by what is occurring around us, we must realize that we consciously choose a possible mode of response to events.

In a famous passage from *Being and Nothingness*, Sartre describes a situation in which a person's life is threatened. What Sartre wants to make clear is that it is our freely adopted values or aims that give this situation whatever meaning it has for us. That the same situation evokes different passions in one person or another bears witness to Sartre's contention that we are not overcome by passions, but rather permit or select passions.

> If I am threatened, I can run away at top speed because of my fear of dying. This passional fact nevertheless posits implicitly as a supreme end the value of life. Another person in the same situation will, on the contrary, understand that he must remain at his post even if resistance at first appears more dangerous than flight; he 'will stand firm. . .' Human reality in and through its very upsurge decides to define its own being by its ends. It is therefore the positing of my ultimate ends which characterizes my being and which is identical with the sudden thrust of the freedom which is mine.[1]

We might argue that Sartre goes too far in affirming our ability to transcend our past. Is it not the case, for example, that our future is conditioned by realities over which we had no control? One person is born to poverty; another person to wealth. One is born with missing limbs; another is physically whole. Sartre, in response, does not deny that these realities are part of our essence or *being-in-itself*, that is, our past. But what meaning these facts have for us is what we choose to give them. One person born without arms grows up in bitterness and self-pity. She resents the cruel trick nature has played upon her, and becomes a recluse in her sensitivity to the difference that separates her from "normal" people. Abandoning all hope of an ambitious career, this individual resigns herself to the passive existence of an invalid.

Compare that choice of response to our facticity with another person's decision to achieve success despite her natural handicap. Human history is replete with examples of those who were determined to succeed despite adversities. If anything, the absence of limbs becomes an occasion for even more dramatic exercise of will power than she otherwise would have developed. What reduced one person to passivity can inspire another to overachievement. In short, we can choose what significance our facticity will have for us.

B. F. Skinner's Behaviorism

In striking contrast to Sartre, the Harvard psychologist B. F. Skinner (1904–) dismisses all talk of human freedom as prescientific. Despite the advances made in areas like physics and biology, he believes, we are reluctant to apply the methods of science to the study of human behavior. Instead, we prefer to mask our ignorance of the real causes of behavior by attributing it to an autonomous self. Our mentalistic vocabulary of intentions, feelings, needs, purposes, and attitudes suggests in the popular mind that the causes of behavior are being discussed. In fact such inner states are at best only by-products rather than causes. Skinner, as a *behaviorist*, appeals to us to focus attention upon behavior as a subject in its own right, rather than as a symptom or by-product of some private world of the mind. Restricting ourselves in true scientific fashion to what is objectively observable, we can move directly from observation of behavior to the investigation of its causes in the genetic and environmental history of the agent. In so doing, we can bypass reference to occult feelings or states of mind. Even were such inner states readily accessible to the observer, they would not be essential to a scientific exploration of behavior, for they are only intermediate between behavior and its prior physical causes.

Given that all linkages between behavior and physical causes are lawful, nothing is lost by omitting consideration of purported nonphysical links. Indeed, important gains are made by this exercise of "Ockham's razor" (the elimination of needless distinctions). Progress towards a science of human behavior until now has been impeded by a mentalism that ignored the conditions of which behavior is a function. Instead, by attributing behavior to an inner self which is not in turn explained, it assumed that for much of human behavior there are no relevant antecedents. It is for this reason, Skinner argues, that "autonomous" or "free" is equivalent to "miraculous," because the investigation of the behavior has not been pressed far enough to reveal real causes. What we don't understand, we attribute to human freedom.

Scientific analysis, on the other hand, takes the human being to be a complex physical system whose behavior can be directly linked to the conditions within which the person has evolved and now lives. In principle, then, the adequate study of human behavior is physiology. Skinner admits that the scientific view of behavior as completely determined by genetic history and environmental circumstances is a view that cannot be proved. But neither can the prescientific view. And there are important reasons for preferring the scientific hypothesis. As we discover more about the effects of genetic endowment and the environment, there is less reason to attribute behavior to the autonomous self. Moreover, from a practical point of view, we are in a better position to affect behavior if we focus attention upon factors such as the environment, which we can change, than by succumbing to a belief that the sources of behavior are inner, unobservable, and inaccessible.

It is Skinner's contention that human beings are not responsible for their behavior, since they are completely determined. Therefore, credit and blame is inappropriate. Control shifts from the autonomous self to the environment. This control is exercised through the reinforcing consequences of behavior. In the evolutionary history of humanity, that behavior which had survival value was *positively reinforcing*, encouraging its repetition. Just as some things were called good because of their positive contribution, other things that were *negatively reinforcing* because they threatened survival came to be identified as bad. All reinforcers, then, ultimately derived their power from the contingencies of survival under which the species evolved. However, in addition to natural reinforcers, there are *conditioned reinforcers* which can shape behavior. For example, society can reinforce through rewards such as tax credits and promotions, or through punishments such as fines and imprisonment. So contingencies of reinforcement (cause-effect relationships that strengthen behavior) can be either natural or social. The latter are effective, however, because they finally derive their power from natural reinforcers. It is evolutionary selection, then, which provides the ultimate explanation for what is good and bad, since it is part of genetic endowment called human nature to be reinforced in particular ways by particular things.

Skinner is curiously inconsistent, however, in his attempt to show that this so-called "scientific" account of behavior establishes that human beings are not responsible agents. For example, even though he states that we are controlled by the environment, he says that it is an environment almost entirely of our own making. Although we are presumed to be incapable of choice because we are determined, Skinner nevertheless exhorts us to select patterns of culture that enlarge the prospects for peace and material prosperity. Whereas Skinner at one point insists that there is nothing for which human beings can take credit precisely because they are not free, at another point he claims that both biological and cultural evolution are subject to intentional design. Trying to reconcile Skinner's disparate claims is complicated by the frequent appearance of opposing statements in his writings, sometimes only a few pages apart. For example, he states, "Whatever we do, and hence however we perceive it, the fact remains that it is the environment which acts upon the perceiving person, not the perceiving person who acts upon the environment."[2] However, later he claims, "As the individual controls himself by manipulating the world in which he lives, so the human species has constructed an environment in which its members behave in a highly effective way."[3]

The vacillating character of Skinner's claims points to the fact that some middle ground should be found between the most extreme views of Skinner and the views of Sartre. Each reminds us of certain very real features of the human situation. On the one hand, it is naive to assume that behavior is not heavily influenced by inherited traits and by the physical and cultural environment. On the other hand, influence is not the same as control. As Skinner uses the term *control*, it means complete determinism, the total lack of freedom and responsibility. Our common-sense experience contradicts extravagent claims that we are controlled in that sense. Rather, as Sartre has emphasized, it is within the power of individuals to decide the significance that facts about their past and present circumstances will have for them. And we frequently witness in ourselves and in others the ability to "rise above our circumstances," even to the extent of a fundamental conversion in our way of life.

Skinner himself in his more moderate passages is forced to acknowledge this potentiality in human beings, for much of his writing is a humanistic appeal for saner use of environmental resources and the restructuring of our social institutions to alleviate sources of unhappiness. Although Skinner says, "Personal exemption from a complete determinism is revoked as a scientific analysis progresses,"[4] on the very next page he asks, "Who is to construct the controlling environment and to what end?"[5] That question makes no theoretical or practical sense unless we have the power to consider alternatives and exercise choice.

Interaction as a Middle Ground

A theory of human freedom should square with our experience, rather than fly in its face. What that experience reflects is the fact that we are both agents and patients. We both do, and undergo. We in turn act and are acted upon. A single word, *interaction*, captures the nature of the relationship between individuals and their environments, physical and social. That word expresses the reciprocal nature of human contact with nature and with other people. It is undoubtedly the case that individuals are influenced and also limited by the forces that surround them. By the same token, it is obvious that individuals can affect those environments with either good or bad consequences. The physical environment can be either polluted or conserved and enhanced by human intervention. And because individuals are part of the community, not outside it, they can participate in shaping those controls by which social interaction is moderated. It is the essence of democratic institutions that people give themselves the laws which they obey.

It cannot be denied that individuals may find themselves in physical and political circumstances in which freedom is reduced virtually to zero. We can be afflicted with a disease that eliminates the capacity to reason and exercise self-control. Or we may be the unfortunate victim of tyrannical social conditions that crush every expression of democratic aspirations. Moreover, it is possible for individuals, by their own action or neglect, to reduce and even destroy their own freedom. Pledging blind obedience to a political or religious leader, developing addictive drug habits, or simply refusing to cultivate self-discipline in the satisfaction of appetites are all examples of self-caused loss of freedom.

The possibility of being unfree, however, is decidedly different from a claim that we all are *necessarily* unfree. To maintain the latter, we must explain away too much of our ordinary experience. In fact, it can be demonstrated that the thesis of hard determinism is not empirical at all. What could count as evidence against the hypothesis? Nothing whatever. Empirical claims, at least in principle, are falsifiable. That is, it should be possible to state what sort of evidence would invalidate the claim. However, Skinner's determinism, although put forth as a scientific hypothesis, is really an *a priori* claim. Nothing can disprove Skinner's view that all control is exercised by the environment, because whatever we might point to as affecting things becomes *ipso facto* part of the environment. "Those who undertake to do something about human behavior . . . become part of the environment to which responsibility shifts."[6] Now, if the word "environment" becomes so all-inclusive that even humans who manipulate the environment are part of it, then the term becomes vacuous. What explains everything explains nothing. If environment is at the controls, what is it controlling? There is nothing with which to contrast it.

Because nothing can function as counterevidence to his deterministic thesis, Skinner's claim is really pseudoscientific, a tautology presented in scientific garb.

Having said this much about the excesses of Skinner's position, we must acknowledge that a balanced theory of freedom should avoid extremes at the opposite end. Because behavior is interactional, the influence of natural and cultural forces is inescapable. We cannot act freely by arbitrary fiat. Conditions must be created for that exercise of will. We are not free to drive a car through the jungle without first having cleared a path. Nor are we free to master a demanding academic program without disciplined study habits and adequate preparatory education. It is foolish, then, to equate freedom with capriciousness or spontaniety. Controls are a necessary condition of action. The ability to exercise our powers when we choose is also an ability to inhibit them. Cannons rolling loose on a shipdeck are in no position to be fired at will.

Habits and Free Action

A misconception more common than it should be concerns the relation that habits bear to free action. The erroneous view is that whatever has become habituated is to that extent not free. However, as we have just seen, without self-controls we are ourselves controlled. This is what we mean by the expression "a slave to passion." The only impulses which we should not inhibit in their spontaneous display are those which issue from sound habits, not those which are independent of habits. Of course, we can cultivate bad habits—bad precisely because they do not free us for exercise of the full panoply of potentialities. But genuine freedom of action means that intelligence is brought to bear upon the upsurge of impulses and the circumstances in which habits operate. Without reflection, there is no way of judging the effectiveness of a possible avenue of behavior. What constitutes an appropriate response to a situation demands a realistic assessment of our own resources and of the situation. In the first place, then, we need intellectual habits, habits of recall or recollection, deliberation, circumspection, and foresight. When intelligence has arrived at a sound judgment about the fitness of a mode of action, then the disposition to act in similar fashion whenever that type of situation occurs is precisely what is meant by habit. Habits not only facilitate the controlled expression of impulse; they also free up our intellectual resources to concentrate on the unexpected.

Having thought through reasonable responses to ordinary kinds of situations, we can make those responses our habits. Then reflection is not needlessly engaged in repeating itself, as though we were to deliberate how to take each step upon a staircase. Intellectual energies remain fresh to cope with what is novel.

A point that cannot be overemphasized about reflective habits is that, precisely because they are reflective, they always remain under our control. If relevant circumstances change, then adjustments in habituated response can be made. In other words, the disposition to reflect ensures that whenever we need to reassess the nature of the response, we are prepared to do so. The habit of holding the door for others passing through at the same time does not prevent us from deciding in an emergency situation that we must forego that courtesy. Remember, too, that a disposition to step aside and allow others through remains a free response. Suppose someone taking advantage of this courtesy were to say, "I shouldn't thank you for holding the door, since you weren't thinking about it. It's just a matter of habit for you." We could swiftly demonstrate to that person the flexible nature of the habit if we slam the door in her face on the next occasion. Acting without thinking is not a problem, provided that we have previously done the necessary thinking. It is readiness to think that is the essential concomitant of habits.

We can also learn an important lesson about freedom in the economic and political order from the interactional character of behavior. Because the impulses of our human nature require appropriate conditions for their expression, it is utopian to assume that economic and political freedom can exist without institutional arrangements that foster that freedom. It is naive to declare that human beings are free, while neglecting the ongoing work of vigilant maintenance and reform of supportive social conditions. The quality of our action depends upon the conditions under which it operates and with which it interacts. Since impulses are malleable, they will be profoundly affected by environmental factors.

Correct thinking about freedom in the social order, then, should view it not as a given to be presupposed, but as a project to be achieved. Moreover, since no social institution is immune to change, the effort to preserve and perfect conditions of freedom is never-ending. It is, of course, the democratic ideal that the potentialities of our human nature be developed within a framework of rights to free speech, assembly, and the like. But these rights remain only abstract symbols unless we pay specific attention to matters like campaign finance reforms, open meeting regulations, and antitrust laws. Once again, our thesis is that it is not controls as such that are hostile to freedom, because some controls are essential for action. Democratic conditions do not automatically maintain themselves. It is critically necessary, then, to create and preserve those social controls which foster freedom.

Rounding out the discussion of freedom and determinism, it is important to recognize the deficiency of any reductionist account of human behavior. The determinist who views human beings merely as complex physical systems tries to reduce their behavior to physiological movements. However, explaining the physiological aspects of an action cannot be adequate. For example, a physical movement such as extending an arm can have a wide range of meanings. Anatomy and physiology do not explain that act as a left turn signal, or a greeting to friends, or a testing of wind direction. The intentional aspects of the act, what give that act meaning in a human context, entirely escape physiological explanation.

Rather than concede the term *cause* to those who refuse to acknowledge anything other than physical causes, it is necessary to insist that *reasons* can function as causes. Human action, while not uncaused, is nevertheless to be explained in important part by distinctive kinds of causes, for example, intentions, ideals, purposes, apprehensions, or ambitions. These are *reasons* for action, indispensable to any adequate account of what is happening, yet clearly distinguishable from physical causes. The intentional act of signaling a left turn by an extended arm presupposes a social convention. We cannot look to the physiologist for an explanation of traffic signals.

In sum, moral action cannot be reduced to physical movements. Adequate explanation of human behavior must recognize as causes not only physical events but also intentional acts. Types of explanation that include reasons as causes are consistent with the ascription of freedom and responsibility to human agents. Although mental phenomena are themselves caused, the difference in kind resists any attempt to reduce mental life to mechanical, physical movements. Reductionism, initially appealing because it simplifies, loses its charm as we realize that we've thrown out the baby with the bath water.

THE NEED FOR CONSISTENCY

The third presupposition of any moral system that we are proposing here states that the system must be coherent or internally consistent. This follows from the fact that the purpose of such a system is to provide moral guidance. It is the point of any logical system to furnish us with a method for discriminating between true and false statements. In a system that is not consistent, anything can follow. If both a statement and its contradictory can be proved within the system, then it obviously lacks utility for enabling us to discover what is true.

Similarly, when we are specifically concerned with the usefulness of a moral system, our purpose is to have a method by which judgments of good and bad, right and wrong, praiseworthiness and blameworthiness can be derived. If the system lacks consistency such that, for example, "Habitual criminals should be executed" and "Habitual criminals should not be executed" are both commanded, then the system cannot fulfill its function. We are being instructed to do incompatible things. Therefore, the system is flawed precisely because it is unable to assist us in discriminating between acts to be done and acts to be avoided.

Although on the face of it this seems to be such an obvious point that some may wonder why it is emphasized, a bit of reflection reveals how frequent are the examples of incompatible value judgments. A parent who teaches her child that "Sweets are not good for you" but then offers the child a sweet as the reward for good behavior is sending contradictory messages. A nation that professes commitment to human rights and then announces a policy of supplying military assistance to despotic regimes is inconsistent in its value system. It is possible, of course, that the conflict is not between beliefs, but is rather between theory and practice. That is, although there may be no contradictions in what we profess, nevertheless, because of weakness or ignorance, we may fail to live up to our beliefs. However, it could also be the case that the examples of conflict just mentioned derive from unresolved tensions in the set of beliefs themselves.

It is important to distinguish this kind of situation from another, which was discussed in the chapter on nonconsequentialist theories. There we discussed the frequent moral dilemma posed by a *conflict of duties*. For example, keeping a promise to one person may be incompatible with saving the life of another person. This conflict does not derive from the fact that we hold inconsistent beliefs. The moral injunction "Keep your promises" is not contradicted by the moral injunction "Help people in distress." However, it is possible that in a particular situation we find it impossible simultaneously to satisfy both injunctions. A promise to meet someone at 3:00 P.M. to discuss an exam can suddenly be in conflict with the desperate need to rush a colleague to the hospital.

This sort of situation leads us to add, in completing the statement of the third presupposition, that a moral system must provide some method for resolving conflicts. It is likely that our moral system will contain a whole host of *prima facie* rights and duties. To call a right or duty *prima facie* is to say that it is based on one morally significant consideration which, however, can be overridden by a weightier moral consideration with which it conflicts. Our right or duty, everything considered, depends on a judgment about *all* the morally significant factors in the situation.

To be able to resolve conflicts among *prima facie* rights and duties requires some sort of prioritizing. One possibility is to rank these rights and duties in an absolute order. We noted earlier that the U.S. Supreme Court has provided an example of that kind of ranking. The case involved a newspaper reporter's refusal to disclose the source of information that had led to the prosecution of an alleged criminal. The defendant claimed a right to confront the accusers. The newspaper reporter claimed a right to protect the confidentiality of the source. The Supreme Court acknowledged in general the value of investigative reporting and the right of reporters to protect their sources. But it concluded that this *prima facie* right is overridden when it conflicts with a defendant's right in a criminal trial.

Whatever may be our own reaction to the order or priorities established by the Court, it seems unlikely that such absolute rankings can be established for all duties and rights in a moral system. For example, in what order would we wish to rank the duties to tell the truth, to return favors, to assist those in distress, and to make reparations? Is it possible to say that whenever telling the truth conflicts with assisting someone in distress, one of the two always take priority? "The question 'Generally, how important is the fact that one made a promise?' deserves the same answer as the question 'Generally, how much does a stone weigh?' "[7]

An alternative to some absolute ranking of *prima facie* obligations would be to adopt a prioritizing principle to which appeal can be made when conflicts arise. For example, the utilitarian principle we considered in Chapter 5 functions in that way. According to Mill, what justifies such secondary rules as truth telling and the like is the happiness principle, and it is this principle which must decide among them when they conflict. It is not possible to decide in the abstract, for example, that we should always tell the truth when that conflicts with protecting the life of another. Rather, we must determine which secondary principle, if observed in this situation, will produce the greatest amount of good, all persons considered. Needless to say, in one set of circumstances this calculation could produce a judgment that the truth should be told, whereas in another set of circumstances the greater good might require that the truth not be told.

To sum up, whether we argue for an absolute priority of rights and of obligations, or defend instead some prioritizing principle such as the utilitarian, it is important to provide within the moral system a method for reaching consistent judgments about acts and agents.

UNIVERSALIZABILITY

Singular moral judgments are never merely singular. Consider a person's decision to swim out and rescue a drowning child. The judgment that this is the right thing to do is implicitly general. The sane presumption is that it would be judged the right thing to do in any other similar situation. Imagine our bafflement were a person to decide that here and now it is right to rescue the drowning child, but in another circumstance relevantly similar to this one, the person maintains that it would not be right to attempt such a rescue. Consistency requires that the judgment made about a particular act having certain characteristics should apply as well to any other act with the same properties.

The implicit universalizability of moral judgments is further made evident in asking *why* we judge this particular act to be right. Suppose the swimmer replies, "Because I was in a position to save the child's life." If the reason justifies this act, it justifies similar acts. Note, moreover, that the reason presupposes a general principle something like "It is right to act so as to save lives."

If the nature of the moral judgment as implicitly general commits the agent to consistency of judgment and action in similar circumstances, it also can be argued that anyone else would be justified in performing the same sort of action. Reasons are, in this sense, impersonal. If what makes this act right is the fact that we are able to swim and a person in our vicinity is drowning, then by implication any person able to swim does the right thing in rescuing a drowning individual. The justifying reason is not peculiar to us. Anyone's ability to swim establishes a *prima facie* justification for attempting a rescue. The suggestion that only we are warranted in so acting reintroduces the incoherent argument for egoism which we considered in a previous chapter.

Although we are implicitly embracing certain rules or principles whenever we judge or choose, this does not mean that an act judged to be right in view of one relevant moral consideration may not be wrong in view of some other relevant moral consideration. We have already discussed the problem of conflicting *prima facie* rights and duties. Nor does the implicit generality of any particular moral judgment mean that moral rules can have no exceptions. In earlier chapters we noted the impossibility of qualifying every moral rule in such fashion that no possible circumstance escapes explicit notice. It is the nature of general rules that they can only prescribe for the generality of cases, with perhaps only the most common sorts of exceptions acknowledged as limitations on their applicability. The rest must be entrusted to the prudent judgment of the individuals in the circumstances. We are reminded here of a true story. Audrey Hughes, age 7, had been taught "not to talk to strangers," and she lived up to this rule so rigorously that she spent two days alone in Utah's Ashley National Forest while three hundred people searched for her. Found perched on a large rock, she explained that she had watched various searchers pass by, but she didn't call out to them because she wasn't supposed to talk to strangers. Of course, even though an extraordinary situation justifies an exception to the rule, the requirement of universalizability is not violated, for that exceptional act is justifiable for any agent in any relevantly similar situation.

We are reminded here of Kant's categorical imperative, which we examined in an earlier chapter. The question "What if everyone did that?" provides a test of the possible immorality of a practice if we find it impossible or undesirable to universalize that practice. A peculiar kind of irrationality has come to infect contemporary thinking about moral justification in a way that conflicts with Kant. Today many would argue, "I can only judge for myself. I cannot say what is right or wrong for someone else."

Tolerance as a Part of Morality

Such a claim must be carefully examined, for it can be interpreted in either acceptable or unacceptable fashion. If the claim simply means that we do not know all the relevant circumstances of another's case, and hence we are in no position to judge her act, then the claim has some plausibility. In fact, we are prudently advised to be cautious in judging the behavior of others for precisely this reason. Nevertheless, it is still possible to say that, insofar as the act of another is relevantly similar to our own, then it bears the same moral evaluation. That our acts are morally indistinguishable means precisely that they may be judged alike. The mere fact that it is someone else's act, not our own, does not invalidate the reasoning that justifies the act. Once again, we emphasize that moral thinking is not idiosyncratic. The function of a moral principle in particular, and of a moral system in general, is to provide guidance in choosing how people should live their lives in a necessarily social environment.

Tolerance, which can be justified as a part of morality, must not be allowed to become the whole of morality, for then there is no morality. We argue falsely from the principle of noninterference with the free choices of others to the principle that all choices are on a moral par. What may be tolerated in the way of behavior is not identical with what we approve. Hence, precisely insofar as we judge an act to be right or wrong for some reason, that reason when relevantly applicable to anyone else's act grounds the moral judgment of the other's act.

Having said this, we should note that the universalizability of moral judgments does not imply lack of individual freedom in choosing how to live the moral life. Given the fact of individual differences in many needs, desires, and interests, we must allow considerable latitude for individualized approaches to the good life within the limits set by necessary moral principles. That is, so long as we respect the universal moral rules without which there can be no progress in the moral life, then we are free to select our own style of life. For one person it is the married state; for another, the unmarried. One person seeks fulfillment through a legal career; the choice of another is domestic. The principle of equal freedom is compatible with universalizability in that the latter specifies only those ways of acting which do and do not comport with moral striving. Within these limits, the extraordinary variety of human interests and desires can be accommodated. For example, we might say that someone is free to choose the married state, provided she doesn't take that as a license to beat her spouse. Or a person is free to become a physician on the condition that she commits herself to saving human lives.

What the principle of individual freedom cannot permit, within a moral framework, is a cult of tolerance that interprets all aspects of human behavior as inherently incapable of judgment. The use of general moral terms necessarily extends analysis of judgments beyond the particular. The final product is a vision of the good life for human beings as such.

THE RELEVANCE OF FACTS

Among the basic presuppositions for a viable moral system identified at the beginning of this chapter was the following: "The system must be compatible with the facts, yet not merely descriptive." To say that it is not merely descriptive calls attention to the distinctive function of a moral system. That function is to state how things *should* be, not merely how they *are*. It is the purpose of a moral ideal to indicate an *optimum* state of affairs; that ideal can be contrasted with a description of the *current* state of affairs. Indeed, the ideal provides a norm for criticism of current conditions. Consistent with the moral ideal, rules prescribe how people ought to behave if they are to realize the ideal. Prescription and description, then, are importantly different concepts.

In previous chapters this difference was operative in distinctions such as the one we made between cultural and ethical relativism, between the desired and the desirable, between psychological and ethical egoism. In each instance the distinction turned on a difference between what *is* the case and what *ought* to be the case. We pointed out that moral judgments do not simply make factual claims; they evaluate the facts. Attitudes of approval and disapproval imply some standard by which acts, persons, and institutions are measured. Clearly, if moral judgments were simply descriptive, we would be denied the means of accomplishing a very necessary task. We would be unable to commend or condemn what we describe.

Remember, too, that moral evaluation is not exclusively a cognitive matter. Since ethics is practical, "the end of this kind of study is not knowledge but action."[8] The purpose of an investigation into the issues of right and wrong, good and evil, in a moral sense, is not simply knowledge for its own sake. In the words of Aristotle, "We are not conducting this inquiry to know what virtue is, but in order to become good..."[9] Moral judgments, then, concern action. Action requires the conjunction of reason and desire, as we saw in the first section of this chapter. Reflection alone will not move us. Discovery of facts must be combined with appeal to our appetites. Once again, the point to be emphasized is that descriptions alone do not set us in motion. The facts must stand in some relation to our inclinations, our wants and needs. This was the significance of claiming, in Chapter 3, that values are relational.

Evaluating Subjective Valuations

Having said all this about the difference between descriptions and prescriptions, it is nevertheless clear that correct apprehension of facts is indispensable for sound moral judgments. We earlier considered at length the view that ethics is "just a matter of how you feel about it," and "moral judgments are basically arbitrary." Were that true, opponents argued, why should it make any difference that we act from *informed* rather than from *blind* desire? Moreover, for what reason would we reject a practice as superstitious? Also, what would enable us to distinguish between rational and irrational persuasion? And finally, how would it be possible to argue that feelings and attitudes are warranted or unwarranted? Clearly, we do these things, and we find it important to do them. Consequently, our ethical theory must square with these realities.[10]

Recall some of the examples used earlier in this book to illustrate that, in moral matters, "thinking something is so doesn't necessarily make it so." The cashier who mistakenly gave incorrect change did not render what justice requires for the customer. The drunken driver who insisted that she was temperate had no case in the face of evidence to the contrary. The swimmer who misperceived her own ability and the conditions offshore was primed for faulty assessment of her duty to rescue someone in the water. In these and many other examples, the point was that we could distinguish between *objective* moral evaluations and *subjective* moral evaluations. That was equivalent to saying that a moral judgment could be right (or wrong) independent of the belief of the person or group making the judgment.

What is relevant in these cases is the nature of the *facts* on the basis of which moral judgments are made. Similarly, identification of superstitious practices, blind desires, irrational persuasion, and unwarranted attitudes requires a determination of facts which, in all these instances, are lacking. In Chapter 3 we argued that we are justified in making moral judgments about persons or acts because of facts about them. Facts are as relevant to "That is an admirable person" as they are to "That is a bad paint brush." Of course, in each case there is implied a rule or standard for determining what counts as a virtuous person or a good paint brush. But we also argued earlier that the adoption of a moral standard itself can (and should) be influenced by facts. A brief review of the bearing that facts have on moral principles and their application is in order.

Discovering Moral Principles

The order of discovery, that sequence of events by which we come to know right from wrong, begins with the moral lessons we learn from parents and others at a very early age. The moral facts with which we are confronted in the beginning are of two kinds. There are the specific judgments about behavior in particular situations, as when we are told how wrong it was to take a playmate's toys without permission.

Also, there are the rules and maxims which are expected to serve as guidelines for making specific decisions. Both individual and general prescriptions, which constitute the moral thinking of prestige figures in our earliest life, later can be subjected to our own critical reflection. With increased experience and the maturation of our personal intellectual abilities, we are able to evaluate customary morality in the light of facts about how well those habituated norms satisfy our desires and square with our own perception of how the world is.

The fact of our desiring this and that provides the starting point for a theory of the desirable. The process of justification requires, however, that those multiple desires must be reconciled with one another within the same individual, and must also be harmonized with those of other people in society. The critical task entails establishing priorities among desires, considering the consequences of satisfying them, and evaluating the resultant "package" of preferences. Moral principles that emerge from this reflective process bear resemblance to those of other people to the extent that needs and interests are common realities. It was argued in previous chapters that facts about those shared essential requirements give rise to the possibility of universalizable moral standards.

What Facts are Relevant?

Claims about human nature, however, have raised difficulties that we sought to clarify earlier in talking about natural law theory, anthropological evidence, and the United Nations Declaration of Human Rights. It might still be asked, nevertheless, to what facts about human nature we should attend. We see plenty of evidence that human beings are selfish, aggressive, and cruel. Why not select those characteristics as indicative of human nature? Certainly it is a fact that humans have the capacity for either cooperative or hostile activity, for behavior that can be either self-fulfilling or self-destructive. What the moral system builds upon, however, are those facts about what we *ideally* can become. Human beings have the potential for that kind of character development which maximizes the chances for happiness in an integrated social context. Rules mandating virtuous acts move us, then, from untutored human nature to human nature in its optimum condition.

Alasdair MacIntyre, in explaining teleological moral thinking, contrasts "man-as-he-happens-to-be   and   man-as-he-could-be-if-he-realized-his-essential-nature."[11] The purpose of a moral system is to serve as the means for the transition from one to the other. The relation between facts and value judgments is clear. What people are capable of, what will satisfy their needs in harmonious fashion, and what steps must be taken in order to achieve this condition are all facts that have fundamental bearing on our moral prescriptions. "To say what someone ought to do is at one and the same time to say what course of action will in these circumstances as a matter of fact lead toward a man's true end. . . Moral sentences are thus used within this framework to make claims which are true or false."[12]

That human beings can be selfish and cruel, then, is no argument against the fact that opposite sorts of behavior produce a social order that we find preferable. What people would do in a starved and tortured condition is no more determinative of general moral principles than what they would do if they wore a *ring of Gyges*. (In Plato's *Republic*, Book II, there is debate about whether people would act morally if a magical ring on their finger made them invisible and, hence, undetectable when they committed crimes.[13]) The moral ideal reflects that potentiality in our human nature which, when actualized, constitutes the best of which we are capable. Human nature can be examined both in its impoverished state and in its perfected state. It is the latter to which the moral system directs us.

Regarding the controversy in Plato, R. M. Hare has pointed out that there are two relevant facts of fundamental importance.[14] First of all, it is a physical fact that there are no rings of Gyges. Presumably, if we are constructing a moral system for this world, as contrasted with some fanciful alternative, Gyges-type situations are irrelevant. Second, it is a social fact that people do not want crime to pay. Accordingly, they have created conditions that lessen the attraction of criminal behavior. It is a supremely relevant empirical fact that the human race "has found it possible to make life a great deal more tolerable by bringing it about that on the whole morality pays. It is better for nearly all of us if social rewards and penalties are attached to socially beneficial and harmful acts; and so it has come about that on the whole they are."[15]

Facts in the Application of Principles

Having said this much about the relevance of facts to selection of moral principles, it remains only to review the ways in which facts are relevant to application of those principles. Recall the structure of a practical syllogism outlined in Chapter 7. What functions as major premise is a moral principle. In order to justify the conclusion that here and now we should act according to that principle, it is necessary to establish a matter of fact, namely, that the present situation *is* an instance of the kind covered by the principle. Does the moral principle, "Indigent people should be given free medical care," apply to the circumstance at hand? That depends on whether the person before me is indeed both poor and in need of medical attention.

Remember, too, that determination of the relative mean in the moral virtues presupposes a decision about many factual conditions. What courage or temperance or justice requires in the present situation cannot be concluded without knowledge about such factors as the agent, the object, the manner, and the means. It is for this reason that the intellectual virtue of practical wisdom must be combined with moral virtue. Also, it is a function of practical wisdom to recognize unusual circumstances that would justify the suspension of an ordinary moral rule. Of course, we are once again talking about the relevance of facts, specifically, those facts which are judged sufficient to warrant exceptional behavior. In general, then, it can be said that what justifies particular moral judgments, whether about persons or their feelings or their actions, are facts about them. Those facts, together with the moral principle that makes them relevant, enable us to draw an appropriate moral conclusion.

Nothing said here should generate a false sense of confidence. Disagreements about what in actuality is our moral right or responsibility are not eliminated by recognition of valid moral principles and a sincere effort to ascertain the facts. However, uncertainties inherent in moral decision making are one thing; the assumption that moral judgments are arbitrary is another. It is the latter claim that collapses under the weight of method, principles, and facts which together constitute a moral argument.

REVIEW QUESTIONS

1. Why is the fact of desiring a necessary starting point in explanation of behavior?
2. What are the tasks of reason in relation to impulse?
3. How is a scientific attitude appropriate to the moral life?
4. Explain: the very possibility of ethics presupposes freedom.
5. Distinguish determinism and indeterminism, as well as soft and hard determinism.
6. Summarize the argument of Jean-Paul Sartre.
7. Explain B. F. Skinner's behaviorism.
8. Why does Skinner consider mentalism a superfluous, prescientific view?
9. What are apparent inconsistencies in Skinner's position?
10. Discuss *interaction* as a theory of the relationship between the individual and the environment.
11. How is hard determinism not an empirical theory?
12. What relationship do habits bear to free action?
13. What social conditions are necessary for economic and political freedom?
14. What is the objection to physiological reductionism?
15. Why is consistency a requirement for any system, and what effect does its absence have on a moral theory?
16. Explain the importance of a method for resolving conflicts in the system.
17. What are alternative ways of ranking *prima facie* obligations and rights?
18. Why are moral judgments implicitly universal?
19. What should be said of tolerance as a part of morality?
20. How is universalizability compatible with the exercise of prudence and the principle of individual freedom?
21. What are objections to characterizing moral judgments and a moral system as "descriptive"?
22. What realities present a difficulty for the view that moral judgments are (a) arbitrary, (b) subjective?
23. Describe the process by which we come to have reflective moral principles.
24. Why do some facts about human nature serve more appropriately than others as the basis for moral principles?
25. What is it about practical syllogisms that manifests the need for facts in order to draw moral conclusions?
26. How are facts relevant to determining the relative mean in the moral virtues?

NOTES

1. Jean-Paul Sartre, *Being and Nothingness*, trans. Hazel E. Barnes (New York: Philosophical Library, 1956), pp. 443–44.

2. B. F. Skinner, *Beyond Freedom and Dignity* (New York: Bantam Books, 1972), p. 179.

3. Ibid., p. 197.

4. Ibid., p. 18.

5. Ibid., p. 19.

6. Ibid., p. 71.

7. Wallace, *Virtues and Vices*, p. 119.

8. Aristotle, *Nicomachean Ethics* (Ostwald), 1095a6.

9. Ibid., 1103b26.

10. "When it comes to emotions and actions, what is said is less reliable than what is done; and, consequently, when words clash with perceived facts, they are scorned and bring the truth into discredit besides." Ibid., 1172a34-b1. Cf. 1179a19-22.

11. MacIntyre, *After Virtue*, p. 50.

12. Ibid., p. 51.

13. *The Republic of Plato*, Francis MacDonald Cornford, trans. (New York: Oxford University Press, 1964), Bk. II (359–360), pp. 44–46.

14. Hare, *Moral Thinking*, pp. 194–95.

15. Ibid., p. 196.

Universal Declaration of Human Rights

Complete text adopted on December 20, 1948, by General Assembly of United Nations

Preamble

Whereas recognition of the inherent dignity and of the equal and inalienable rights of all members of the human family is the foundation of freedom, justice and peace in the world,

Whereas disregard and contempt for human rights have resulted in barbarous acts which have outraged the conscience of mankind, and the advent of a world in which human beings shall enjoy freedom of speech and belief and freedom from fear and want has been proclaimed as the highest aspiration of the common people,

Whereas it is essential, if man is not to be compelled to have recourse, as a last resort, to rebellion against tyranny and oppression, that human rights should be protected by the rule of law,

Whereas it is essential to promote the development of friendly relations between nations,

Whereas the peoples of the United Nations have in the Charter reaffirmed their faith in fundamental human rights, in the dignity and worth of the human person and in the equal rights of men and women and have determined to promote social progress and better standards of life in larger freedom,

Whereas Member States have pledged themselves to achieve, in co-operation with the United Nations, the promotion of universal respect for an observance of human rights and fundamental freedoms,

Whereas a common understanding of these rights and freedoms is of the greatest importance for the full realization of this pledge,
Now, Therefore,

The General Assembly Proclaims

This universal declaration of human rights as a common standard of achievement for all peoples and all nations, to the end that every individual and every organ of society, keeping this Declaration constantly in mind, shall strive by teaching and education to promote respect for these rights and freedoms and by progressive measures, national and international, to secure their universal and effective recognition and observance, both among the peoples of Member States themselves and among the peoples of territories under their jurisdiction.

Article 1. All human beings are born free and equal in dignity and rights. They are endowed with reason and conscience and should act towards one another in a spirit of brotherhood.

Article 2. Everyone is entitled to all the rights and freedoms set forth in this Declaration, without distinction of any kind, such as race, colour, sex, language, religion, political or other opinion, national or social origin, property, birth or other status.

Furthermore, no distinction shall be made on the basis of the political, jurisdictional, or international status of the country or territory to which a person belongs, whether it be independent, trust, non-self-governing or under any other limitation of sovereignty.

Article 3. Everyone has the right to life, liberty and security of person.

Article 4. No one shall be held in slavery or servitude; slavery and the slave trade shall be prohibited in all their forms.

Article 5. No one shall be subjected to torture or to cruel, inhuman or degrading treatment or punishment.

Article 6. Everyone has the right to recognition everywhere as a person before the law.

Article 7. All are equal before the law and are entitled without any discrimination to equal protection of the law. All are entitled to equal protection against any discrimination in violation of this Declaration and against any incitement to such discrimination.

Article 8. Everyone has the right to an effective remedy by the competent national tribunals for acts violating the fundamental rights granted him by the constitution or by law.

Article 9. No one shall be subjected to arbitrary arrest, detention or exile.

Article 10. Everyone is entitled in full equality to a fair and public hearing by an independent and impartial tribunal, in the determination of his rights and obligations and of any criminal charge against him.

Article 11. (1) Everyone charged with a penal offense has the right to be presumed innocent until proved guilty according to law in a public trial at which he has had all the guarantees necessary for his defense.

(2) No one shall be held guilty of any penal offense on account of any act or omission which did not constitute a penal offense, under national or international law, at the time when it was committed. Nor shall a heavier penalty be imposed than the one that was applicable at the time the penal offense was committed.

Article 12. No one shall be subjected to arbitrary interference with his privacy, family, home or correspondence, nor to attacks upon his honor and reputation Everyone has the right to the protection of the law against such interference or attacks.

Article 13. (1) Everyone has the right to freedom of movement and residence within the borders of each state.

(2) Everyone has the right to leave any country, including his own, and to return to his country.

Article 14. (1) Everyone has the right to seek and to enjoy in other countries asylum from persecution.

(2) This right may not be invoked in the case of prosecutions genuinely arising from non-political crimes or from acts contrary to the purposes and principles of the United Nations.

Article 15. (1) Everyone has the right to a nationality.

(2) No one shall be arbitrarily deprived of his nationality nor denied the right to change his nationality.

Article 16. (1) Men and women of full age, without any limitations due to race, nationality or religion, have the right to marry and to found a family. They are entitled to equal rights as to marriage, during marriage and at its dissolution.

(2) Marriage shall be entered into only with the free and full consent of the intending spouses.

(3) The family is the natural and fundamental group unit of society and is entitled to protection by society and the State.

Article 17. (1) Everyone has the right to own property alone as well as in association with others.

(2) No one shall be arbitrarily deprived of his property.

Article 18. Everyone has the right to freedom of thought, conscience and religion; this right includes freedom to change his religion or belief, and freedom either alone or in community with others and in public or private, to manifest his religion or belief in teaching, practice, worship and observance.

Article 19. Everyone has the right to freedom of opinion and expression; this right includes freedom to hold opinions without interference and to seek, receive and impart information and ideas through any media and regardless of frontiers.

Article 20. (1) Everyone has the right to freedom of peaceful assembly and association.

(2) No one may be compelled to belong to an association.

Article 21. (1) Everyone has the right to take part in the government of his country, directly or through freely chosen representatives.

(2) Everyone has the right of equal access to public service in his country.

(3) The will of the people shall be the basis of the authority of government; this will shall be expressed in periodic and genuine elections which shall be by universal and equal suffrage and shall be held by secret vote or by equivalent free voting procedures.

Article 22. Everyone, as a member of society, has the right to social security and is entitled to realization, through national effort and international cooperation and in accordance with the organization and resources of each State, of the economic, social and cultural rights indispensable for his dignity and the free development of his personality.

Article 23. (1) Everyone has the right to work, to free choice of employment, to just and favorable conditions of work and to protection against unemployment.

(2) Everyone, without any discrimination, has the right to equal pay for equal work.

(3) Everyone who works has the right to just and favorable remuneration ensuring for himself and his family an existence worthy of human dignity, and supplemented, if necessary, by other means of social protection.

(4) Everyone has the right to form and to join trade unions for the protection of his interests.

Article 24. Everyone has the right to rest and leisure, including reasonable limitation of working hours and periodic holidays with pay.

Article 25. (1) Everyone has the right to a standard of living adequate for the health and well-being of himself and of his family, including food, clothing, housing and medical care and necessary social service, and the right to security in the event of unemployment, sickness, disability, widowhood, old age or other lack of livelihood in circumstances beyond his control.

(2) Motherhood and childhood are entitled to special care and assistance. All children, whether born in or out of wedlock, shall enjoy the same social protection.

Article 26. (1) Everyone has the right to education. Education shall be free, at least in the elementary and fundamental stages. Elementary education shall be compulsory. Technical and professional education shall be made generally available and higher education shall be equally accessible to all on the basis of merit.

(2) Education shall be directed to the full development of the human personality and to the strengthening of respect for human rights and fundamental freedoms. It shall promote understanding, tolerance and friendship among all nations, racial or religious groups, and shall further the activities of the United Nations for the maintenance of peace.

(3) Parents have a prior right to choose the kind of education that shall be given to their children.

Article 27. (1) Everyone has the right freely to participate in the cultural life of the community, to enjoy the arts and to share in scientific advancement and its benefits.

(2) Everyone has the right to the protection of the moral and material interests resulting from any scientific, literary or artistic production of which he is the author.

Article 28. Everyone is entitled to a social and international order in which the rights and freedoms set forth in this Declaration can be fully realized.

Article 29. (1) Everyone has duties to the community in which alone the free and full development of his personality is possible.

(2) In the exercise of his rights and freedoms, everyone shall be subject only to such limitations as are determined by law solely for the purpose of securing due recognition and respect for the rights and freedoms of others and of meeting the just requirements of morality, public order and the general welfare in a democratic society.

(3) These rights and freedoms may in no case be exercised contrary to the purposes and principles of the United Nations.

Article 30. Nothing in the Declaration may be interpreted as implying for any State, group or person any right to engage in any activity or to perform any act aimed at the destruction of any of the rights and freedoms set forth herein.

Bibliography

The following bibliography consists solely of works to which reference has been made in this book.

ALLPORT, GORDON W., *Becoming*. New Haven: Yale University Press, 1955.
___ , *Pattern and Growth in Personality*. New York: Holt, Rinehart and Winston, 1961.
___ , *Personality*. New York: Henry Holt and Co., 1937.
___ , *Personality and Social Encounter*. Boston: Beacon Press, 1964.
ANGYAL, ANDRAS, *Foundations for a Science of Personality*. New York: The Viking Press, 1969.
___ , *Neurosis and Treatment: A Holistic Theory*. New York: The Viking Press, 1965.
ANSCOMBE, G. E. M., "Modern Moral Philosophy," *Philosophy*, 33 (1958), 1-19.
AQUINAS, ST. THOMAS, *Summa Theologica*, trans. Fathers of the English Dominican Province. New York: Benziger Brothers, Inc., 1947.
ARISTOTLE, *Ethica Nicomachea*, trans. W. D. Ross. New York: Random House, 1941.
___ , *The Ethics of Aristotle*, trans. J. A. K. Thomson. Baltimore: Penguin Books, 1966.
___ , *Nicomachean Ethics*, trans. Martin Ostwald. Indianapolis: The Bobbs-Merrill Co., Inc. 1962.
ASHMORE, ROBERT B., "Deriving the Desirable from the Desired," *Proceedings of the American Catholic Philosophical Association*, XLIV (1970), 152-60.
BAYLES, MICHAEL, "Mill's Utilitarianism and Aristotle's Rhetoric," *The Modern Schoolman*, LI (January, 1974), 159-70.
BENTHAM, JEREMY, *An Introduction to the Principles of Morals and Legislation*. New York: Hafner Publishing Co., 1948.
BUTLER, JOSEPH, *Fifteen Sermons Preached at the Rolls Chapel*, ed. W. R. Matthews. London: G. Bell and Sons, Ltd., 1914.
CAMPBELL, KEITH, *Body and Mind*. Garden City, N.Y.: Doubleday and Company, Inc., 1970.

CICERO, *DeOfficiis/On Duties*, trans. Harry G. Edinger. Indianapolis: The Bobbs-Merrill Company, Inc., 1974.

COLEMAN, JAMES C. et al., *Abnormal Psychology and Modern Life* (7th ed.). Glenview, IL: Scott Foresman and Company, 1984.

DEWEY, JOHN, *Human Nature and Conduct*. New York: The Modern Library, 1957.

——, *Theory of the Moral Life*, ed. Arnold Isenberg. New York: Holt, Rinehart and Winston, 1960.

——, *Theory of Valuation*. Chicago: University of Chicago Press, 1939.

DONAGAN, ALAN, *The Theory of Morality*. Chicago: University of Chicago Press, 1977.

ERIKSON, ERIK H., *Childhood and Society*. New York: W. W. Norton and Company, Inc., 1963.

FOOT, PHILIPPA, *Virtues and Vices and Other Essays in Moral Philosophy*. Berkeley and Los Angeles: University of California Press, 1978.

FRANKENA, WILLIAM, *Ethics* (2nd ed.). Englewood Cliffs, N.J.: Prentice-Hall, Inc., 1963.

FROMM, ERICH, *Man for Himself*. Greenwich, CT: Fawcett Publications, Inc., 1947.

GRIFFIN, JAMES, "Toward a Substantive Theory of Rights," in *Utility and Rights*, ed. R. G. Frey. Minneapolis: University of Minnesota Press, 1984.

HALL, EVERETT, "The 'Proof' of Utility in Bentham and Mill," *Ethics*, LX (1949), 1-18.

HARE, R. M., *Freedom and Reason*. New York: Oxford University Press, 1965.

——, *The Language of Morals*. New York: Oxford University Press, 1964.

——, *Moral Thinking*. Oxford: Clarendon Press, 1981.

HART, H. L. A., *Law, Liberty and Morality*. New York: Vintage Books, 1963.

——, "Legal Positivism," *The Encyclopedia of Philosophy*. New York: Macmillan, 1972.

HOBBES, THOMAS, *Leviathan*, ed. Michael Oakeshott. Oxford: Basil Blackwell, 1960.

HORNEY, KAREN, *Neurosis and Human Growth*. New York: W. W. Norton and Company, Inc., 1950.

HUDSON, W. D., ed., *The Is/Ought Question*. New York: Macmillan and Co., Ltd., 1969.

HUME, DAVID, *An Inquiry Concerning the Principles of Morals*, ed. Charles W. Hendel. New York: The Liberal Arts Press, Inc., 1957.

——, *A Treatise of Human Nature*, ed. L. A. Selby-Bigge. Oxford: Oxford University Press, 1975.

JAMES, WILLIAM, "The Moral Philosopher and the Moral Life," *The Will to Believe and Other Essays in Popular Philosophy*. New York: Dover Publications, Inc., 1956.

KANT, IMMANUEL, *Foundations of the Metaphysics of Morals*, trans. Lewis White Beck. New York: The Liberal Arts Press, 1959.

——, *Religion Within the Limits of Reason Alone*, trans. Theodore M. Greene and Hoyt H. Hudson. New York: Harper and Row Publishers, Inc., 1960.

KIERKEGAARD, SØREN, *The Point of View for My Work as an Author*, trans. Walter Lowrie. New York: Harper and Row Publishers, 1962.

KLUCKHOHN, CLYDE, "Ethical Relativity Sic et Non," *Journal of Philosophy*, 52 (1955), 663-77.

——, "Universal Categories of Culture," in *Anthropology Today*, ed. A. L. Kroeber. Chicago: University of Chicago Press, 1953.

LASCH, CHRISTOPHER, *The Culture of Narcissism*. New York: W. W. Norton & Co., 1979.

LEOPOLD, ALDO, *A Sand County Almanac*. New York: Ballantine Books, 1970.

LINTON, RALPH, "The Problem of Universal Values," *Method and Perspective of Anthropology*, ed. Robert F. Spencer. Minneapolis: University of Minnesota Press, 1954.

MACBEATH, A., *Experiments in Living*. London: Macmillan and Co., Ltd., 1952.

MACCOBY, MICHAEL, *The Gamesman: The New Corporate Leaders*. New York: Simon and Schuster, 1976.

MACINTYRE, ALASDAIR, *After Virtue*. Notre Name, IN: University of Notre Dame Press, 1981.

MARIN, PETER, "The New Narcissim," *Harper's*, 251, no. 1505, (October, 1975), 45-49.

MASLOW, ABRAHAM H., *Motivation and Personality* (2nd ed.). New York: Harper and Row Publishers, 1970.

——, *Toward a Psychology of Being*. New York: D. Van Nostrand Company, 1968.

MCCLOSKEY, H. J., "A Non-Utilitarian Approach to Punishment," *Inquiry*, VIII (1965), 249-263.

____ , "An Examination of Restricted Utilitarianism," *The Philosophical Review*, LXVI (1957), 466–485.

MEDLIN, BRIAN, "Ultimate Principles and Ethical Egoism," *Australasian Journal of Philosophy*, 52 (1957), 111–18.

MILL, JOHN STUART, *On Liberty*, ed. David Spitz. New York: W. W. Norton and Company, Inc., 1975.

____ , *Utilitarianism*, ed. Oskar Piest. Indianapolis: The Bobbs-Merrill Company, Inc., 1957.

MOORE, G. E., *Principia Ethica*. Cambridge: Cambridge University Press, 1959.

MURDOCK, GEORGE, "The Common Denominator of Cultures," *The Science of Man in the World Crisis*, ed. Ralph Linton. New York: Columbia University Press, 1945.

PERRY, RALPH BARTON, *General Theory of Value*. Cambridge, MA: Harvard University Press, 1967.

____ , *Realms of Value*. Cambridge, MA: Harvard University Press, 1954.

PLATO, *The Republic of Plato*, trans. Francis MacDonald Cornford. New York: Oxford University Press, 1964.

PRICHARD, H. A., "Does Moral Philosophy Rest on a Mistake?" *Mind*, XXI (1912) 487–499.

RAND, AYN, *The Virtue of Selfishness*. New York: The New American Library, Inc., 1964.

RAWLS, JOHN, "Two Concepts of Rules," *Philosophical Review*, 64 (1955), 3–32.

ROGERS, CARL, *On Becoming a Person*. Boston: Houghton Mifflin Company, 1961.

SARTRE, JEAN-PAUL, *Being and Nothingness*, trans. Hazel E. Barnes. New York: Philosophical Library, 1956.

SKINNER, B. F., *Beyond Freedom and Dignity*. New York: Bantam Books, Inc., 1972.

SMITH, JANET, "Can Virtue be in the Service of Bad Acts; A Response to Philippa Foot," *The New Scholasticism*, LVIII (Summer, 1984), 357–73.

SOLZHENITSYN, ALEXANDER, "A World Split Apart," *Vital Speeches of the Day*, 44, No. 22 (September 1, 1978), 678–684.

SORABJI, RICHARD, "Aristotle on the Role of Intellect in Virtue," *Proceedings of the Aristotelian Society*, n.s. 74 (1973–74), 107–129.

STONE, CHRISTOPHER D., *Should Trees Have Standing?* Los Altos, CA: William Kaufmann, Inc., 1974.

THOREAU, HENRY DAVID, *Walden or Life in the Woods*. New York: Harper and Row, Publishers, 1965.

WALLACE, JAMES D., *Virtues and Vices*. Ithaca, N.Y.: Cornell University Press, 1978.

WARNOCK, G. J., *The Object of Morality*. London: Methuen and Co., Ltd., 1971.

Index